The Revolutionary Potential of Peasants in Latin America

Gerrit Huizer
Institute of Social Studies
The Hague, Netherlands

Lexington Books
D.C. Heath and Company
Lexington, Massachusetts
Toronto   London

Published simultaneously in Canada

Printed in the United States of America

International Standard Book Number: 0-669-75440-4

Library of Congress Catalog Card Number: 70-165589

Table of Contents

Acknowledgement

Since I was working with various agencies of the United Nations while the material for this book was collected I am heavily indebted to these agencies, particularly I.L.O., for the possibilities they gave me to work on the subjects covered by this book. Opinions expressed are of course my own responsibility. I am also greatly indebted to many friends and colleagues who have given me their advice and support. Amongst them I want to mention: Judith Adler, Desmond Anker, Luis Antezana, Solon Barraclouch, Anton Blok, Jeremy Boissevain, Thomas Carroll, Arthur Domike, Ernest Feder, German Guzman Campos, Andrew Gunder Frank, Benno Galjart, Horacio Labastida, Henry Landsberger, Clodomir Santos de Morais, John Powell, Anibal Quijano, Rodolfo Stavenhagen, Marvin Sternberg and last but not least Wim Wertheim, who supervised this book as a Ph.D. Thesis.

I want to dedicate this book to Guadalupe Campos of village San Luis, El Salvador and many other peasants whose distrust and friendship taught me about the dignity and revolutionary potential of the repressed.

Introduction

This study has grown over the past 15 years as a result of involvement in development work in several countries of the Third World, mainly in Latin America. This explains why the main bias behind this study is the desire to find practical and feasible solutions for the problems that the peasants in most countries of the Third World have to face. The great majority of these peasants are dominated and exploited by a relatively small class of large landowners. The United Nations and other international agencies have indicated that this situation is a major obstacle to the social and economic development of the countries of the Third World, particularly in Latin America. The land-owning elites generally spend their considerable earnings conspicuously and in ways highly detrimental to the national economies, rather than invest them in a manner that would stimulate development.[1] It seems that only a radical change in the large estate system would free economic resources presently monopolized by a small privileged group for personal consumption. Such change will at the same time free the energies of the peasants to participate in a national development effort that gives them a just share in the benefits. In order to bring about the needed radical change in the traditional estate system, as recommended time and again by the United Nations, plans have been made and laws have been promulgated in many countries. In most countries, the results have been highly disappointing.[2] In the meantime over the last decade, a whole literature has appeared on the reasons for the lack of success of development programs and projects that were undertaken in the context of the traditionally structured societies. The passive reaction of the peasantry to these development efforts have given the impression that the traditional peasant subculture or peasant mentality is a main obstacle for development. On the surface, this explanation seems appropriate, but once one gets more profoundly involved in peasant life and in efforts to stimulate them towards new possibilities, this explanation proves to be erroneous. Resistance to change of the peasants is mainly a reaction of self-defense against the resistance to change of the traditional elites which fear to lose their domination over the peasants. It appears that peasants can be mobilized quite well, if this is done to change the present status quo for a system under which peasants can reasonably expect effective improvements. This discovery and its consequences for action is the main theme of this book.

The way this discovery was made has been highly empirical and practical, often through some kind of involvement in the life of the peasants. Value judgments and other subjective factors have from the outset been an integral part of the study.[3] Some degree of identification with the peasants' lot was not only necessary to understand (in the sense of *verstehen*) their motivations, but was also a simple act of human solidarity with those who are repressed. This identification, however, does not seem to diminish the scientific value of the findings.

The risks of the methods can be compensated to a large extent by giving what has been called the natural history of our conclusions.[4] The present book is partly structured along the lines of this natural history. Based on historical evidence and some recent anthropological and sociological studies, it will be shown in the first chapter that peasant distrust and resistance to change in Latin America, rather than being a symptom of a natural or traditional incapacity and unwillingness to change, can be explained as the result of several ages of repression. Peasant resistance to the introduction of the large estate (hacienda) system in the past was violently crushed but continued to spring up again on several occasions. Only through the exercise of overt or covert repression of the peasants could the hacienda system establish and maintain itself, and thus create for the peasantry living under its sphere of influence what has been called the culture of repression or internal colonialism. As part of this system, the so-called patronage seems to be one of the means through which the landowners try to keep the peasantry under their domination.

In the second chapter, three cases are described where resistance to change and distrust of the peasants were encountered as an obstacle to the usual kind of community development efforts. In these cases, the implications of peasant distrust could be studied empirically, using the methods of participant observation and participant intervention.[5] Through these methods, I could watch and experiment with factors related to peasant distrust, and could discover gradually its good reasons and the fact that distrust can be turned into a mobilizing force for social change. The first field experience described took place in 1955 when I spent almost a year in a small village in El Salvador doing community development field work. In the effort to implement some community improvement projects, I found that the distrust of the peasants and their initial refusal to participate in the project was related to the fact that they lived under the hacienda system in a culture of repression. Their distrust proved to be justified. The changes introduced into the village were only piecemeal and the possibility for more substantial change was purposely blocked by the landowners and the government agencies controlled by them.

The second experience consisted of two years of community development work in Sicily (1959-1961), where conditions similar to those in Latin America prevailed. It was clear from the outset that the peasant distrust—called amoral familism by one scholar—was justified, facing the overwhelming control of the *mafia*. Through trial and error, I learned that this distrust could be overcome once the peasants had a chance to unite effectively and in concrete ways outside the sphere of influence and control of the *mafia*.

From the experience in Sicily, the feasibility of rallying people against the real obstacles to change, the traditional system, could be concluded. The possibility of organizing peasants effectively as part of community development against the interests that exploited them was studied more carefully during a few years of field visits to evaluate community development and similar projects in Mexico and Central America.[a]

However, a clear proof how peasant distrust and resistance to change can be turned into well-organized peasant action was the experiment carried out during a year of community development work in the Punitaqui area in Chile (1965-1966). Once peasant attention was focused and initial efforts were channelled against the forces of landlord control (and were clearly to the benefit of the peasants) enthusiastic participation resulted.

The three experiences described, in addition to a careful look at similar situations in some Latin American countries, suggest that the theories of Banfield, Foster and Erasmus about the resistance to change of the peasants are short-sighted. Resistance to change rather than being an inherent peasant characteristic and an impediment to development and change can be the beginning of effective peasant action for change. In fact, peasant distrust can be one of the most important promoters of change and development if it is utilized as a force that brings peasants together in a common struggle, opposing the traditionally vested interests of landlords and other repressive forces. The growth of several strong peasant organizations that were crucial in the promotion of radical change in some Latin American countries was a result of these forces, as will be described in Chapters 4 and 5.

The organizations dealt with are the agrarian movements in Mexico, Bolivia and Venezuela. Others are the regional peasant organizations in Peru (particularly in the Convención valley and in the Central highlands) and the peasant leagues in the Northeast of Brazil. Also, the violence occurring in Colombia and Guatemala as a result of the manner in which the traditional elite tried to maintain the status quo will be briefly described since it appears to have a radicalizing effect on the peasantry.

A large part of the material of these chapters regarding large-scale peasant organizations has been collected as a contribution to a study on the role of peasant organizations in the process of agrarian reform in Latin America, jointly undertaken by the International Labour Office and the Comité Interamericano de Desarrollo Agrícola (CIDA), of which I was in charge for almost three years from 1966.[b] The methods used during the collection of this material were only

---

[a]In that period, 1962-1965, a large part of the general ideas behind this book took shape. This was expressed in several articles (see bibliography), but particularly in a polemical article "Some Notes on Community Development and Rural Social Research," which appeared in *América Latina.*[6]

[b]Most of this material appeared in a CIDA document (no. UP-G5/071), published in 1967 under the title *On Peasant Unrest in Latin America*, partly also published in 1968 by CIDA's Mexican counterpart, Centro de Investigaciones Agrarias as *Los Movimientos Campesinos en Mexico*. Preliminary generalizations based on material have been presented and discussed at a meeting of CIDA study directors. ILO permitted me to present these generalizations as a paper to the Second World Congress of Rural Sociology that took place in August 1968 in Enschede, Netherlands.

to a small extent participant observation and participant intervention, but consisted mainly of interviews, conversations and consultations with peasant organization leaders and members all over Latin America. Experiences of one group were contrasted with those of another in personal conversations with leaders or in group discussions. Thus, learning and advising were intertwined, and a good deal of comparative insights could be obtained. Some of the main questions around which this operational research was focused are reflected in Chapters 4 and 5, but are more directly dealt with in Chapter 6. These are the questions *where, when* and *how* effective peasant organizations can be created.

In addition to overall peasant distrust and resentment, a number of specific conditions exist which seem to make a peasant organization feasible. These are the factors that practically all the described large-scale peasant organizations have in common: (1) modernizing influences that bring frustration rather than real improvements to the peasants; and (2) closeness to urban areas which enhances the chance of able leadership from within or support from outside. It will be shown that peasant organizations have been started where acute grievances existed. The availability of charismatic and uncorruptible leadership was essential to bring the peasants to united action regarding grievances and frustrations. In order to be effective at a later stage, the support of urban allies who could help to establish a regionwide organizational structure was needed.

The best way to utilize peasant distrust as a positive force was to engage the peasants in a struggle through organized action for their most basic demand: land. The approach used in response to the increasingly violent reactions of the large landowners against the growing peasant movements was an escalation of demands and tactics of struggle. How this was done by most existing organizations is described in the last part of Chapter 6.

Finally, in Chapter 7, the effects of the peasant movements as political forces will be evaluated, particularly highlighting the possibilities for future radical or revolutionary peasant action. It appears that practically all situations presently existing in Latin America, contain considerable revolutionary potential: (1) the merely repressive regimes maintaining the status quo are increasingly considered as illegitimate; (2) the regimes that have neutralized a strongly organized peasantry are creating new frustrations; (3) the populist regimes that try to introduce change, (but change not radical enough to satisfy the basic peasant demands) are creating uncertainty and high expectations with an explosive effect. The overall presence of distrust and resentment among peasants under the traditional hacienda system and the frustrating effects of modernization seem to make the peasants ready for militant organization as soon as they can find sympathetic and able allies to guide and support them.

The Revolutionary Potential of Peasants in Latin America

1 The Background of Peasant Distrust in Latin America

Historical Factors

The present situation and the potential for organization of the peasantry in Latin America has to be seen in the perspective of historical developments.

The colonial period brought forms of social organization to Latin America which persist in many areas. Although there is considerable variation from country to country and from region to region, on the whole, the social system in rural Latin America is characterized by the latifundia or the *hacienda* (*fazenda* in Brazil) system. The fertile valleys or coastal lowlands, during the precolonial civilizations cultivated by the indigenous groups, were transformed into large estates belonging to the conquerors and their heirs. In some areas, they were used for pasture, elsewhere for plantation agriculture. The indigenous peasantry was in part sent as cheap labor to the mines in which the conquerors were most interested, or were driven into subsistence agriculture on the mountain slopes if they did not want to work on the estates. Once a certain equilibrium was established by armed force, legal provisions were made in several countries to give the indigenous population minimum guarantees for survival. Regulations were issued which protected the remainder of indigenous *comunidades* from complete extinction. Several cases are known where recourse to such legal protection was in vain and where the peasants took up arms to defend their rights against usurpers. Mostly, such self-defense activities were countered by the armed forces of the landowners or the national army, and smothered in blood.[1] Sometimes, they reached such proportions that region or nationwide protest movements developed into a kind of internal war. The movement led by the Indian leader, Tupac Amaru, in the Andean Highlands at the end of the eighteenth century is a case in point.

After the end of the colonial epoch, the local white or mestizo elite in most of the Latin American countries expanded its wealth and power in an aggressive way, mainly at the cost of the indigenous peasants. Thus, the process of pushing back the indigenous peasant population towards more remote and even more barren agricultural areas was initiated. The I.L.O. report on indigenous peoples made the following statement.

With the advent of the republican form of government the existence of the remaining aboriginal communities was endangered by the fact that the substantive Latin American legislation, informed by the European doctrine of economic

1

liberalism, disowned the principle of corporate ownership of the land and refused to grant them legal status. This facilitated the alienation of communal land, either by purchase or by appropriation on the part of powerful landowners, with the result that many of the members of the *comunidades* became tenants or peons on the haciendas. Unfamiliar with the official language and bemused by a money economy, the Indians parted, often unknowingly, with land and water rights which had suddenly acquired a scarcity value.[2]

In Colombia, the first law calling for the division of communal lands belonging to indigenous peasants was promulgated in 1821. In Peru, Bolivar decreed in 1824 that all Indians were to be proprietors of their plot and that the comunidas had to be divided individually among their members, the surplus falling to the state in order to sell.[3]

In Mexico, the official bias was directed against the existence of the so-called *ejidos*,[a] which had enjoyed protection under the colonial rule. The weakening of the Indians as groups, through the introduction of the individualist tenure systems, resulted in their incapacity to resist the expansive tendencies of the large haciendas.[5] The agrarian struggle of the traditional system started in 1825, with an uprising of the Yaqui Indians in the state of Sonora.[6] More reactions came in 1834 in Ecatzingo in the state of Hidalgo, in 1836 in Oaxaca, and in 1840, the first signs appeared of what later became the "caste war" in the state of Yucatan. Between 1841 and 1844, there were several rebellions to defend the communal lands in the state of Guerrero, and later in Puebla and Oaxaca. In the central valley of Mexico, uprisings took place between 1846 and 1864, particularly in the San Louis Potosí area. The regenerating army in this region, consisting mainly of peasants who decided to obtain justice by their own effort, proclaimed in May 1849 the *Plan de Rio Verde*, a precursor of later land reform legislation.

In 1847 began the caste war in Yucatan which lasted until 1901. Sometimes, the revolts were against usurpations of land, on other occasions, against certain forms of taxation that were imposed.

In most countries, anticommunal legislation was enacted or confirmed during the second half of the eighteenth century. In Guatemala, such measures were taken in 1870. In El Salvador, the law of this type, promulgated in the same period, was called Law of Extinction of Ejidos and Indigenous Communities (Ley de Extinción de Ejidos y Comunidades Indígenas). In Mexico, new land tenure laws of 1835 prohibited civil and ecclesiastical corporations from possessing or administering land. This prohibition endangered the whole traditional system of collective ownership or use of the land since the *comunidades* and *ejidos* were regarded as corporate bodies.

[a]*Ejido* can be defined as commonly owned land, originally at the exit (the word ejido is claimed to come from the Latin "exitus") of a community, the extension of which was generally one *legua* (about three miles) or more, where the Indians could raise their cattle separated from that of the Spaniards. After the Revolution, the term was introduced in the land reform legislation of Mexico.[4]

A process of disintegration of the remaining *comunidades* began through the alienation, concession, sale and auction of their lands. More uprisings resulted in Mexico: in 1856 in the states of Michoacan, Queretaro, Veracruz, Puebla and Jalisco. Later, the social bandit Manuel Lozada became famous as the defender of the peasants in the western parts of Mexico until his death in 1873.[7]

In 1876 in Mexico, an Act was passed granting concessions to private companies for marking out large tracts of land in specified parts of the country, which made it possible to seize properties without registered titles. This led to the disappearance of still more *comunidades*. It has been estimated that nearly 2.273.000 acres of land belonging to *comunidades* passed into the hands of estate owners by the occupation and appropriation. The number and extent of the large estates increased and many of the former members of the *comunidades* and ejidos became peons on them.[8]

In 1877, another wave of revolts broke out in Queretaro, Hidalgo, Michoacan, Guanajuato and Guerrero. When the peasants tried to defend their land through legal process in Hidalgo, threats and assassinations were the response. After protests and petitions from at least 56 communities were in vain, the communist war broke out in that area and extended later into San Luis Potosi.[9] By 1910 in most of the states of Mexico, about 95 percent of the rural families were landless, while one percent of the population owned 70 percent of the arable land.

Likewise also in Bolivia, the new liberal legislation provoked a strong reaction from the local population. Thus, the Indian uprisings of 1869-1871 were the consequence of a decree of 1866 followed by a law in 1868 which declared all lands to be state property and obliged the Indian communities to pay heavy taxes or lose the right to their lands. This measure resulted in a significant loss of land (as well as lives) in the indigenous communities where the measure was enforced.[10] In 1895-96 and 1899, similar occurrences took place as a consequence of the so-called *Leyes de Exvinculación* which pretended to abolish communal property and introduce private ownership instead. Since Indian groups had no guarantees once their traditional structure was broken, they became easy prey of the extending latifundios.[b]

One study indicated that in Bolivia between 1861 and 1944, more than 2,000 peasant rebellions or movements occurred over land problems and against the imposed servitude.[12]

As in other Latin American countries, most of the resistance movements, since they were scattered and not organized on a large scale, were bloodily repressed. Only few of these rebellions became widespread and had a considerable national impact, e.g., the peasant movement led by Zarate Willka in 1898-1899 in the Bolivian highlands which helped a Liberal government come to power. However, after the change of regime, the promises of justice to the indigenous

---

[b]This process was going on as late as 1920 when a *comunidad* in Taraco was transformed into a hacienda by President Ismael Montes. The inhabitants were driven away by military forces under Montes' command.[11]

peasants were forgotten, the leader Willka assassinated and the peasant armies overcome by the government's army.

In the countries or areas with a smaller indigenous population, where relatively few comunidades existed, developments took place which for the peasantry during the nineteenth and twentieth century had effects quite similar to those suffered by the *comunidades*. Many peasants, either escaping from the repressive hacienda system (runaway slaves) or being pushed by the expanding estates into less accessible areas, had settled, as squatters, *conuqueros*, or *sitiantes* in marginal areas. Once these areas became valid, the estates often moved into them with property claims, dislodging those who had opened up the area and lived there as subsistence farmers. This process, which took place to some extent in the coastal areas of Peru, Colombia and Venezuela when plantations were created there, was particularly visible in Brazil. At times, this process was complicated by a crisis in the market of the plantation crops, sugar or cacao, for example, that had considerable repercussions on the labor market and thus on the situation of the marginal peasants.

Thus in the coastal belt of the Northeast of Brazil, after the few indigenous communities had been extinguished, the best lands were occupied in the colonial period by the rapidly extending sugar plantations (*engenhos*) which produced for the world market. The dryer inlands were occupied by large cattle ranches. When the traditional sugar estates could no longer effectively compete on the world market, a crisis occurred and many workers were dismissed. The abolition of slavery in 1882 was relatively painless for the landlords for this reason, particularly since they received indemnification for the slaves. The marginal areas, where some land of inferior quality was still available for subsistence farming, were soon occupied and peasants went farther westward into the remaining areas in the dry *sertao* region, where risks of severe drought existed. Many of them migrated to the South to find work in the newly created coffee estates or in the growing urban centres. The extension of the estates in the Northeast went on in spite of the decadence of the old *engenhos*, since modern sugar factories (*usinas*), built often with foreign capital, were introduced and the government took measures to protect the sugar industry. More and more land was taken up.

Since the number of independent subsistence peasants had increased considerably after the abolition of slavery, a stronger pressure on the marginal land that did not belong to the estates resulted. These peasants generally lived precariously, rather like permanent squatters (*sitiantes*). They formed a social stratum between the owners and workers of the estates and the fact that some estate workers could become independent by joining this group has been noted as a factor preventing the outbreak of revolts on the estates.[13] They enjoyed a minimum of economic independence, although they lived in the shadow of the neighboring estates. Coexistence was not very peaceful. The continuous extension of the estates made the life of this group increasingly difficult. Many of the *sitiantes* were dislodged and had to move farther away to the dry lands, the *sertaos*. It was particularly this group of peasants (rather than the workers or sharecroppers who formed part of the estates) who sometimes joined protest movements.

One of the factors that aggravated the already precarious land tenure situation in the marginal areas were the droughts that occurred at times in those areas. The drought of 1877-1879 in particular had a tremendous impact. The protest movements that resulted took the form either of small bands of rural bandits (cangaceiros), rebellious groups without a clear cause, or large-scale rebellions of fanaticos as occurred in Canudos (1893-1897)[c] and Contestado (1912).[14] These movements of fanaticos had religious and messianic overtones, but were partly a reaction to the increasing pressure on the land.[15] The religious movement headed by Father Cicero in the area of Juazeiro from 1872 onwards had a moderating influence. It tried to solve the basic issues of land tenure, against which the peasants reacted through the construction of a Holy City where many found work as artisans.[16]

The cangaceiros could be considered as an independent counterpart of the capangas, the private armies that the estate owners maintained from the time that they had to defend their estates from the expelled Indians who did not respect private property. These capangas often fought the family rivalries between the estate owners (fazendeiros) over boundaries or over the political control in a region. Sometimes, they made themselves independent from the estate owners and operated on their own account, as rebellious bandits, the cangaceiros.[d] Social banditry has been noted as one of the more primitive ways through which peasants have protested against their conditions.[18] This should be seen, however, against the background of the overall lawlessness existing in the rural areas where power imposed the laws at will. Although messianic movements, jacqueries or social banditry were not the most effective means to defend the peasants' fundamental interests in conserving their lost land, in view of the lawlessness imposed by the landed elites and educated classes, the peasant reaction seems understandable. It was extremely difficult to find an appropriate response to the violence with which alien systems of land use, property and economic activity were introduced.

In several cases where peasants got involved in the armed struggle between competing factions of the landed elite, or between specific caudillos, their participation seems to have been provoked in part by promises of justice or land reform. This was the case with the beginning struggle between Liberals and Conservatives in Colombia[19] and with the recruitment for some caudillo armies in

---

[c]The movement in Canudos became famous through the book of Euclides da Cunha, Os Sertaos.

[d]It was noted, however, that at times they all united against a common enemy, such as the famous Coluna Prestes, the armed column, headed by the Communist Party Leader Luis Carlos Prestes which operated in 1924-1926 in large areas of Brazil. Father Cicero and his movement supported the efforts to combat the revolutionary Prestes column, and tried, in vain, to use the campaceiros leader Lampiao for this purpose.[17]

Venezuela,[20] both in the later part of the last century. The peasants got very little out of such struggle, as in the case of Zarate Willka, in Bolivia, mentioned above, or the beginning stage of the Mexican Revolution, as will be shown later. The fact that the peasants were often utilized against their own basic interests says more about the clever domination by the landlord class than about the alleged ignorance of the peasantry.

Similar phenomena have been studied in other parts of the world, and show the same tendencies. In Sicily, for instance, in the course of the nineteenth century, peasant rebellions protested against a new landed elite that came up and drove from the estates the peasants who had expectations of benefiting from antifeudal reforms that were initiated in those days. Contrary to the *jacqueries* and brigandage of earlier days, the peasant movements became increasingly instrumental and well directed but even the strongly organized Fasci movement, starting in 1893, did not succeed in achieving a land redistribution. The new elite, related to the old one and intertwined with the Mafia, relied on force and corruption to counter the peasant movements. Many peasant leaders, starting their revolt as social bandits were assassinated, others were coopted by the Mafia and used by the elite in exchange for a good position in the dominant system to control the peasantry by violence.[21] The way the hacienda system in Latin America operates and maintains itself, including the violence and corruption, seems not to be essentially different from the ways the Mafia operates in Sicily.

On the whole, it is clear that the hacienda system which had been established in the rural areas of most of Latin America was enforced in circumvention of traditional law, and the rules of fair play. For that reason, the legitimacy of the new structure, the latifundia-minifundia complex, has remained questionable until today. In several countries, lawsuits concerning land property have been going on for many decades. Most of such lawsuits were lost by the peasant communities because they lacked funds to continue paying lawyers and other costs involved in the suit. Such cases were decided automatically in favor of the large proprietors. Resentment and a strong feeling of injustice remained alive among the peasants who had become serfs or workers on their former lands. Apparently, they conformed to the newly established order.

The summary of studies carried out in seven Latin American countries by CIDA emphasized the following.

Unquestionably, force has been used to maintain this social order. The numerous rural uprisings since the Spanish Conquest hardly give credence to the myth of a universally respected benevolent paternalism. But an equilibrium is no less real because it is maintained by arms. Not until the present century has the dominance of the landed class in rural Latin America been seriously threatened. Social revolutionary processes are threatening the old order throughout Latin America.[22]

Peasant Attitudes under the Hacienda
System: The Culture of Repression

Before analyzing the conditions for and growth of several peasant organizations, the general conditions of the peasantry living under the latifundia-minifundia complex or the hacienda system should be described, highlighting some of the points about which misunderstanding appears to exist. In the summary of former CIDA studies, it was emphasized

Plainly speaking, ownership or control of land is power in the sense of real or potential ability to make another person do one's will. Power over rural labor is reflected in tenure institutions which bind workers to the land while conceding them little income and few continuing rights.[23]

The CIDA studies show with a wealth of data the existence in Latin America of the latifundia-minifundia complex,[e] emphasizing that although this stereotype is oversimplified, it does not exaggerate reality.

Based on the CIDA data, a recent document of FAO's Indicative World Plan summarized that there are 8.700.000 landless peasants (agricultural workers) in Latin America, 5.300.000 peasants who own altogether 4 percent of the agricultural land (minifundistas), 7.000.000 small and medium farmers who own 56 percent of the land, and a group of 440.000 large landholders who have 40 percent of the land. The IWP document then pointed out

Furthermore the majority of the active rural population has little independent economic or political power, quite apart from the weakness inherent in the small size of their holdings, since the minifundia and to a certain extent also the medium-size holdings, are part of the latifundia-minifundia complex in which the latifundista or patrón is dominant.

The FAO document continues

The conquerors and the conquered have remained for four hundred years locked in the latifundia-minifundia complex, which gives little incentive for improvement of agricultural technology. . . . Many of the landowners have not been under economic pressure to raise productivity per hectare or per man. A great deal of the income generated in the agricultural sector has been transferred outside the (Latin American) region or gone into conspicuous consumption.[24]

The situation of most of the peasants who work under the hacienda system has been summarized by Thomas F. Carroll, who noted that only a small fraction of the workers is paid on a cash basis. Most of them work under a system

---

[e]It should be noted that the *fazenda* and *engenho* system prevalent in large areas of Brazil are included in this complex, but that the modernized plantation system existing in some areas of the Caribbean is not.

...in which the worker is paid in the temporary or traditional usufruct of a parcel of land and certain other privileges. In return, the *colono* must serve a specified number of days on the estate and fulfill other customary obgliations, such as making available members of his family for certain tasks in the field or in the owner's household. This system is often combined with sharecropping or with tenancy on a cash rent basis.[25]

It should be noted that in many cases, these conditions also prevail in what the CIDA summary called multi-family medium farm units.

There is considerable variety in the conditions of work of the peasants on the estates in the different countries. This system of servitude or semiservitude is called huasipungo in Ecuador, colonato in Bolivia and Central America, yana-conaje in Peru, inquilinaje in Chile, and similar kinds of obligatory gratis work are called cambao in Brazil. Such obligatory work consists of normal agricultural tasks on the land of the estate, but in many areas, it includes all kinds of services in the homes of the estate owners both in town or on the estate. Usually, in former days and occasionally until today in some countries, this includes the rendering of daughters for the sexual pleasures of the landlord. In areas where the role of the patron and of the peasants on his estate are well defined by tradition and have functioned for a long time, there is little open resistance from the peasants. However, the system easily lends itself to abuses and such instances cause a great deal of resentment. In order to check such resentment and prevent it from becoming open resistance, the status quo is maintained by severe sanctions. Minor errors or offenses of peasants are punished disproportionately.

A recent summary of CIDA studies noted that one of the tools of power is to create an artificial climate of uncertainty and insecurity among the peasants as a means for maintaining this power. Peasants continuously face not only the uncertainties of plagues and diseases, but also those imposed on them by the rural power elite. There are a number of institutional arrangements which instill in peasants the knowledge that they always live uncertain of where the next day's bread is to come from and uncertain of whether they will still have a job. The effect of this uncertainty and insecurity—occurring as they do at the margin of subsistence—is intimidation of the peasants. They are restrained from making demands—even when entirely justified—for fear of losing their slim livelihood. That the fear of losing everything is not imaginary has been proved on many occasions where the landowners imposed their will upon the peasants and made their power felt. This may be for economic reasons or just to keep the peasants in their place. One powerful landlord, an important politician in his country, had the homes of his resident workers burned down and used tractors to shut irrigation canals bringing water—without which nothing can be grown—to the workers' garden plots and posted armed guards to stop the workers from opening the ditches at night. This forced the workers to abandon their plots.[26] In Ecuador, complaints addressed to the leaders of workers' organizations testify to some of the physical punishment threatened or received by the Indians of the Altiplano.

Here are a few examples: burning the huts of the workers; giving an Indian worker on domestic duties 10 blows and putting him in irons for allegedly having taken some clothes; accusing Indians of stealing milk, sugar and toys and threatening to break their necks or to give them a beating.[27]

Many peasants suffer heavy economic losses through the imposition of punishment for real or alleged misdeeds. On one Ecuadorian estate, it was the practice to make the workers work off free of charge the penalty imposed upon them for alleged violations. This is enforced through taking from the workers personal belongings as pawns (hats, ponchos, utensils, etc.). The control is extremely severe and punishments are meted out freely by suppressing the wage payment for alleged violations or failure to work. The men are often abused by the foremen and overseers and their livestock damaged if it trespasses on the (unfenced) land of the landlord. The loss of an animal belonging to the owner and in care of the worker is counted at its market value against his wage. Since he cannot pay it off in cash, his belongings are taken from him (including his own livestock) and the value of the property confiscated is estimated at a low price.[28] Through such means, the peasantry is kept in a constant fear under a permanent threat of violence and a climate which the anthropologist Holmberg defined as culture of repression is created.

Holmberg and his collaborators of the Cornell University research team which studied a typical estate in the Peruvian highlands, found among the peasants who lived under the hacienda system an almost pathological mentality.

The Vicos manor serf suffered from a number of forms of fears—so many, and often so serious that we entertain some doubts as to whether the local subculture ever really worked out effective escapes from danger that permitted the serfs to enjoy a state of relaxation. In the most general terms of interpersonal interaction, the serf regards all human relationships as hostile, since they are basically power-orientated.[29]

The fears mentioned by Holmberg as present among the peasants were (1) fear of death by capital punishment; (2) fear of the pain of corporal punishment; (3) fear of incarceration; (4) fear of disapproval of the landlord; (5) fear of property loss; (6) fear of hunger; and (7) fear of the supernatural. It was noted that behavior of the serf peasants is often defined by the strongest of competing fears. A peasant whose animal is taken away by the estate owner will not complain since fear of patronal disapproval or even incarceration is stronger than fear of property loss or hunger. The whole complex of complementary or, at times, competing fears makes the peasants seek to avoid any danger and risk involved in contact with outsiders and new situations. The culture of repression reinforces itself through these fears, and makes the introduction of changes extremely difficult.

Many examples were given by the scholars of the Cornell-Vicos project to demonstrate that the peasants had sound reasons for their many fears.

Vicos serfs usually did not complain even when whipped and kicked for fear the patron would have them sent to jail in Carhuaz, which he did in fact to those who protested. On an adjacent manor, the operator persuaded several serfs to supply him and his companions with their daughters for sexual exploitation by holding the men in his manorial jail until they yielded, on at least one occasion.

And regarding the most repressive aspects:

In 1960 members of the Project witnessed the deaths of three serfs attached to a manor just across the river from Vicos. They were shot by a contingent of national police cooperating with the manor leasee, and five other serfs were hospitalized with wounds. This was not an isolated incident: the national capital city press openly reported several similar incidents during that year.

This shooting occurred when the peasants in question tried to agitate for measures on their estate similar to the reform programme successfully carried out in Vicos by the Cornell University team. Such rebellion was punished immediately. It indicates however a slumbering will to change deep under the apathy and conformism generally shown by peasants. About this conformism, Holmberg made the following observation

Serfs, like other subordinated groups, have worked out a feigned behavior to confound authority figures. Although possessed of an earthy sense of humor and great conversational ability, the Vicos serf forgot his picaresque good humor, his conversational sparkle and courtesy when he found himself before his patron or other Mestizos. Serfs presented themselves as the most foolish and incapable of beings.[30]

The exaggerated conformity and servility of the peasants in the Vicos estate and elsewhere in the haciendas of Latin America can be interpreted as a counterpoint element in the culture of repression. In societies where the predominant set of values is more or less imposed by those in power, conflicting sets of values may function as a kind of counterpoint. These conflicting values may be dormant and hardly noticeable, but they form a basis for consensus among repressed groups and are a potential threat to the stability and legitimacy of the predominant system as a whole.[31] The values conflicting with the dominant ones are expressed sometimes in folktales and legends that contain and protect elements.[32] Apparent passivity and the feigned laziness of the peasants on estates are a form of protest and resistance they seem to utilize since all other forms of protest are blocked by severe sanctions. The peasants, considered as inferior by the landowners and supervisors on the estate, as well as the Mestizo townspeople and government officials, can only preserve some form of self-esteem by picturing their superiors as boogeymen, who are to be distrusted as dangerous and contact with whom should be avoided. As was observed by one collaborator of the Vicos project

If contact were unavoidable, however, a kind of passive nonco-operation in the interaction situation would be adopted. If the Mestizo wanted him to work, the Vicosino would have to be instructed repeatedly in the same things. 'Dimwittedness' was the sanctioned mental state; lack of initiative and brightness its manifestation in behavior. Despite their fears, however, the Vicosinos were not entirely passive under the manorial system. Obliged to work three days a week without effective remuneration, they took what they could whenever possible. The agricultural custom of gleaning and the patterns of work rhythms aptly illustrate this opportunism. Anyone was allowed to glean the manor fields after harvest. This being the case, Vicosino peons engaged in the harvest generally left uncounted numbers of potatoes behind for the gleaners who followed. The manor thus lost a very large per cent of its harvest.[33]

Also for the Puno area in Peru, it was noted that the structural violence inherent in the prevailing social climate was supplemented by the outward subservience and conscious resentment of the peasants.[34] This is the way the peasants maintain a certain dignity, while at the same time submitting to the way of life imposed upon them. This situation is potentially explosive and at times when abuses become particularly acute, e.g., when an estate changes owners, the peasants may take vengeance. Fear of this always threatening vengeance, on the other hand, explains part of the harshness of the repressive attitude of the landlords.

The sociology of conflict indicates that mutual aggressiveness and expressions of hostility within underprivileged groups may serve as a safety valve to maintain the prevailing social system. The frequent homicides, often related to drunkenness, which occur among the peasantry in many Latin American countries can be seen in this light.[35] Feasts, traditionally organized among indigenous and mestizo peasant groups, where drunkenness and homicide occur with considerable frequency, may thus partly have a safety-valve function. These traditions are probably tolerated or even stimulated by the rural elite and local church authorities precisely for this reason. They neutralize the feelings of hostility and resentment which exists among the peasantry regarding their inferior and repressed status. It is for this reason that some peasant organizations include a campaign against alcoholism among their initial activities.

Only little difference exists in this respect between the situation of peasants who are serfs or workers on the estates and the peasants who own minifundia or who are members of the free comunidades. This difference is limited by the fact that although the independent peasants have some land and a certain freedom, they are often in many ways tied to the regional economy by forms of commercial exploitation which make them not much better off than the peasants on the haciendas. Gonzalo Aguirre Beltrán and other Mexican anthropologists have demonstrated that many indigenous communities lived under precarious conditions after they were despoiled of their best lands. The isolated areas where they withdrew are generally dominated by the white or *ladino* people of the commercial urban centres, *metropoli*, who keep the indigenous groups in debt-bondage and other forms of economic exploitation. The areas where this situation prevails were called refuge zones. Aguirre Beltrán distinguished several mechanisms of domination in the relationship between the *metropoli* and the refuge zones: (1) the racial segregation, which separates the white town dwellers from the peasants who are mainly Indian or mestizo with a strongly Indian influence; (2) political control which leaves the native peasants without any participation; (3) economic dependence through a monopolistic and monopsonistic control of the local market; and (4) unequal treatment of the peasant population in the supply of educational and other facilities and unequal access to justice.[36] On the whole, the members of small peasant communities live in a relationship of subordination to the rural elite, be they the large landowners of the area or the merchants and moneylenders.

A recent United Nations Report summarized the overall Latin American situation in which the peasantry both free and on haciendas lives as internal colonialism.[37] Gonzalez Casanova and Stavenhagen have noted that internal colonialism arose as a result of the expansion of the capitalist economy during the second half of the nineteenth century, accompanied by the ideology of economic liberalism, as a new form of colonialism.[38] That the situation of internal colonialism was never completely accepted is clear from the way the hacienda owners felt they had to repress or terrorize the peasants of their estates or of surrounding communities. The few cases summarized from CIDA studies above and the findings of the Vicos study team are indicative. The resistance of the peasants, however, was on the whole unsuccessful, as discussed below.

It should not be felt, however, that even in the nineteenth century the *Sierra Gamonal* (owner of a hacienda in the highlands) constituted a stable, traditional all-powerful, landed aristocracy. In the first place, Indian unrest and resistance against land encroachment never ceased. Life in the Sierra was closer to the United States frontier relations with its Indians than is generally supposed. The main point about this Indian resistance is that it was largely sporadic, unorganized, and 'conservative.' This is, it had no revolutionary goal of remodeling society, but only of protecting or attempting to take back traditional landholdings.[39]

In large areas of Colombia, Venezuela and particularly Brazil, a similar frontier situation prevails. The latifundio system was here created not at the cost of existing indigenous *comunidades*, but by appropriating large virgin areas and evicting the squatters, *conuqueros* or settlers who had been cleaning and cultivating small plots in those areas.

The establishment of cacao *latifundios*, particularly in the Ilheus region of Bahia, still the major cacao producing area of Brazil, was accompanied by the ruthless 'extermination' of small landholders and cacao growers often through violence and fraud and it is said that traces of these practices are still found today.[40]

13

Fights and violence over land was reported by historians from most areas of Brazil, particularly in the period when they were opened up for large-scale commercial agriculture.[41]

It seems that the resistance of peasants against this process was even more scattered and piecemeal than the resistance of the *comunidades*. While the latter had a good deal of cohesion on their own account, there existed fewer horizontal ties among the peasants in more recently opened areas. They were mainly migrants, in part probably former slaves, and there was among them little of the kind of solidarity and security that existed in the indigenous *comunidades*. It may well be that for this reason the peasants in those areas could be dominated more easily by the large landowners. Once the latter controlled land and other resources in a specific area, the only way for the peasants to have some kind of security was complete submission to the landlord as a *patron*. Ties to the all-powerful master had to be strong, since they were the only channels to the outside world for the peasants. They were completely at the mercy of the *patron*.

Descriptions of the situation in the haciendas of Latin America indicate that generalizing is risky. There are cases where the relationship between the landlord and his peasants is warmly paternalistic, but elsewhere the relationship has been characterized as blatantly exploitative. As a characteristic for the exploitative kind of relationship in the colonization area of Yungas in Bolivia, it was noted that in such cases the landlord rarely served as a godfather to the children of the peasants.[42] It can be seen in many cases, however, that even if the landlord serves as a godfather to the children of peasants, this is often more a means to tie them to him so that they can be more easily exploited and dominated. The peasants themselves seem to have little awareness of this subtle form of domination. Particularly in the more isolated haciendas, or those that maintain a tight control over their subjects, people accept their situation, practically forced to make the best of it. Charles Loomis, who studied with his collaborators some hacienda and adjoining communities in the area of Turrialba in Costa Rica, introduced the term patron-configuration for this mentality and defined this as "an imminent tendency for people in both religious and lay matters to feel more secure if important decisions are handled by people with authority."[43]

In the course of their investigations, Loomis and his collaborators discovered the existence of different classes through sociometric techniques, but they did not study the quality of those differences.[f] Little or no attention has been given, e.g., to the condition of distrust and suspicion[46] that was encountered by the researchers and was demonstrated also by the fact that the majority of the people did not respond to the extension service existing in the region. Loomis probably did not look for counterpoint elements in the system, since his main interest was in the prevailing structure,[g] although they noted its implications:

[f]They discovered in Attiro, a labor class belonging "to the 'proletariat' class in a Marxian sense," a "skilled supervisory" class and a "proprietary" class,[44] each class constituting a "subsystem of interaction."[45]

[g]An indication of Loomis and his collaborators' preoccupation with the status quo may be found in their statement on the function of the social status and communication structure.[47]

In all societies, social status and related prestige are rewards for potential service, and are supposedly in relation to the contribution made by the individual or group according to the norms and ends of society. This relationship is basic to cooperation. In fact, probably the most effective way to destroy cooperation is to reward those who, according to the norms of society or the group, are the least effective or the most destructive. Of course, in noncommunistic societies, the wealth resulting from the contribution of one generation may carry over to another.

Other forms of ascribed or inherited status may depend less upon the individual contributions and the esteem attached to role performance than to the manner in which the customs regulate the distribution of privileges and status. Nevertheless, whether a society relies for its motivation more on achievement or more on ascription, one of the important functions of status is to assure recruitment of competent people for positions of responsibility. Variations in social status also provide a means whereby those with high status can be made accountable and responsible for the welfare of many.

Later another advantage of well-defined social status differences is mentioned: "This reduces the uneasiness and anxiety which could arise from not knowing what to expect from persons of either inferior or superior rank who are not in one's family or friendship group."[48] A similar statement was made by Loomis' collaborators, Leonard and Clifford:[h]

Large families, poor health conditions, low incomes, little education, and a lack of a conception of education as a status-elevating device, all contribute toward perpetuating the situation in which the laborere finds himself. He sees himself as the ward of the patrón, who, like the Good Father, will take care of his children. This concept is strongly imbedded in the thinking of the people, and is reinforced by the attitude of the administrative elite. 'We need peons,' said the owner's son, 'not degrees or diplomas.'[50]

Some authors have characterized the form of domination existing in the hacienda system as a patronage or clientele system.[51] Patronage, clientele, following or dependency has been defined by Galjart as "a dyadic contract between social unequals, according to which the socially higher ranking person dispenses protection in exchange for the political support and prestige given by the lower ranking party."[i]

One could easily doubt the appropriateness of the term patronage, as defined by Galjart, for the whole complex of patron-worker relationships under the haci-

---

[h]Los símbolos de clase funcionan para evitar confusión y conflicto entre los miembros de la sociedad, a la vez que limitan la posibilidad que tienen de cambiar su posición social.[49]

[i]Later, Galjart offered a slightly different definition. "The patron-client relationship can be

enda (or fazenda) system. As one specialist on Brazil indicated, this relationship was essentially economic and highly exploitative, although it had some other elements.

It involved a sense of *noblesse oblige* and paternalism on the part of the employer towards the worker which had survived out of the paternalism of slavery and the monarchy. On the part of the worker it involved a sense of loyalty to the patrão.[53]

Patronage in the sense of protection and favor-supply seems to be only one aspect of the hacienda system, and not the essential characteristic. This comes out even in the description of the Brazilian patronage system given by Galjart.[54] First, he portrayed a rather idyllic type of rural life before the 1930s in which the landlord, if his peasants were a true following (clientele) to him, gave a variety of favors, including an occasional gift or a trousseau, in which peasants received some protection and in which possibilities of upward mobility existed for those peasants who had good relations with their masters. That another side of the picture existed in the old days did not escape Galjart as comes out in his remarks that a conflict of peasants with their landlord could "cost them their land,"[55] or in what he described in a footnote about the landlords' power, that shows itself in a variety of ways.

. . . in wages paid in tickets which could only be used in the shop on the fazenda, instead of in money; in the purchase by the owner of the harvest of his sharecroppers against lower than prevailing prices; in low wages and high rents; in oral contracts of short duration; in the obligation imposed on sharecroppers to work a number of days per week for the owner, mostly for lower than prevailing wages, sometimes for no wages at all; in the simple swindle with weight and measurements. An important result of the fact that the peasants lived on the fazenda was that the owner to some extent could manipulate their social contacts; a visitor whom he did not like was not admitted.[56]

In another context, Galjart observed how landlords in Brazil before 1964, when people enjoyed theoretically certain civil rights, could maintain their control and patronage by organization of the voting and expulsion of workers who became members of unions. If things would become difficult, the influential landlord would receive support from the police or the army.[57]

Altogether it seems that, although idyllic aspects of patronage may have existed in the past, they were disappearing as a result of the entrance of alternatives. The landlords, facing modernization and competing influences among their peasants, showed their true face by harshly punishing nonconformity of peasants.

That the term protection in Galjart's definition of patronage is somewhat out of place comes out further in his own description of how patronage or the patronic syndrome grew in some areas in Brazil. Among the factors which contributed to the growth of patronage were: (1) the fact that large tracts of land were granted to entrepreneurs with monetary resources who then dislodged the squatters, transforming them into dependent workers; and (2) small landowners had to seek protection of one big owner against the danger of being dislodged by other big landowners.[58] The situation described by Galjart was clearly an imposition by the rich upon the poor, who then had no choice but to conform to this situation. Protection was enforced loyalty. One wonders if the application to this situation of the term patronage, as defined by Galjart is not a form of euphemism, introduced in order not to use such terms as exploitation, repression or domination.j If one wants to utilize the term patronage for the hacienda system, it seems necessary to qualify it as exploitative, repressive or authoritarian patronage, indicating that there is little voluntariness on the side of the client in his relation with the *patron*.

It is quite unlikely that the case of the Japanese farmer and his sharecropper living in the place where Galjart[60] did his fieldwork in Brazil (between whom "in spite of the exploitation, relations are rather pleasant ") is typical for the hacienda system in Latin America or Brazil as a whole. It has been indicated that there were an increasing number of factors that interfered with the idyllic picture of patriarchal benevolence if this had existed at all. The fact that many large proprietors were absentee owners who left the management of their estate(s) to an administrator with whom the peasants had no emotional ties is one factor. The increasing possibilities that peasants get some kind of facilities, such as medical help or school education for their children through government programs, made them less dependent on the *patron*. There was also a decrease in personal contact between landlord and peasants because many traditional estates became transitional through concentration of ownership, some degree of rationalization of the production, or change of ownership.[61]

A particularly important factor in some areas of Brazil, is the fear of the landlords in the face of the possibility of representative peasant organizations. Many landlords react to this possibility even before it appears, in such a violent way that idyllic aspects of his relation with the peasants, if it existed, disappear. CIDA reported several cases of violent and criminal acts by landlords that made it more than clear to the peasants that he was not their protector.[62] Particularly, the employment of private police, the *capangas*, increased the hostilities between landlords and peasants that started to occur for various reasons.[63]

However, some elements of patronage, as defined or noted by Galjart, may have remained: the upward mobility offered to those few who were outstanding

jJuliao noted how the use of certain terms has implications for the subject one is dealing with. Specific words may have an emotional impact while other words, indicating the same thing do not. Thus, the term peasant, *campones* was not used in the Brazilian press, with the exception of the leftist periodicals. In the legislative assembly of the state of Pernambuco, the deputee Juliao was asked to use a less aggressive word such as ruricola to indicate the countrymen.[59]

among their peers, and who otherwise might have become leaders of resistance. Such peasants could become overseers on the fazendas or even *capangas*.

The more the traditional patronage system felt itself endangered by modernizing influences, education, roads, cheap and easy transportation and other means through which the peasants could broaden their horizon, the more repressive the system became.[k] This comes out in one, possibly extreme, case of estate regulations which prohibited workers from the following activities.

1. carrying arms of any type;
2. drinking aguardente or any other alcoholic beverage;
3. playing cards or any other game;
4. spending their free time anywhere except on the property;
5. hunting or allowing strangers to hunt;
6. fighting with their neighbors or anyone else;
7. attending sick friends;
8. holding a dance without the permission of the owner;
9. spreading gossip;
10. feigning illness to avoid work; and
11. raising their children without learning to read and write.

In addition, anyone who does not comply has twenty-four hours to leave.[64]

If in the definition of patronage emphasis is laid on the elements of protection, it should also be stressed that such patronage is only one element in the overall traditional hacienda system, and that one of the main functions of patronage then seems to be to cover up blatantly exploitative elements in this system. This becomes particularly clear in the use of the modern forms of patronage, the channeling of government services to peasants.

While on one hand the reaction of the landlords to modernizing influences, undermining the isolation and stability of the hacienda system, was an increase of repression, on the other hand, such modernizing forces could often be used and controlled in such a way that they function to consolidate the landlord's position.

Some landlords have attempted to strengthen their power over the peasants through favors distributed to them through a clientele or patronage system, as a reaction to the appearance of representative peasant interest groups, competing with the landlords monopoly. Utilizing and channelling through the traditional patronage system some facilities supplied by the government, the emergence of new peasant leadership was hindered. One observer noted the following.

---

[k]One very striking example of the terror was given by the Uruguyan journalist Edgardo Carvalho in his introduction to Francisco Juliao's book, *Escucha Campesino*. The capangas were reported to have branded a peasant who had joined the peasant leagues with the initials of his landlord before the eyes of his wife and children.

Had 'revolutionary-type' organization developed influence in this area, it would probably have established block and subzone groups which would have enlisted recruits and galvanized them into action. But traditional type politics in this subregion of northeast Brazil minimized the importance of organization. Instead, more informal relationships, which include personal and kinship relations and granting of personal favors in return for political support have been relied upon. It is apparent that certain local leaders discourage popular participation, because this could threaten the existing status quo politics.[65]

For that reason in different parts of the northeast of Brazil, community improvement projects have been promoted by local estate owners or political leaders related to them by family or friendship ties. Such improvements using public funds were introduced as "favors" obtained by the patron through his political influence at the national level, and then distributed to the community or communities of his clientele with or without promoting self-help activity at the village level. Even if self-help activity is promoted, care is taken that this activity is kept within certain limits and under the patron's control. Stimulating and training vigorous community leadership is avoided or prevented. Only the loyal community members and local leaders are stimulated and used to control a willing clientele.

Paulson noted about the landlords' attitude

In short, 'reforms' that have the obvious political impact of increasing potential influence of various groups in the community could not but imply a diminution of his own prestige. The traditional leader's rule-of-thumb guide must be highly pragmatic: support an action unlikely to have consequences that challenge his own position; oppose any action that seeks to redistribute power or prepare persons who will recognize that the only means to enlarge their opportunities is by changing the status quo.[66]

Paulson also came to the following conclusion.

Thus an effective development programme cannot overlook the need for changing the structure of society in the area, which inevitably involves it with potentially volatile political factors. The fear of these political dimensions associated with structural change is a main reason for the marginal impact of many development programs on the community.[67]

This seems to be an exemplary case where landlords tried to keep their peasants in line through the distribution of favors, out of fear of competing groups that offered not only some benefits, but the overthrow of the whole traditional system.

Since the peasant is heavily dependent on the relationship with his patron and on the degree of favor he enjoys in this relationship, the horizontal solidarity among the peasants tends to be weak. It is clear that in order to create viable and representative peasant organizations, the link with the patron has to be changed drastically, if not broken. In this sense, the introduction of new forces from which the peasants can gain some security, benefit or favor, such as community development projects, cooperatives, credit societies, can have an important function to break the overdependence of the peasants on the patron. But an important condition for the effe tiveness of these agencies is that they are and remain outside the control of the traditional rural elite, which is often not the case. It is understandable that wherever community development projects and similar efforts are promoted by agencies of a government that is controlled by the traditional elite, the peasants will show the kind of distrust and resistance to change that many development efforts seem to encounter. A great deal of literature exists on resistance to change of the peasants and a number of concepts, to be dealt with in following chapters, have been introduced regarding this topic. The terms amoral familism, the image of the limited good and encogido syndrom have been created to explain or describe the distrust as a general characteristic of the traditional peasants.

If one takes into account the ample description of the existence and frequency of resistance to change and related phenomena in traditional communities, one might be inclined to see development and organizational efforts in the rural areas as a hopeless undertaking. Only few scholars seem to have studied these phenomena while trying to overcome their impact in a pragmatic way. This is probably due to the bias among many social scientists that action disturbs a scientific and objective view. A few policy-oriented social scientists and development workers of national and international agencies have had experiences which have enriched the more theoretical knowledge. It seems that there is not a characteristic and generalized peasant mentality which is basically different from the mentality of other people. Peasants are apathetic or organizable under certain circumstances—circumstances which should be seen in their historical context.

Some observers give the impression that characteristics such as distrustfulness, lack of innovative spirit, fatalism, family-orientedness, dependence on government, and lack of cosmopolitan orientation are part of a generalized subculture of peasantry,[68] without stressing the fact that such a subculture may be determined by culture of repression as it prevails in the rural areas in most of Latin America.

**Case Studies of Peasant
Distrust and Its Functions**

A Field Experience in Central America:
The Rationality of Distrust

That peasant distrust is not merely a negative reaction to development efforts but that it is related to a justified resentment towards the overall repressive system under which peasants live was carefully studied firsthand during an experiment in peasant organization that I was able to carry out in a Central American village. During that experiment, it could be seen that distrust was the main motivation for lack of participation of peasants in community improvement efforts. This distrust can be overcome through the application of a community development approach to win the peasants' confidence. However, the representatives of the predominant social system, the officials in the service of a government dominated by the large hacienda owners, were unwilling to apply consistently these community development techniques which are designed to stimulate active peasant participation. They blocked the experiment that was carried out and thus confirmed the peasants' distrust and feeling that minor changes did not mean a real and significant improvement in their situation.

The methods used in this intensive field experience were participant observation supplemented gradually by a great deal of participant intervention. Through empathy with and active involvement in the life of the peasant community, I could become well acquainted with the implications, psychological as well as social, of peasant distrust.[1]

Thanks to a UNESCO scholarship, I spent the year of 1955 as part of a team of volunteers,[a] assisting the Administración del Valle de la Esperanza in El Salvador in its community development efforts.[3] This Salvadorean government agency had already been working for some years in the region, mainly concerned with reconstruction and development made necessary by a severe earthquake in 1951. (The Administración was an autonomous organization which coordinated the efforts of the divisions, each of which represented one of the ministries of the country, like public works, agriculture, education, health, etc. These divisions worked, however, rather independently within the structure of the Administración.)

Initially, I worked some time as a member of the team in the small town

---

[a]The organization which sent volunteers of several nationalities to assist government agencies in certain community development projects was the American Friends Service Committee.[2]

where the Administración had its headquarters, assisting the director of the Agricultural Department in activities such as the establishment of a poultry-raising cooperative. This cooperative was a typical example of betting on the strong, since the credits given to it were managed by a board headed by the two richest merchants of the town. This pattern in which the wealthy citizens dominate new organizations created with help of the Administración has also been noted in the region by Carlos Campos Jiménez.[b]

The fact that smaller farmers also participated in this cooperative was to a great extent due to the fact that they had to conform to the pressures of the few bigger ones, who were at the same time money-lenders and merchants, and thus could easily assume control of the cooperative. The volunteers team was not in a position to influence this situation.

One of the other efforts in which the team assisted the Administración was to start a sanitation program in a nearby small village, San Luis, with the active participation of the villagers. This project was the construction of a drinking pipeline of several kilometers from a well in the mountains to the center of the village. Previously, the people had used the contaminated water of some wells in the nearby riverbed. In a public meeting called by one of the directors of the Administración, the villagers had more or less agreed to do the manual labor, while the Administración would contribute the pipes, other equipment and technical supervision. However, the villagers did not actually take up their assigned work when the project was initiated. This puzzled both the Administración and the voluntary team. When visits to the village made in a jeep by the team to convince the population did not change this reluctance to work, it was decided that I should go and live in San Luis permanently in order to find the reasons for this attitude and possibly help get the project under way.

It was quite obvious that one of the first things I had to do when going to live in San Luis was to win the confidence of the people. The fact that I was a foreigner, (not placed socially) and especially the fact that I went to live in a hut like that of everybody else in the village (something Salvadorean upper- and middle-class people generally do not do) helped to gain the confidence of my neighbors.

It seems to me not quite right to speak about techniques in order to describe the way confidence was won. I relied mostly on a general human sympathy for the villagers, and used the following approach.

---

[b]Jiménez[4] describes some community organization efforts. As negative factor he mentions, among others, the authoritarian attitude of certain local leaders, stiff egoism, delay in the initiation of the reconstruction and distrust, and the fact that the Comites Pro-Reconstrución, formed in each town on the initiative of the Administración, only represented the economically upper and upper-middle class.[5] The community organization was especially difficult in población 4, where the Comité was practically imposed by one local leader who manipulated a reduced group of persons to that effect[6] Campos Jiménez describes a small town: "the great majority of its inhabitants are not owners of land, and they work as 'peones' in the big estates in the area, the owners of which live in other towns."[7]

1. It was essential to accept the people as they were, and not take an educator's attitude. So I enjoyed being taught about local practices in many fields. I very seldom criticized their primitive (as they called it themselves) way of life, and I was always eager to find something to admire, for instance, when I visited their houses. Thus, even my lack of fluent Spanish in the beginning was a help.
2. To share, first passively and gradually more actively, the community life: sitting together with the men in the center of the village or with one of the families at home, playing guitar and singing, telling endless stories about Holland or listening to the local musicians and storytellers. I also participated in fiestas, funerals, hunting parties, etc., so that the villagers got the feeling, and started to say: "He belongs to us."
3. To share the simple meals of a neighbor family, especially during the first weeks, and to insist on eating the same things in order to learn about their food habits.
4. Contrary to the habits of most local government officials, to keep every promise or appointment, and if this was impossible, to carefully explain why and apologize. Also contrary to what was usual, I never carried any weapon except the machete, big knife, that the peasants themselves use, and I always directed myself to the villagers with the polite form *Usted*, unless I knew them very intimately, while government agents generally use *tu*.

The village of San Luis consisted of 78 cottages, mostly straw huts and, for the rest, mud-walled houses, spread along a dirt road where only jeeps could pass in the dry season. This road connected the village with two small towns, in one of which the headquarters of the Administración del Valle de la Esperanza, the regional development agency, was established. This small town was also the municipal center to which San Luis belonged. Although the difficulty in passing the road made the village rather quiet and isolated, the distance to the municipal center was not far and could be walked in less than an hour, making frequent visits easy for the inhabitants.

There were between 400 and 450 inhabitants in the village during the time that I was working there in 1955. The fluctuations were due to a few births and deaths, as well as to people (especially the men) moving out to the plantation regions in the coffee harvest season. Some of them came back to their family, some did not.

There were 78 families, 70 of which were classified as poor by the Administración. The families that were not poor owned some land (5 HA or a little less) that was just enough for subsistence farming. However, even these families all had income from other sources, such as a son or unmarried brother working in some kind of job in one of the nearby small towns. The 70 families classified as poor had very little land or none at all, and were dependent for the most part on income earned from work as agricultural or unskilled manual laborers.

It is well known that much of the land in El Salvador that is now in the hands of the large owners formerly belonged to the communities. The "Ley de Extinción de Comunidades" (1881), the "Ley de Extinción Ejidos" (1882) and other liberal reform laws required the distribution of communal land to individual members of the community. As a consequence to these laws, in a few years most people through the free play of forces had lost the land they should have possessed to a small group of the economically strongest people.

Such things had also happened in San Luis. Some of the older people in the village still remembered the time that each family was living decently with enough land for everybody, and that little by little the land had to be given up to the one big landlord who finally owned practically all the lands of San Luis.

This landlord lived mostly in San Salvador, the capital of the country. He and his manager were typical patrones. Within the limits of the hacienda system, however, they did not treat their villagers badly and were respected for this reason. The manager enjoyed considerable respect among the villagers because they depended on him for work, if there was any. The simple fact of being able to give people at times the opportunity to work gave the manager great power over the villagers. This power was constantly emphasized, however, by the conspicuous carrying of a pistol. Sometimes, he impressed people by showing how well he could use his weapon by shooting birds. Since he participated at times in the social life of the village, the people did not express dislike for him.

The land of the hacienda was very extensively cultivated. Most of it was rather hilly and used for grazing. The milk that was produced went to the nearby towns in the form of cheese. Some of the land was rented to those villagers who could afford to take the risk of cultivating land not belonging to themselves. The villagers told me that the rents were not exorbitant.

In general, the hacienda did not provide much work to the villagers, which obliged most of the men to look for work elsewhere. They usually went as seasonal workers to the coffee plantations outside the area or to the construction sites of the Administración in the surrounding towns (where practically half of the houses had been destroyed during the 1951 earthquake). There was little overt hostility towards the local landlord in San Luis. People did resent, however, that he did not take care to exploit his lands better, so that they would have more work.

On the other side of the river that passed San Luis, lived some *colonos* of the hacienda, a type of agricultural laborer who has to be ready to work for the hacienda at all times, since he is completely dependent on it. His house and a little plot of land were made available to him in exchange for his total availability. These people lived too far away to belong to the village. The San Luiseans distinguished themselves, as free men (who may work or stop work at will), with pride, from these slaves who had sold themselves and their families for life to the hacienda.

Apart from the contrast between the world of the landlord and that of the rest of the villagers, there was not much differentiation or stratification among the peasants of San Luis. Notwithstanding the fact that some of them had enough land to support themselves more or less independently and most of them had little land at all, they all strongly felt that they lived in the same poverty.

From the first days of my participation in village life, it was quite clear that the main quality of life in San Luis for the peasant class was suffering, or as people themselves called it: tristeza. Both the villagers and the officials of the Administración expressed their amazement about the fact that I cared to share this kind of life for some time.

The differences between those who had practically enough land to support (very modestly) their family and those who had hardly any or no land at all, disappeared in the face of this general suffering from insecurity. The little security of those better-off was always being threatened by the dangers of sickness and plagues (a year before I came to the village, a chicken plague had killed off all the chickens), indebtedness, government interference, violence, and the growing family which meant the need of splitting up the small plot of land among several sons.

When after a few weeks, I felt that I was accepted within the community, I started to try to find out the reasons for the people's negative reaction to the promises of the government officials. This could be done in many personal talks, especially in the mornings when most of the men came together to relax in the center of the village. Thus, I discovered that they suspected that the water system would, in the end, not lead up to the village, for the benefit of everybody, but would go to the *hacienda*. Although the speeches of the officials made them inclined to believe and hope for the best, they had been disappointed so often that in spite of some initial enthusiasm, they maintained their distrust. The existing resentment expressed itself in all kinds of statements that I either heard or overheard. The main tendency of these arguments as regards the voluntary work can best be expressed more or less in the words of the villagers. They would say:

Why are officials of the Administración earning twenty times as much as we do and tell us to work for nothing?

The government obviously has lots of money. Look at the wages of higher officials, cars and trucks running around all the time. See all the construction that is taking place in the towns, etc.

When they don't want to pay us our modest wage, certainly somebody is filling his pockets with part of the money that is supposed to go for this (sanitation) project

It isn't true that we can afford to do voluntary work because we are often unemployed. We need to hang around in case some odd job comes up somewhere

You cannot work if you don't earn money for food. How can government officials know that working with an empty stomach is bad for your health and increases the risk of becoming sick, which would be disastrous in our condition.

(Agricultural workers get habitually besides their wage of ₡ 1.25 (0.80 dollar cents) a day, a meal consisting of *tortillas* and some beans; workers in government constructions get ₡ 2.–, and no such meal)

Why should we pay taxes on the small piece of land or the ox cart we happen to have and besides that, work for nothing in order to have the government bring some improvement to our village.

When I tried to see the Administración through the eyes of the villagers, I found this feeling justified. Even the lowest paid government workers, such as the drivers of the jeeps who spent many hours a day just waiting, earned ₡ 6.– to ₡ 8.–, which was several times the wage the agricultural laborers received. With the higher officials, there was often still more conspicuous waste of time as evidenced by the many hours I had spent with some of them just chatting in their offices. If there is any value at all in the well-known stereotype of people in tropical countries being lazy, it was certainly more true for those officials, than for the peasants, who are always blamed for it.

In addition to this, it was well known among the villagers that most of the higher officials of the Administración were either large landholders themselves or related to them through family ties. The government officials who came to the villages for agricultural extension or community development activities were always armed with a pistol, a factor which did not contribute to winning the people's confidence, and which only emphasized the rigidity and potential instability of the rural power structure. Since the peasants could not openly disagree with or protest against the government officials, they feigned agreement with what was proposed, but expressed their opposition by not showing up to do the voluntary work. An additional factor in this passive refusal to collaborate was found to be the simple fact of undernourishment from which many peasants suffered between the coffee harvest seasons. This resulted in a half-conscious economizing of physical energy and feelings of insecurity and apathy. (As an experiment, I tried to live for several weeks on the same diet as my neighbors and rather soon found myself suffering from some of the same phenomena, recalling former experiences of undernourishment during World War II in the Netherlands.)[8]

Some of the psychological factors related to undernourishment, which clearly formed a barrier to cooperation, were the feelings of powerlessness and inferiority that accompanied it. The obsession of a screaming stomach, completely occupied by getting fed, may explain why the villagers said that they live just like animals.

I found that sometimes the dehumanizing effects of malnutrition were even stressed by some programs of the Administración. The home economics demonstrators came to the village to tell people how to improve their diet in order to be healthier, however, without giving them the means to do so. No need to say that such programs often worked against fostering goodwill for the Administración. It was another proof how middle-class people, from an urban environment, trained in rather sophisticated forms of social work, are often out of touch with village life.

It was not only undernourishment that made people feel inferior and un-capable of real self-help. The detrimental effect of unemployment on people's self-esteem should not be underestimated. The fact that they spent most of the year just idly waiting, in the hope that somehow somebody would give them work, had a considerable impact on their personalities. This was further aggra-vated by the fact that they had to take whatever came up and that they had no rights at all, since there were so many people available who could take a job if they would not do so. These factors created strong feelings of hostility, towards better-off classes and towards society as a whole. This form of aggression that was turned inward was one of the reasons for much of the drunkenness for which the area was ill-famed. The most distressing fact was that people them-selves knew so well the impact of the three above-mentioned factors, and other problems on their life.

From the intimate reactions of people, it became quite obvious that under a surface of apathy, indifference and distrust, there was a strong resentment, if not hatred, directed towards the powerful, which created a climate of slumbering explosiveness. Government officials warned me often about the dangers of living among the peasants.

Peasant unrest had existed in El Salvador since the creation of large latifundia but became particularly strong after the liberal government (1881-1882) promul-gated the decrees of extinction of communities and ejidos. In 1885 and 1898, resistance movements against the despoliations occurred. In the later movement some judges who had been helpful in dividing the lands of the villages were severely punished by cutting off their hands. The most violent reaction was the uprising of 1932, during which more than 60,000 peasants with primitive weap-ons revolted against the prevailing system. In the few following days, a great number of peasants were killed. Leftist political groups claimed that there were 30,000 people killed and the government that there were only fifteen thousand.[9]

Many years after this massacre, the rural areas were still under severe control by the *Guardia Nacional*. It often happened that quiet gatherings of the peasants for social purposes in the center of their community were broken up when the arrival in the neighborhood of a police patrol, generally three heavily armed men, was announced by someone. In the rural areas, it was legally forbidden to gather in one place with more than five persons. The formation of peasant asso-ciations is legally prohibited.[10]

Interestingly enough, it seems that the fear of the traditional elite for any form of change is one of the tension-creating factors. While the massacre of 1932 brought about a considerable deactivation of political participation or a depoliti-zation of the peasantry,[11] the fearfulness of the elite and the preventive measures always taken to keep people down, kept alive among the peasants considerable awareness of their basic interests, in spite of the servility shown at the surface. There was at times more talk about the possibility of land reform by those who feared this than by the peasantry, but the fact that the elite was constantly armed and on the watch for any move of the peasants and was willing to block or repress it immediately, contributed to the highly explosive social climate.

In this overall climate, the distrust of the peasants seemed to be rational and justified and their passive refusal to participate in a project which had been proposed by representatives of a government related to the landholding class could be seen as a logical response. Not showing up at work when they were expected was the peasants only way to affirm themselves and to say no to a society in which they had very little stake. People were partly aware of this themselves. Nevertheless, after living among the villagers for some months, it was not difficult to convince them to try how far they could go in benefiting from the services the government offered. Voluntary work on the sanitation project, and later on the improvement of the road connecting the village with the nearby town, was undertaken and carried out with some degree of enthusiasm, when the villagers saw that they, rather than the landlord, effectively benefited from these projects. On a few occasions, it was necessary to protest against cheating or tactless activities of the government officials regarding the voluntary workers. As a socially unplaced person, I could deal with the officials at their own level, while at the same time identify with the peasants. I attempted to convince the peasants that, if they would have good reasons, they could possibly stand up to defend their own interests.

A representative village committee had been formed with whom I discussed all problems that arose (the bad treatment by some technical supervisors, the fact that one official tried to steal from funds) before I took steps to remedy the situation at the bureaucratic level. The villagers' natural reaction in both cases was to abandon the whole project and withdraw from participation. Because the problems were solved, the projects could be carried on and resulted in a greater self-confidence among the villagers and their committee. It remained to be seen, however, if the authorities would let the representatives defend the village's interests by themselves without my mediation. I had already been warned by the higher officials to be careful not to stimulate the peasants too much. There was a danger, they indicated, that the peasants might become *bravo*, bold. In order to keep them in their place, the introduction of a charitable program was suggested by these officials rather than the continuation of the community self-help efforts.

A test for the possibility of the village leaders to defend their village's best interests came when the government officials in charge changed a promise to build a school in the village. They reduced the government contribution and demanded a much greater contribution from the people than originally proposed. When the village committee was stimulated to try on its own to arrange for a meeting with the government official in question to discuss the issue, the peasant representatives were humiliated and practically thrown out of his office. The peasants were well aware and so they told me that this was proof that basically nothing had changed for them, and that their habitual distrust was justified. Their resentment increased as a result of this experience in which they had participated with considerable cohesion and expectation.

As was indicated earlier, certain forms of community development, particularly those which are part of the traditional patronage system, tend to confirm the status quo, rather than to bring about social change. The case of San Luis demonstrated clearly the different ways in which this kind of patronage can function. Galjart, in an earlier mentioned article, offered my intervention in San Luis as an example of a patron, be it, as he says, an unusual patron.[12] The pressure group which—as a new patron—I had helped to create in the village to defend the peasants' interests was so suspected by the traditional power elite that its functioning was blocked immediately. The old patrons did not want to give place to new more democratic ones. The fact that my stay in the village was known to be temporary probably implied that the negative reaction of the elite to local representation which I tried to organize, remained relatively moderate. Normally, such reactions are, as Galjart indicated, "slander, dismissal of the most conspicuous advocates of the project, complaints at higher political levels, even ambushes."[13] They anxiously tried to maintain their monopoly of power and (traditional) patronage as soon as a minor threat appeared. It should be emphasized, in the light of the resistance to change, lack of solidarity and other obstacles ascribed to the peasants by scholars, that it was relatively easy to rally them and bring them into action.

The only satisfaction I could initially give the peasants, when creating a new following, was to identify with them, to be on their side and to treat them as equals. Only later, the effective defense of their interests could be taken up at the bureaucratic level, whenever there was trouble in the carrying out of the projects. Particularly in moments of difficulties and tensions, there was a strong group feeling among the villagers, a solidarity which was expressed for example when they walked out *en bloc* when a supervisor offended one of them on a job for which they received some pay. Also, the way they talked among each other about the government officials after the latter had gone back to town, revealed a common and strong resentment, which they never showed when townspeople were present.

It was not difficult to stimulate them to participate in decisionmaking once I had proved that I was on their side. They were prepared to take the risk of facing the Administración through their own representatives. The fact that I had, in their name, acted a few times against corruption committed by officials (a thing which I, as a foreigner, could do without much risk), gave them a tremendous satisfaction and helped them to rally and try to do the same. They were accustomed to being told off and humiliated by any officials or townsman and the only response they could make was to withdraw in anger and resentment and passive refusal to collaborate. Seeing government officials backing up and giving in to their justified demands or complaints, was a source of pride and pleasure, which became the subject of conversation for days. After a few of such occurrences, it became easier to rally the people for voluntary work, and it was even possible to make them act on the possibility of standing up for themselves, without my role as intermediary. Those experiences seemed to prove the hypothesis that it is easier to rally people *against* what they consider an enemy than merely in favor of something. As Coser has said, "Conflict with another group leads to the mobilization of group members and hence to increased cohesion of the group."[14] Particularly since resentment and hatred toward the elite was strongly felt, this counterpoint element could be taken up as a point of departure for action and channelled as far as possible. In the context of the Salvadorean society, it was understandable that this approach would not be tolerated by the authorities. The strength of a common negative feeling, and hatred toward the rich and powerful, is not the same as solidarity—willingness to make contributions and the existence of common objectives[15]—but if properly channelled, this negative feeling may easily become solidarity.

A Relevant Field Experience in Sicily:
To Overcome Amoral Familism

From the experience in San Luis, El Salvador, I had learned (1) that the peasants' distrust could be overcome, at least temporarily, by sincerely identifying with their interests and by winning their confidence; and (2) that the development agency was not really identifying with the peasants' interests and that the peasants' distrust and their refusal to collaborate with the agency was only too justified. A next step would be to find out if peasants are willing to participate in development activities which are not controlled by the forces they rightly distrust. An experiment to this effect could be carried out during a period of community development work in Sicily where conditions were similar to those in Latin America. In Southern Italy, the concept of amoral familism originated as an explanation for peasant distrust as an almost insurmountable obstacle to community development efforts.

Banfield defined the content of amoral familism as follows: "Maximize the material, short-run advantage of the nuclear family; assume that all others will do likewise."[16] This ethos, predominant among South Italian peasants according to Banfield, leads to what he called political incapacity.[17] He thus saw few chances for success of any cooperative effort: "In a society of amoral familists, no one will further the interest of the group or community except as it is to his private advantage to do so."[18] After recommending some community development measures for the village he studied, he ended on a cheerless note.

Finally, it must be said that there is little likelihood that any such measures will be tried. Even if it were certain—which it is not, of course—that they would work, they probably would not be tried. Nations do not remake themselves in fundamental ways by deliberate intention any more than do villages.[19]

I had an opportunity to test Banfield's hypotheses and discover their limitations during two years (1959-1961) of field work in community development as a collaborator of the Centre Studi e Iniziative per le Piena Occupazione (Centre for Study and Initiatives towards Full Employment) created in 1958 by the Italian social reformer Danilo Dolci. I was in charge of community development work in Partinico, an agro-town[20] of 25,000 peasants where the headquarters of Dolci's center was established. In the course of those two years, it became clear that the amoral familism and political incapacity of the peasants could be overcome once activities were promoted that were outside the control and domination of the *mafia* and the traditional elite.[21] It appeared that unity and cohesion can grow in peasant groups once they oppose the forces that are the cause of their distrust.

The fact that even highly distrustful peasants such as those in Sicily can be organized effectively under certain circumstances was discovered by the trial and error approach which is characteristic of community development: to identify the people's strongly felt needs and to rally people around these issues to work for possible solutions.

The process of my experiments in Partinico will be briefly described.[22] The first important step was to become acquainted with the peasants of Partinico. In the social center that was part of the building where the headquarters was established, meetings were organized in which the agricultural technician attached to the center gave instructions useful to peasants. Movies were also organized for them. In the rather distrustful, not to say hostile, climate of Partinico, my getting to know the people at these meetings helped in establishing friendly relationships with many other inhabitants. I followed the communication lines which existed between them and others, and thus was able to penetrate into the life of the town.

The peasants very often clustered together in small groups in the *corso* (main street) or the *piazza* (town square), where in the evenings, and also often in the mornings, because of the high degree of underemployment, the men passed their time. It seemed that aside from a strong solidarity with the family and close relatives, there also existed relations of the type that have been called family-friendship groups.[23] Becoming friendly with one person in such a small group gave easy access to relations with the other members. These informal groups usually consisted of from 5 to 10 members.[c] Some of the members were relatives or had mutual godfather relationships. Most of them also belonged to the

---

[c]Apparently, Banfield did not notice this kind of group in Montegrano, the South Italian village he studied.

same political party, the same trade union and more or less the same income group.

The fact that these small informal groups were often slightly overlapping, with a certain person being a member of two or more of such groups, facilitated a penetration into the community. People who participated in many such groups, the more popular persons, proved to be useful in this respect. Especially on Saturday evenings and Sundays, when practically all the men of the town could be found in the corso and the piazza, these key persons could be easily detected.

Through the formal discussions at the meetings of peasants in the social center and the informal talks in the small groups in the main street and the town square, the Iato River irrigation scheme planned for the area came up as the strongest focus of interest. The day laborers in particular saw in this project a solution to their problem of frequent unemployment. They realized that the construction would provide many jobs and even more thereafter because of the intensification of agriculture in the region.

Soon these formal and informal discussions led to the initiation of a large-scale civic campaign. The objective was to pressure the (autonomous) Sicilian government through a petition to execute the plans and to start the construction of the dam. Everybody knew that the funds had been made available to the Sicilian agency responsible for the project, but the project was held up by bureaucratic slowness and the opposition of the *mafia*.

The mafia opposed this irrigation project[24] because it threatened its monopolistic control of the water resources of the area.[d] The civic campaign was only moderately successful. The *mafia* organized a countermovement among the farmers who were to lose some of their land because of the creation of the irrigation water reservoir. The construction of the dam could be started only after the problem of reimbursement of these farmers was definitely solved several years later.[25] In the meantime, the mafia had managed to get a position of control in the executive agency of the project. During the campaign, the *mafiosi* used some of their traditional techniques of intimidating people. The vineyard of one of the leaders of the campaign was destroyed.

During the many meetings and informal discussions which took place as part of the campaign in favor of the irrigation project, other important issues related to the Sicilian economic and social structure came up. The most frequently mentioned problem was the possible effect of increased agricultural production on the future market situation. The farmers were used to getting very low prices for their products. This, they told me, was not only due to competition and other economic factors, but mainly because of the strong monopoly of the *mafia*. They feared that in the end they would be worse off, since this control would

---

[d]Later, shortly before I left Sicily, a revealing incident occurred related to the water control. One of the most active local farmers (a member of the first wine producers cooperative) wanted to form a group with some other farmers who had plots of land next to his to take advantage of the water of a small stream which passed through those lands. After some initial steps were taken, the *mafia* made known that the group would run into trouble if the plan were carried out. Thus ended this small project.

persist. The main local market for agricultural produce, especially for fruit and vegetables, was Palermo, with 600,000 inhabitants. However, this market was solidly controlled by the *mafia*. The local farmers saw the need for a strong co-operative movement to cope with the need, but they were firmly convinced that the formation of such a cooperative was not possible. To prove this point, they related many past failures of coops, because of deceit and corruption. They were also convinced that the mafia would not leave them in peace if they could eventually overcome their own intragroup difficulties. Cases of leaders who were assassinated by the *mafia* when their efforts to organize the people were successful were too well remembered.[26] And if people would not remember such events, they were constantly reminded of the *mafia* control by such acts of warning as a destroyed vineyard. (In about ten years following 1945, 33 local peasant and labor leaders were assassinated by the *mafia* in Sicily. Among them were outstanding leaders who became popular heroes, such as Turiddu Carnevale and Accursio Miraglia.)

This constant threat of violent reprisal against any action which might threaten the traditional power system seems a better explanation for the difficulty in bringing about change in Sicily than political incapability or amoral familism.[e] The fact, however, that the creation of a simple cooperative was seen by the people as an act of struggle against strongly hated and resented forces made such an initiative look challenging. The problem was to find a feasible opportunity.

In spite of the dangers, there were among those farmers who had been outstanding in the campaign for the dam, a few who cherished the idea of starting a cooperative to sell their wine. Wine was the main product of Partinico, but it gave the producers a low remuneration. Its good name on the national market was deteriorating because of the baptizing process (mixing with water and chemicals) used by the big wine merchants who controlled the market.

When these farmers were told by some of the foreign specialists who visited Dolci's project that the wine they produced in their own small cellars was not inferior but of excellent quality, they saw that the so-called wine crisis[f] about

---

[e] . . . my chief impression was that the Sicilian small farmer reacts in his economic behavior in a rational way to irrational conditions, which he does not believe it possible to change," and: ". . . the 'small man' in Sicily is largely resigned and afraid, because a great number of reasons and a great deal of practical experience have taught him to be so. It seems that after the Second World War, there was an upsurge of hope and a wish to change conditions. However, during the fifties, resignation again spread, because the forces of the old 'establishment' succeeded not only in frustrating more basic changes, but even in consolidating and strengthening their power. In this region, people prefer to obey and pay the illegal forces, because these are able to 'punish' by violating property or even life without the risk of effective redress by the forces of law.[27]

[f] Today, particularly in political circles they talk about 'the wine crisis,' but not about the wine racket. The wine 'crisis'—a fine word you'll hear from the lips of a thousand speakers at public meetings—is not a crisis at all; it's a crisis only for the wretches who produce the wine after enormous sacrifices. The 'crisis' is discussed in Italian, good Italian, by men with enormous stomachs and bulging cheeks; it's discussed in luxurious lounges and by people who are too clever by half. The poor peasant watches this act year after year, and year after year he kids himself, while the large-scale cultivators and big wholesale dealers are building up for themselves a solid monopoly. It's not my place to say anything more about the real wine-growing crisis; it's a big field, a field of politics and the political aims of well-known political figures who grow fat on it.[28]

which everybody was always talking, could at least partly be solved by themselves. Discussions about the formation of a cooperative were initiated among the family friendship groups clustered around some of the most courageous and somewhat better-off peasants. It seemed that, if possible at all, a cooperative would have to be formed with people who had already much in common, such as a combination of closely related and overlapping family friendship groups. With the key persons, the discussions were intensified and as an incentive, I told them that I would try to find a market for their products in Holland outside the *mafia* sphere of influence when I went there on home leave. They continued to hesitate until, a few hours before my departure, the most dynamic person of the group brought me some samples of wine to take with me. Since Sicilian wine is of high quality, it was not difficult to find a merchant in Holland who was interested, and an order for the first barrels was immediately sent to Partinico. This outside economic incentive proved to be a catalyst. By the time I returned, the cooperative had been instituted with the help of the Centro's agricultural technician. Since post-war Italian legislation facilitates cooperative organization, the legal aspect did not present many difficulties.

The new cooperative, starting off with 14 persons, which soon increased to 30, consisted mainly of middle farmers, who could afford taking some economic risks, such as renting together a big wine cellar, a necessity in order to get a great quantity of uniform, typical wine, which can be regularly exported under a certain trade-mark. The local government wine expert offered his services free to the new cooperative to control quality and proper processing.

This modest but surprising success had a double effect: a certain sense of pride among the Partinicans about the proved quality of their product, and a decrease in skepticism regarding cooperatives. Other family friendship groups of small farmers came together to follow the example. They did not have the direct material incentive of exporting wine to Holland. But in addition to cheating the *mafia*, competitiveness between this cooperative and the other one probably helped to bolster the new group.

Later a vague plan developed that when enough farmers would form cooperatives, which could then join together, they would be able to take over the big communal wine press (processing plant), built officially for cooperative use. This plant was, for the time being, managed by the government.

A great question was if the first and second cooperative and eventually other groups, would be able to merge. The fact that one consisted of middle farmers with center or rightists political inclinations, and the other small farmers who were mostly Socialists, made this doubtful.[g]

Also, tensions and difficulties with the cooperatives were to be expected. So, after some time, a conflict arose between the president and the vice-president of

---

[g]The process of legal recognition of the second cooperative took much longer than the first one, probably because of the fact that most members were Socialist and thus opposed to the Christian-Democrat authorities in power in Sicily in those days, while the others were politically independent.

the first cooperative, the real reason for which was almost impossible to detect. Some people strongly believed that it was due to a *mafia* maneuver to split up the group when it was growing in strength. As usual, the dissident president had his following. The internal discussions and reciprocal accusations of dishonesty unfortunately interrupted the trade with Holland, which made future success of the cooperative practically impossible.

The second cooperative, which started in a less spectacular way, kept growing slowly but steadily over the next few years. According to letters I received after I left Sicily, it became a flourishing enterprise.[29] Perhaps the more disciplined forms of organization which accompanied the growing left-wing political movement in Sicily had a favorable effect on this group. As was noted, the members of the second cooperative were practically all Socialists.

Applying the usual community development approach, it was found that in spite of the seemingly amoral familist atmosphere, certain organizational and united efforts of peasants can be successfully undertaken. These efforts proved to be of such a kind that they implied, in addition to possible economic benefits, a weakening of the prevailing repressive social system as a whole. As could be seen from the campaign in favor of the irrigation project, a potential existed for opposition against, and even conflict with the *mafia*, and the traditional elite. The irrigation scheme, however, was still a rather abstract and far-away possibility. Those who participated most strongly in the campaign were the agricultural laborers who had nothing to lose and had badly needed employment possibilities to gain from the project.

Among the small and middle farmers, more fearful of the *mafia* because they have something to lose, immediate economic gain obtained through new market facilities that were not controlled by the *mafia* was a strong incentive to get together. They opposed the system that was very disadvantageous to them through the formation of some cooperatives. It was an attack on the prevailing system. It should be noted that in addition to the factor of economic gain, a certain personal bravery, the awareness of standing out by challenging the *mafia*, helped to stimulate the new groups in their initial stages. Another factor was competiveness, which helped the second cooperative to come to life.[30] Thus, certain counterpoints or weak spots in the ethos of amoral familism were discovered and used to start breaking the vicious circle of backwardness and political incapacity. Banfield did not clearly see these possibilities.

In addition to these forces (personal pride, competition, and profits existing within the amoral familism), other factors were encountered that could be utilized. Such a factor was the consciousness that the local people had about the background of their political incapacity. The people knew they had sound reasons[h] for their general and mutual distrust, in the concrete and all-pervasive in-

---

[h]Even Banfield called the distrust he discovered among the peasants of Montegrano healthy, although he used the qualification pathological a little before;[31] I was acquainted with several cases where farmers who had improved their techniques and as a result of that had a better produce than the average, became the victims of thieves who were protected bv the *mafia*.

fluence of the ruling groups and the *mafia*. Even Banfield mentioned as one of the explanations that people in Montegrano gave themselves for their backwardness:

Political behavior reflects class interests and antagonisms. The upper class gives the village no leadership because it lives by exploiting the peasant and can do so only by keeping him in poverty and ignorance. The lower class hates the upper and seeks for revenge upon it. Collaboration between the classes is impossible, although nothing can be done without it.[32]

It is not clear if the last part of this phrase is part of the opinion of the people of Montegrano, or a comment by Banfield. The experience in Partinico agreed with the first part, but certainly not with the second idea that nothing can be done without collaboration between the opposed classes. On the contrary, it seemed that once class enemies are clearly defined, they can—as a negative reference group[33]—indirectly serve the formation of new and cohesive interest groups, representing formerly repressed sectors of the population.

The civic campaign in favor of the dam and the cooperative were not very important as such, but they channelled the diffuse existing antagonism towards the *mafia*. Some peasant leaders were well aware of this and willing to take the risks involved, as they said. When the first cooperative showed its signs of weakness, the second cooperative offered to help the first one to overcome the dividing interference of the *mafia* through a merger of both cooperatives. Banfield vaguely noticed the potential influence of class antagonism towards ruling groups when he noted the following.

Class antagonism does not explain Montegrano's political behavior either. If it did, one might expect the peasants uniting in action against the upper class. But there is no such action, nor is there likely to be. Class and status relations do, however, influence the situation profoundly in ways that are diffuse, indirect, and hard to identify. Like poverty and ignorance, they are general conditions, which, so to speak, form the causal background.[34]

Since he was only an outside observer and did not intervene or participate in any processes, he could not see the causal forces in operation, and the new awareness growing among people regarding the ways to defend their interests. Friedmann noted:

This new kind of awareness marks the passage from a static, hierarchic society to a dynamic one of social polarization, from an acceptance of the historical elements as necessary parts of the objective environment to a transfer of these elements into the subjective field: the peasant begins to see that among the causes of *'la miseria'* are the interests of men who are not essentially different from himself and certainly not outside of his own field of action. As he accepts, thus, the possibility of eventually overcoming the human causes of *'la miseria'* he begins to participate in the making of history.[35]

The community development experience in Sicily confirms some of the findings of Silverman, which are critical of Banfield's hypotheses.[36] Silverman found that the characteristics of the predominant social system as expressed in the agricultural system are the basis of the ethos of amoral familism. It was also indicated that amoral familism can be changed by modifying crucial aspects of the predominant social structure. Silverman did not suggest how these changes could be brought about, but the experience in Sicily gave some clues. An essential element in the introduction of such changes appeared to be to direct them purposely against the forces controlling the social and agricultural system, utilizing the counterpoint elements contained in the predominant ethos or value system. These elements were discovered by trial and error as part of the community development experience. Some of these counterpoint elements have been noted by scholars.

One recent study argued strongly against the amoral familism concept, indicating that there are many examples of southern Italians joining their fellows in all kinds of groups: to fool the government; to carry on black market activity; to send relatives as emigrants abroad; or occupy a latifundia.[37] These examples are all more or less clear counterreactions to the overall establishment, being either an escape or a protest action.

It appears that in a society with a traditional structure which hinders development, the best way to create new institutions and organizations in which peasants actively participate is purposely to use the traditional dominating power holders as a negative reference group. New groups are formed in conflict with those who stand for the status quo. Conflict can thus be an important stimulus for the creation of new and participatory institutions, replacing archaic ones, which are no longer considered legitimate by a large sector of society. This interpretation of conflict is consistent with the work of J.M.G. Thurlings.

Admittedly conflict is without doubt aimed at upsetting the existing order, but in our opinion, it is directed just as much towards the establishment of a new order, however temporary that may be. . . . The commonest cause of conflict seems to be the necessity of finding a new form of society. When the existing order is attacked in the conflict, that is not because it is an order but because it is no longer regarded as legitimate by the protesting party. Viewed in this light, conflict is not only a mechanism of destruction but also an institutionalizing mechanism.[38]

A Field Experience in Chile: Distrust
Turned into Effective Participation

During my experience in Sicily, I had learnt by trial and error that peasants can overcome their distrust and get organized particularly when their group or organization is directed against the causes of the distrust. A few years later, I was able to apply this approach in a systematic way as an experiment, in a relatively short time bringing highly distrustful peasants into effective organized action for their own benefit. Through this experiment, it could be shown that distrust and resistance to change was an asset to effective organization, rather than an obstacle. Distrust, if well understood and appreciated, can be transformed into a dynamic force which can unite the peasants to bring about a real improvement in their conditions and challenge the traditional power structure that attempts to maintain the status quo.

The experiment in which this was tried was undertaken while I worked in a community development and agrarian reform project in the Punitaqui valley in the province of Coquimbo in Chile. I worked for one year (1965-66) in that area as a United Nations expert assisting the Chilean government in the setting up of this project that initially encountered serious distrust and resistance from the local population. Looking for the counterpoints in the prevailing system[i] and building unity around those points proved to be a relatively easy way to mobilize the peasants.

On the 14th of August 1964, an agreement between the government of Chile and the United Nations' World Food Programme had been signed to execute a community development project in the Punitaqui valley in the province of Coquimbo. As stated in this agreement, the objective of the project was to develop the agricultural potentiality of the 16 communities in the Punitaqui valley with assistance from the World Food Programme (WFP) in the form of surplus food.

The Punitaqui valley belongs to the parts of Coquimbo province where in the so-called *comunidades agrícolas* a type of communal land tenure is predominant. The region is also characterized by a very adverse climate. Severe droughts were suffered over many consecutive years to such an extent that the government had to take emergency measures, such as food distribution.

The Punitaqui Project was an experimental attempt to develop 16 *comunidades agrícolas* which were relatively favorably located close to the urban center of Ovalle and to the Panamerican Highway. There also existed the possibility to improve the agricultural situation through various forms of irrigation, for instance on the basis of the already functioning Cogoti-Recoleta scheme. The latter had to be improved and extended with the water from the La Paloma dam, 25 kilometers south-east of Ovalle, which would be ready in the course of 1968. The job description included the following passage.

Advise the Zonal Director of Agriculture for the Second Zone and other authorities connected with the promotion, coordination, implementation and evaluation of the community development project for the Estero de Punitaqui, Department of Ovalle, Province of Coquimbo (World Food Programme, Republic of Chile, agreement dated 14 August 1964) *on the application of community development principles and methods, taking into account the necessary preliminary steps of community motivation, organization and education which are prerequisites for obtaining proper and effective implementation of such programs.*[40]

---

[i]Wertheim emphasized that sociologists concerned with development should have a great deal of sensitivity to the counterpoints in the prevailing system.[39]

One of the reasons for my assignment to the Punitaqui project was the fact that almost for a year after the agreement between the Chilean authorities and the United Nations' World Food Programme had been signed, virtually nothing had happened. The main event had been a meeting in Ovalle where a good number of high Chilean government officials (including the minister of agriculture and technicians of several United Nations agencies) had tried to explain the project to representatives of the *comunidades*. This meeting had a negative effect since one of the two largest *comunidades* in the area decided not to participate in the project designed for them and the other one remained aloof.

The reason for this was that in the planning of the project the *comunidades* had hardly been consulted. Among the proposals introduced by the technicians was a campaign to diminish goat breeding in the area, which was highly resented by the peasants, since they depended mainly on their goats for bare subsistence. Other factors which stimulated distrust among the peasants were the implications of the presidential election campaign of 1964, and the change in plans and personnel that occurred as a result of the entrance of the new Christian-Democrat government in that year. The *comunidades* were generally affiliated to the Federacion Campesina e Indigena de Chile, supporting the Communist-Socialist opposition coalition.

Another circumstance not favorable to the initiation of the project was the fact that its initial director had been transferred because of corruption and that the interim director lived in Santiago. When I arrived in June 1965, I found a group of young and able professional staff of the project severely demoralized, distrusted by the *comunidades* and lacking proper direction.

The Punitaqui area can be seen as a typical case of internal colonialism.[41] The *comunidades* in that area had, since the second half of the last century, lost most of their fertile valley lands to shrewd large landholders in the region who knew how to get property rights to large tracts of communal land through legal manipulations. Some of the lawsuits through which the communal peasants (*comuneros*) tried to defend their rights were still going on in 1965. Most of the law suits had been lost however many years before, because of the incapacity of the *comuneros* to continue paying lawyers to defend their cases in the courts which traditionally tended to be on the side of the landed elite.

The new situation became legalized in many cases. On the spot, it was said that in more or less similar ways, the *comunidad* Punitaqui had lost more than 2,000 hectares of its best lands at the beginning of this century. Although this situation had been legalized, a feeling of injustice and resentment about this fact continued to exist, as could easily be discovered. In some *comunidades* in the Punitaqui valley, litigations were still going on. The *comunidad* Potrerillo Alto won back about 1,000 hectares of flat irrigable lands through the insistence of its leaders, and another few hundreds of hectares were still disputed. The *comuneros* of Potrerillo Alto proudly narrated on various occasions how they once, only a few years ago, chased the neighboring landlord away, in spite of the fact that he threatened them with a pistol, when he actually started to move the fences. Six other *comunidades* in the valley had such affairs on hand. Only one, however, had won back most of its lands a few decades ago under the leadership of its representative who in 1955 was a provincial leader of the leftist Federación Campesina e Indígena de Chile.

Tentatively, it could be said that in the *comunidades* where this kind of problem existed and was being faced, cohesiveness and also a degree of politization was stronger than where such was not the case. The deep distrust of any outside interference was clearly related to these experiences.

In those cases where law suits had been lost or given up, the *comuneros* remained on the eroding slopes of the mountainous parts of their original *comunidades*. There a few gulches that facilitated some irrigation allowed a minimum subsistence agriculture to some inhabitants and, in exceptional cases, the surplus of some marketable products such as oranges or lemons. Most *comuneros* lived in conditions close to destitution. In addition to the loss of good land in the area came the loss of other valuable resources. An important gold mine in the town of Punitaqui brought in the first decades of this century ample employment possibilities to the *comuneros*, which compensated somewhat for the loss of good agricultural land. After some time, however, the mine was exhausted, while the fortune gained by its owner had disappeared in travel, conspicuous living and other ventures, according to the local tales. In the meantime, the woods which had covered part of the mountains in the area had been used as fuel for that mine, and the comuneros were finally left with barren, eroding mountains, good only for the grazing of goats. Increasingly, severe droughts possibly related to the deforestation eliminated even part of this last resource.

There were still a few copper and mercury mines left in Punitaqui, but they were producing at a limited capacity. Apart from these, there were a large number of small mines in different parts of the *comunidades*, which the *comuneros* would like to exploit for their own benefit. This, however, in most cases was impossible, because the sites where such resources existed were generally claimed by mining companies, which preferred to keep them as a reserve. According to the current mining legislation in Chile, such mines could not be exploited by others than the claimants, who only had to pay a relatively small fee to the government to maintain their claim as legally valid. The fact that this legislation was under consideration for modification, was a cold comfort for the *comuneros* who had such unused mines in their own *comunidad* while suffering under-employment and living at the subsistence level.

A similar situation which aroused strong feelings of resentment among the *comuneros* was the fact that the lands which they actually possessed could not benefit from the nearby government-built Recoleta and Cogoti irrigation schemes, because the *comunidad* had as yet no legal personality. Especially in bad years of drought, when whole wheat crops were lost because of lack of water, while the irrigation canal to the surrounding *fundos* (estates) went right through some *comunidades*, this situation created indignation. One result of this whole situation was a strong distrust among the peasants of any outside intervention, particularly since the government had generally been on the side of the mining and large landholding interests (one of the large landholders in the area, in 1966, still disputing with a neighboring *comunidad* over a large plot of land was the former vice-president of the country).

From the frustrating experience that the peasants had, one could expect a high degree of militancy if organizations were created to defend their legitimate interests. This could be easy, particularly since remnants, in some places active nuclei, existed of the internal government structure of the *comunidad* (which had played or still played an active role in the defense of the community boundaries). Also, the fact that many *comuneros* had experience as members of mineworkers' unions could be helpful in this respect.

Already in the early fifties, the *comunidades* had formed a federation to defend their interests, which in 1961 became one of the founding organizations of the communist-socialist *Federación Campesina e Indígena de Chile*. It is possibly partly due to the strong denunciations by this federation, supported by sympathy demonstrations of the Central Unica de Trabajadores (CUT), the overall trade union confederation in Chile, that in the land reform law (No. 15020) of 1962 a special article was included to legally regulate and protect the existing *comunidades agrícolas*, providing among others for a legally recognized internal government structure, and for a definitive fixation of boundaries. Practically no implementation had been given to this legislation by 1965.

It is important to note that a traditional form of organization existed in practically all *comunidades*. A few times a year, the *comuneros* arranged for a community meeting to solve common problems. Each *comunidad* has an *administrador*, elected at such a general assembly, who often served his community for many years. In the larger communities, the *administrador* was assisted by a board of delegates from the various sectors which made up the *comunidad*. Some *administradores* were charismatic personalities who lead their comunidad against many odds in a successful way. Others were old men, without much initiative, whom people followed out of tradition. Some used their position of power for personal benefit, some for the benefit of all, and some combined both approaches.

In many communities, a tradition persisted of common voluntary work. Through such efforts over the years, many kilometers of roads, irrigation canals, and schools were constructed. Most schools in the area owe their existence to such common efforts. The tradition was not very strong however. The last few years, it had been revived somewhat since the Ministry of Agriculture had stimulated a common cultivation of wheat on parts of the communal land. The harvest was divided according to the days of work which each *comunero* had put up. Because this cultivation was done on a large scale, machinery could be used on credit from the government. Unfortunately, the adverse climate made any wheat cultivation a risky affair, and indebtedness to the government because of bad harvests added to the existing feeling of distrust.

When in 1964, the community development project was initiated in the area, the peasants and their representatives generally declared, in meetings with government officials or among themselves, that they did not want to have anything to do with it. One of the material incentives of the project was the rations of the World Food Programme which would be distributed among those *comuneros* who would work voluntarily on community projects. Several communities refused this alms distribution scheme, denouncing it as humiliating, and as a device of the government to avoid a real solution of the problems of the *comunidades*. Others accepted the food distribution, however, not as a stimulus to do community work, but as an emergency measure after another drought had killed off a large part of the goats on which they depended for survival.

I tried a new approach in community development, turning the justified resentment and distrust of the *comuneros* into active collaboration in the project. This was not too difficult once the peasants were challenged to give content to the project themselves, so that it would satisfy their basic needs and grievances. A first thing to do was to establish communication with the local leaders and to win their confidence. This was achieved through a straightforward discussion of their most strongly felt grievances. These were not the felt needs for schools, roads and other facilities which were often discussed at meetings, but, as in most rural areas of Latin America, were the felt injustices regarding land tenure. However, this obvious grievance initially had to be brought up questioningly in private conversations, in order to be discussed at all. Resentment about these injustices was so deep that the subject was not discussed with foreigners, particularly not with those who come in the context of a government program. Showing understanding and some measure of appreciation for these grievances was an essential element in establishing the needed communication. An interesting comment in this respect by a communist peasant organizer was quoted by Hobsbawm.

There are three things you have to do to get anywhere with peasants. The first is, you must live exactly as they do. If you can't stand the food, you can't organize peasants. Second, you have to talk to them not just about *the* land, but about this land, which used to belong to them in their grandfather's day but was taken over by Hacienda X. Third, you must always be teaching them something. I am not an intellectual, so I teach them football. But learn something they must— they insist on it.[42]

I found that the—on the whole well-intentioned and dedicated—technicians of the project had never talked frankly with the *comuneros* about their grievances, and were afraid to do so, although they had some kind of understanding of the situation, when asked about it. The technicians were taken along on visits to all the *comunidades* and they became aware of the basic grievances of the *comuneros* while present at, and participating in, the initial discussions I had with the local leaders or at community assemblies. Soon the technicians participated fully in the open dialogue with the *comuneros* and learnt through this experience that partial technical solutions would be ineffective and that the full collaboration of the *comunidades* could only be achieved by focusing on an overall solution, including the land tenure situation. The *comunidades* would never be able to solve their problems without recovering the fertile lands they had lost in the past which were in modern days extensively and inefficiently utilized by a few large landowners. Once the technicians of the project saw this structural problem clearly and were willing to discuss the concrete solutions of it with the *comuneros* in their meetings or assemblies, confidence was established and participation of the *comunidades* in the project, including the utilization of the World Food Programme facilities, could be started.

The project technicians were well aware that by taking sides with the *comuneros* against some local vested interests, they would create some opposition in the town of Ovalle, but, politicized as they were during their (recent) student years, they took this with good humor and even some pride, after they had overcome their initial hesitation. Opposition soon started in the local newspapers *La Provincia* and *El Limari*, but the new Chilean director of the project, nominated later, was allowed by these papers to answer the criticisms in their columns, which resulted in a better understanding on the part of the urban middle class people in Ovalle.

Some misunderstandings had to be overcome on both sides. Government technicians too easily blamed the resistance on the part of the *comuneros* on political troublemaking, rather than on injustice and deceit suffered in the past (and sometimes recently). The comuneros too easily lumped all government officials together as bureaucratic parasites who cheat the common people. Initially, it happened not unfrequently at community assemblies that local leaders strongly criticized the government, including the local agencies and the Punitaqui Project, in speeches filled with political terminology used in communist and socialist circles. The technicians had an inclination to withdraw from such uncomfortable situations, which, however, would have meant the end of the Project. Guidance was given to help them understand the background, and the often justified reasons for the resentment which obviously was the basis of the violent verbal expressions. By analyzing the political statements and initiating a discussion of problems during or after such meetings, the involvement of the technicians and the community leaders in a common effort could be promoted. This demanded some mental effort, especially on the part of the technical field personnel. Thus, the implications of agrarian reform and rural structural change became normal topics of conversation, somewhat out of the sphere of political demagoguery or academic agrarian economics.

In spite of the fact the new government had made some strong statements regarding land reform, this subject had been taboo among Chilean middle-class people for so long that it needed some encouragement to adapt to it as a concrete and practical possibility. That the local landholders expressed themselves rather vocally against this possibility kept the subject in the sphere of agitation, which facilitated a rallying of the *comuneros* and most of the technicians. The fact that an improved land reform law was under discussion in the national assembly facilitated a frank exchange of views, since a legally feasible final solution favorable to the peasants came in sight as unavoidable.

An additional but equally important factor which helped the peasants to overcome their distrust was to transfer the management of the World Food Programme facilities at the community level over to their elected representatives. After the initial fear and distrust had disappeared, it was not too difficult to convince the project personnel to give considerable active participation and decisionmaking-power to the community representatives. In each community, the leaders and the community assembly were given the responsibility of managing the food ration distribution to those *comuneros* who wanted to participate in the work for the community projects. Moreover, these projects were to be chosen not by the agency but by the community itself in its assembly. The community organizations could thus be considerably strengthened.

It should be noted that tension continued to exist in some *comunidades* because private and semiofficial social welfare agencies tried to stimulate new leadership in competition with the existing, mostly communist or socialist leaders. These efforts were generally unsuccessful, since the leftist leaders were respected for their militancy in the defense of the community interests. (Interestingly some of the most politicized *comunidades* were at the same time well-known as Catholic ceremonial centers where the yearly saints festivity was celebrated with great fervor and in which the communist-oriented leaders had an important share.) A few *comunidades*, such as Salala, where a German priest lived and developed such activity, were Christian-Democratic with conservative tendencies. It was a policy of the project to work through the leadership as elected by the *comunidad* whatever their political coloration, without any discrimination—which was against well-entrenched political traditions in Chile. This helped to affirm the confidence of the *comunidades* in the project's management. It also prevented the food distribution program from becoming involved in political patronage.

Thanks in part to their former syndical or political organization experience, the local leaders did very well in the administration of the WFP supplies in the communities (to the surprise of the technicians). These and other arrangements showed the peasants that at least the project technicians working in the area were on their side, and were willing to act accordingly. Several other obstacles had to be overcome. When, for example, in the municipality of Punitaqui a committee was formed where the urban center of Punitaqui would integrate and coordinate efforts with the surrounding *comunidad*, it was obvious to any sociologically minded observer that the conservative town mayor and his friends had prepared a committee where the local urban interests would be dominating. These vested interests were those of middle farmers, small mining employers, merchants and other middle-class representatives. The representatives of the *comuneros* at the constituent meeting would not have opposed this kind of arrangement, but would simply have boycotted the committee, later withdrawing from further contacts. Such events seemed to be normal. To the surprise of the technicians and the *comuneros*, however, it was possible to suggest at that meeting that the arrangement proposed by the town mayor seemed to be somewhat out of proportion, and that it might be worthwhile to hear the opinions of the *comuneros* of Punitaqui for whom the Project was specifically designed more carefully. Then the *comuneros* proposed an arrangement which would do sufficient justice to their interests. This was accepted by all present and institutionalized.

Such incidents, besides helping to win the confidence of the *comuneros*, helped the field workers of the Project to become more aware of the sociological, not to say sociostructural, aspects of their work.

Another aspect in which assistance and encouragement could be given was the introduction or improvement of democratic group techniques. During most community meetings, I generally fulfilled a rather passive role as an observer, later discussing with each technician who directed a meeting the details of his approach, and helping him to overcome his paternalistic tendencies.

Altogether, after a few weeks of intensive work in all the 16 communities, local committees had been formed or revived, and were strengthened by giving them the responsibility for the monthly emergency distribution of food from the World Food Programme (between August 1965 and January 1966), and the responsibility for the organization of the community works and the proper distribution of food rations as a stimulus for participation in those works. Thus, over the next few months, 7 roads were improved or repaired, 8 schools were built, 5 irrigation canals were constructed or repaired, 2,000 lemon trees were planted and steps toward the formation of multipurpose peasant cooperatives were made in several *comunidades*. It should be noted that although a number of these projects would have been undertaken without the special stimulation from the World Food Programme, the availability of food helped significantly to increase such efforts.

Unfortunately, the determination with which the Christian-Democratic government had announced an effective agrarian reform program, benefiting 100,000 peasants between 1964 and 1970, soon proved to be less strong than it had originally appeared. It took two years simply to get a new land reform law approved in the national congress and then the implementation suffered from delays. Promises made regarding the legislation of the boundaries of the *comunidades*, making it possible for them to benefit from the irrigation facilities that were under construction, were executed very slowly and so were the activities concerning the expropriation of the estates in the area to the benefit of the *comunidades*. Other frustrations were that the materials to be sent by the government agencies to complete the construction of schools and other facilities undertaken by the *comunidades* with local materials, arrived with great delay, causing new resentment among the *comuneros*. In all these setbacks, the technicians of the project were strongly on the side of the *comuneros* and did all possible to compensate for the mistakes made at the bureaucratic level in Santiago. This helped to maintain to some extent the enthusiasm that had been created but that could not be fully utilized, because of the above-mentioned complications at the national level.

Shortly before I left the project in 1966, The Federación Campesina e Indígena de Chile (FCI) had organized in Ovalle a regional congress where the participation of the *comunidades* in the project and the pressure in favor of the needed solution of the land tenure injustices were strengthened. Although this congress had a lot of political implications, several technicians of the project were willing to participate in the preparatory meetings in the *comunidades* as well as in the congress itself, to explain the purpose of the project and its orientation towards a definitive and radical solution if the *comuneros* would be willing to push forward. All the former resentments and doubts were brought out again, but now as things past, and the wholehearted participation of the *comunidades* in the project, and pressuring, together with the technicians for the needed reform measures, were agreed upon and applauded.

Apparently, it was the Communist and Socialist party line to critically support the government's reform program facing opposition from vested interests, pushing it beyond its slow pace wherever possible.[43] Great care was taken by the national leaders of the Federación not to go too far beyond the most strongly felt local needs. Although they stimulated the *comuneros'* thinking towards increasing collectivization of agriculture as part of the agrarian reform program, they did not push this issue when they found that there was little response at this moment. No resolution regarding this point was accepted, while the resolution regarding the distribution of the estates in the area to the *comunidades* on a partly communal, partly individual basis, as foreseen in the land reform law, received overwhelming applause.

During the next few years, the Punitaqui project slowly increased its impact. Several of the estates that were claimed by the *comuneros* at the congress were expropriated, and first steps for the settlement of *comuneros* on those lands were made. However, later new conflicts arose over the question of whether the *comunidades* would have to pay for the lands that would be assigned to them under the reform program. They claimed that the lands had formerly been theirs and that they did not need to pay as was usual in the *asentamientos* (land reform settlements) in other areas, where estates were distributed among its former workers. It is not surprising that in 1969 one of the *comunidades*, tired of discussing this issue with the land reform agency (CORA), simply occupied the several hundreds of hectares that it had claimed for many years. (The local newspaper indicated that the FECH (Federación de Estudiantes de Chile) helped the peasants in the organization of the event.)[44]

It should be noted that on the whole opposition of the large landowners was relatively weak, although initially they made a great deal of propaganda for their cause in the local and national press. The well-organized peasant pressure, supported by the project technicians, has as a side effect that local middle-class public opinion turned away from the landowners. This, in addition to the fact that they were to be reimbursed according to the law, made them give in. There is little tradition of violence in Chile and on the whole a greater respect for orderly procedure than in most other Latin American countries. For this reason as well, peasant action was less radical than it could have been under other circumstances. It took a long time before the peasants decided upon such a radical act as the seizure of claimed lands. During the above-mentioned congress of the FCI, it was clear that the leaders tried to instill moderation and self-control in their followers.

Summarizing the Punitaqui experiment, it could be said that the relative ease with which the peasants of the Punitaqui area could be brought to effective action once they were convinced that this action was part of a broader, overall solution of their main problems and strongly felt needs, shows that there is a considerable potential for peasant mobilization. Of course, it cannot be emphasized enough that such mobilization only occurs if the peasants see their efforts as a step towards a radical and real solution. This generally means that a conflict situation that has existed for many years, such as the inequality of land tenure, has to be brought into the open and more or less radically solved in favor of the peasants. They also have to be given effective participation in the management of the process of change. Once this opportunity is given to them, they will prove able to cope with such responsibilities.

Whether peasant organizations, created to channel a mobilization of the people towards the solution of basic problems, will use radical or moderate means of action seems to depend mainly on the reaction of those who have to give in to their demands. If this reaction remains moderate, more or less within the legal possibilities, peasants will struggle for the solution of their conflict with the traditional elite step by step in more or less institutionalized ways, as long as the process goes on without creating too much frustration.

The factors which contributed most to the mobilization of the distrustful community leaders were: (1) agreement with their good reasons for distrust and the assistance to them in expressing this in concrete and effective complaints; (2) the trusting of considerable decision power to the community leaders regarding projects to be executed, as well as the management of the available resources; and (3) the direction of the project in such a way that a basic conflict with the traditional elite over land (which was behind the attitude of distrust of the peasants) would be definitively solved in favor of the latter.

3 Resistance to Change Reconsidered

The potential of conflict as a stimulus to overcome the effects and causes of amoral familism, political incapacity and resistance to change among the peasants has generally not been emphasized by anthropologists and sociologists concerned with rural life in underdeveloped societies. It should be noted in this respect that in historical accounts of the peasantry in some highly developed countries with a troubled agrarian history stress is given to the almost innate rebelliousness of the peasants rather than to peasant inertia.[1] It seems however that while the history of mankind is full of wars and struggle, social scientists have dedicated little attention to the forces motivating people to participate in such uninstitutionalized activities. They have been too preoccupied with social structure[2] to see the importance of social conflict.[a] In some cases, anthropologists have been unwilling or unable to deal with controversial subjects rather than face difficulties with the local authorities.[b] They often studied the evolutive and static aspects of development and consciously or unconsciously neglected the dynamic, radical or even revolutionary tendencies. They may thus have overlooked the almost innate rebelliousness of the peasants which also exists in Latin America, although it may be less obvious than in Eastern Europe at the beginning of this century.

Several anthropologists and rural sociologists have given special attention to the envy, jealousy and difficult interpersonal relations which exist in peasant villages under the prevailing social structure. It appears, however, that these jealousies and internal conflicts in peasant communities largely disappear when the peasants are able to face in a united way the forces which have kept them in a submissive and backward state. The striking changes in the personalities of the peasants, once they see the old traditional and repressive social structure break

---

[a]In this respect, Wertheim noted regarding a related subject:

There is often a considerable discrepancy between the significance of a social phenomenon and the attention paid to it by sociology. One greatly neglected phenomenon is that of corruption. Though a favorite subject for club conversation and newspaper headlines, it has so far received remarkably little attention from professional sociologists. As a result, the current concept of 'corruption' is still enmeshed in emotional reactions and popular notions; it hardly reflects any real understanding of the historical roots and social significance of the phenomenon.[3]

[b]Some anthropologists working in Latin America have confidentially told me this, others have less consciously practiced some type of self-censorship.[4]

down have been noted in Mexico and Bolivia in areas where the culture of repression was ended by a successful peasant revolt which made way for a more open and dynamic atmosphere. The change from a submissive, resentful and apathetic attitude to one of self-confidence as one of the main factors in agrarian reform will be dealt with later.[5] This is the case particularly if the change in power structure was brought about through the organized intervention of the peasants themselves. The crucial point is how to utilize the distrust existing among peasants in many areas in Latin America, as part of the culture of repression, as a point of departure for active struggle for change.

Even a superficial acquaintance with the areas where Foster and Erasmus, two of the more renowned scholars who studied the peasants' resistance to change, did their main field work, reveals that also in those areas severe social conflicts existed which brought the peasants out of their apathy and showed their innate rebelliousness. A brief description of some of these facts may give new insights into the potentialities of peasant distrust and resistance, overlooked by the above-mentioned scholars.

Foster: The "Image of the Limited Good"

Foster,[6] who introduced the term image of the limited good, did much field-work in the municipality of Tzintzuntzan in the state of Michoacan, Mexico. In the following passage, he lists factors which have an adverse effect on economic life.

The kinds of behavior that have been suggested as adversely influencing economic growth are, among many, the 'luck' syndrome, a 'fatalistic' outlook, inter- and intra-familial quarrels, difficulties in co-operation, extra-ordinary ritual expenses by poor people and the problems these expenses pose for capital accumulation, and the apparent lack of what the psychologist McClelland has called 'Need for Achievement.'[7]

He explained local distrust through the fact that only a scarce and limited amount of good were available to the villagers and that those who tried to take in an inappropriate share of this limited good are scorned and criticized. This image of the limited good was given as a reason why peasants are reluctant to get ahead individually and to show more initiative and entrepreneurial spirit than their neighbors. Foster gave little attention to the fact that the state of Michoacan has been touched strongly by the Mexican Revolution and particularly by the agrarian struggle and its aftermath. This struggle went on for years at the cost of many lives, but Foster only refers to the efforts of the clergy to intimidate and discourage the peasants from participating in the agrarian movement without giving a description of this struggle or an analysis of its effects on the peasants' attitudes.

Some of these facts came out in studies carried out by others in the area of Tzintzuntzan. Thus, one study dealing with the village of Cucuchucho in the municipality of Tzintzuntzan gives some data on the agrarian struggle that was unsuccessful because of the strong opposition of the traditional interests.[8] In 1935, Nemesio de la Cruz and other inhabitants, altogether 25, started the proceedings for petition of land and denounced unused lands of the hacienda Santiaguito. The *cristeros* (antireform bands often led by priests and armed by the landlords) were strong in the area and for that reason the community asked military protection. Soon, the peasants themselves received arms although they had not yet received land. Nemesio de la Cruz was attacked when the petition was officially taken into consideration and an engineer had come to measure the land. He defended himself but through legal intrigues and paid witnesses he was accused of assault and punished with five years in prison. This was done to intimidate the agrarianists. He was imprisoned in Morelia, far away from his followers, rather than in the local jail of Patzcuaro. Threats of excommunication in addition to the other threats finally brought about the dissolution of the petitioning group, and forced the group to sign a declaration to renounce its activities. After Nemesio left prison, life in Cucuchucho was made impossible for him and he worked for a while in Patzcuaro. Later, he went as a migrant worker, *bracero*, to the United States. Cucuchucho is still known for its conservative and distrustful attitude and the sinachist movement has a strong impact.[9]

In Ihuatzio, another part of the municipality of Tzintzuntzan, (and studied by Rudolf van Zantwijk) the support of Catholic priests and bishops to the antiland reform movement was also successful. The remaining influence of this conservative movement in Ihuatzio, although diminished considerably (from 80 to 30 percent) between the thirties and today, was partly ascribed by van Zantwijk to the influence of a particular local priest. The impact of the conservative approach in this area was also in part a result of the fact that community leaders feared the loss of traditional forms of organization and their function in it, as a result of the agrarian reform or other development efforts. However, the maintenance of traditional Tarasco Indian institutions could be seen as a defense against complete loss of social status and dignity which would occur once the standards and norms of the mestizo population would be accepted.[10]

Traditionalism is thus related to the overall social structure in the country as a form of protection against the danger of pauperization. Van Zantwijk noted that, depending on different and often accidental local circumstances, the result of the agrarian struggle varied from place to place. He observed that in other communities in the same region the result of the struggle was different from the one in Ihuatzio,[11] or Cucuchucho, for that matter.

Foster apparently did not take into account the hard realities of the agrarian struggle in the area he studied and the fact that peasant leaders risked their lives for the common good on many occasions. The communities where the image of the limited good prevailed suffered severe physical and spiritual repression by a combination of the landed elite and the religious authorities. It would have been interesting if a comparative study had been made of the peasant attitudes in those communities where the peasants' struggle for land has been effective and successful and those where this was not the case.

Successful agrarian struggle went on in an area not far from Tzintzuntzan in the same state of Michoacan. In that region, an effective peasant movement was created by Primo Tapia, a peasant who had worked as a migrant worker in the United States. He started to form in 1921 a peasant syndicate in his village and its surrounding areas in order to petition for the restitution of the communal lands as stipulated by the land reform law. As an obstacle against the execution of the reform legislation, the landowners organized the so-called white syndicates which were controlled by them. The Catholic clergy gave its support to the landlords by preaching submission and conformity with the status quo. Also white guards, organized by the large landholders, intimidated the peasant agrarian committees which petitioned for the restitution of land. However, in spite of these obstacles, the movement gained strength and in 1922 formed a league in the state of Michoacan. In the meantime, several of the leaders had lost their lives. In 1924, the league became so strong that several haciendas were distributed according to the law. The opposition continued however and in 1926, the league suffered a severe setback when Primo Tapia was taken captive and shot.[12]

The municipality where Primo Tapia's movement had its origin and main impact was studied by the anthropologist Friedrich, who noted the continuation of the struggle for land and power in the villages long after Tapia's assassination. The old elite tried to reestablish itself and initiated factional struggle in the communities which resulted in a sizeable death toll over the years. As Friedrich noted

A total of 77 political homicides have interrupted the life of the *pueblo* during the past 36 years, and the three 'bad years' from 1937 to 1939 witnessed 21 politically motivated homicides and several times more armed encounters and exchange of gunfire.[13]

It is possible that in the communities where the agrarian struggle was represented at its initiation once and for all, a state of apathy and suspicion resulted as described by Foster. It seems that in those communities the suspicion and resistance to change was particularly felt when later small-scale community improvement efforts were undertaken. Aníbal Buitron, who worked in the same area that Foster studied noted the following.

The exploitation which these people have suffered and the subhuman conditions in which they live, made them timid, suspicious, resigned and apathetic. They have lost all hope, they lack all initiative or fear to exercise it, and they do not have the courage to break with the traditions which throttle them. To expect people who live under such conditions to take part in the efforts to improve their living standards at their own initiative is to expect the impossible. These people will not climb out of the bottom of the well until some outside force raises them at least to the landing where the ladder starts.[14]

It could now be asked how the peasants living under these circumstances would have reacted if the visitors from the development agencies would have come to help them to struggle against the repressive system, rather than with minor improvement schemes which hardly relieve but rather emphasize the state of frustration in which the peasants live. It calls attention that wherever Foster—and Banfield for that matter—speaks about change, he means gradual, piecemeal change of the community development type, as it is usually applied. He hardly sees the counterpoint elements which exist in the resistance to change and certainly does not notice them as possible points of departure for radical overall change, breaking through the culture of repression. The resistance to change existing among peasants could be interpreted as a resistance to minor changes within a social system from which they have no expectations for essential betterment, as we will see later.

Erasmus: The 'Encogido Syndrom'

It is known that often community development and similar efforts only serve to strengthen the peasantry in their basic distrust. Evaluation of several development programs has indicated that the main benefits go to those who are already better-off. A number of such programs purposely applied the approach which has been called betting on the strong.[15] Other programs are carried out so half-heartedly that the beneficiaries feel that no real change will result from it. (This was the case with several of the projects carried out in the Patzcuaro-Tzintzuntzan region as could be verified on several field visits there.) There are cases where betting on the strong leads to relative deprivation among the peasants, and thus indirectly provokes these peasants to unite against the traditional elite or the newly privileged ones. Coser indicated about this concept:

The notion of relative deprivation has been developed in recent sociological theorizing to denote the deprivation that arises not so much from the absolute amount of frustration as from the experienced discrepancy between one's lot and that of other persons or groups that serve as standards of reference. Whether or not superordinate groups or persons are taken as standards of reference by subordinate groups or individuals depends, at least in part, on whether the unequal distribution of rights and privileges is considered illegitimate by them. Negatively privileged groups or individuals may not develop the awareness that they are deprived of rights and privileges. In a caste society, for example, members of the lower caste, considering this system justified for religious reasons, may not feel frustrated by it. If the privileges of the superordinate group are not considered legitimately attainable by their subordinates, lower-status people compare themselves only with each other and not with members of the higher-status groups.[16]

One obvious case was the regional development project in northwestern Mexico (states of Sonora and Sinaloa) that served a minority of rather wealthy farmers instead of the peasants in the area. In this region, Charles Erasmus carried out his fieldwork which concerned resistance to change.[17] Here also a great amount of distrust existed among the peasants. Erasmus used the term encogido syndrom to characterize the peasants' attitude. The *encogido* is a personality type which is, according to Erasmus, prominent among the rural lower classes in Latin America. Erasmus derived this term from popular usage in the area he studied.[18] The term was used in conversation by people to classify neighbors or acquaintances. The *encogido* is timid and withdrawn, and avoids persons of higher status except for a few who act as intermediaries between him and the broader society. The opposite personality distinguished by people in the area was the *entrón*, a person who pushes himself and is not afraid to interact with higher status persons for economically advantageous contacts. Erasmus noted that a word used in some parts of Venezuela for the *encogido*, is *patronizado*, subjugated to the *patron*. It is the *encogido* personality which holds the image of the limited good, invidious sanction or keeping the Joneses down, as Erasmus puts it. Erasmus, more or less like Banfield and Foster, emphasized the fact that the peasants, the Joneses, keep each other down. A further look into this situation and its wider societal implications, shows however that keeping the Joneses down is to a large extent the result of an outside force, the expression of the culture of repression. Erasmus did not see this. From the description by Erasmus, one may get the impression that the *encogido* syndrom is a more or less pathological state of mind, incompatible with the need for development and the great obstacle to becoming part of the middle-class mentality of keeping up with the Joneses, the ideal according to Erasmus.

Erasmus, addressing himself to American policy makers, sees individual competitive middle-class emulation as a way to integrate the peasantry into the national development process. His agreement with the method of betting on the strong comes well out in his book.

At this point one might ask whether it is necessary to spark development through invidious emulation and conspicuous ownership. Why not skip this stage of crass materialism and go straight into a benevolent development in which people learn unselfishly to help themselves by helping each other Certainly some of the extremes of conspicuous ownership can be avoided by a coercive form of government that rewards conspicuous production. But coercive methods are the ones we (sic!) most wish to avoid. Expansion of the middle classes seems the most reliable way of providing the sanctions to make government benevolent for the greatest number, and invidious emulation is the major stimulus for middle-class growth,

and

... Strengthening the middle classes wherever we can will promote the kinds of social sanctions we approve and will help to broaden the economic base and increase the desire for popular education.[19]

In Sonora, different rates of change between town and country or Indian and white do not justify giving priority to adult education programs called by such names as self-help, fundamental education, extension and community development. The fact that development is not likely to be uniform means that everywhere there are many people at the bottom of the social ladder who cannot keep up with the rest.[20]

Erasmus saw a confirmation of the success of individual competitive middle-class emulation as a way to rapid development in the northwest of Mexico, where in the early fifties huge irrigation schemes were introduced. The newly irrigated lands were, on the whole, not distributed according to the law as part of the land reform program to the mass of landless peasants living in the area, but to friends of the government in lots of three hundred hectares (the maximum limit for private land property of irrigated land, planted with cash crops). These farmers were legally called small proprietors. They formed the rising middle class in the region. In this area, a more or less radical peasant organization had existed since the Cardenas regime when initial agrarian reform was introduced in the late thirties. These organizations were since 1949 affiliated to the *Union General de Obreros y Campesinos de Mexico* (UGOCM), an independent leftist organization headed by Jacinto Lopez and related to the Popular (Socialist) Party of Vicente Lombardo Toledano.[21] When studying this area in 1958, Erasmus observed that the conspicuous consumption patterns of the rising middle class emphasized the contrast between privileged and underprivileged.[22] He hardly noticed the peasant movement which sprang up in this area as a reaction to this development. This movement covered large parts of the states of Sonora, Sinaloa, and Baja California, and was one of the main incentives for the acceleration of the agrarian reform program during the government of President Lopez Mateos (1958-1964).[23]

Erasmus neglected to see the massive mobilization of a large sector of the peasant population, opposing a relatively small group of profiteers, and described the situation as follows.

Even under conditions of rapid development as in northwestern Mexico there are some social sectors or 'pockets' [sic!] that do not keep up with the rest. In Sonora, for instance, the rural population in general and the Indian sector in particular have lagged behind.[24]

In addition to the sharpening social contrasts noted above, it should be mentioned that a strong feeling of injustice predominantly among the peasantry in the area because part of the middle and large landownership of irrigated land existed in circumvention of the law: a considerable number of large landholdings consisted of several small properties which were exploited as one unit. The existence of such properties was difficult to prove, but was revealed in the patterns of the use of irrigation. Thus, various neighboring properties proved coincidentally to belong to relatives and were coincidentally exploited in common.[25]

Although such facts were hidden in cadastral archives in forms which were not easy to unravel, the peasants who lived in the area, landless, waiting for their chance to receive some share of the new developments, knew every detail of this situation, and felt strongly frustrated or embittered that no official action was taken to their benefit. It has happened that in Sinaloa, peasants were forced to leave lands which were included in the irrigation scheme of the Miguel Hidalgo dam.[26] It was in those areas where later neolatifundios of thousands of hectares were created.

With assistance of the UGOCM, the formation of new land reform settlements, as stipulated by the agrarian reform law, had been petitioned by local committees. Many of the petitioners were migrants from some of the overpopulated states of Mexico, who had been working in the region for several years in the construction of the irrigation works or as peons, in the hope of receiving land in the newly irrigated areas. In the state of Sinaloa alone, about 250 group petitions were under consideration in the land reform department of years. Many of these held-up petitions had already obtained the presidential resolution, the last step in the reform process before the actual assignment of the land, but no land had actually been distributed. On March 30-April 1, 1957, the UGOCM organized in Los Mochis, Sinaloa, a congress of its affiliates in the northern region.[27] Approximately 1,500 peasant delegates attended, many of whom represented committees of petitioners for land, mainly those peasants who had been expecting to receive the irrigated—or soon to be irrigated—lands which fell into the hands of new large landholders. During the meeting, a series of resolutions were discussed and unanimously accepted. These provided that if the problems of the petitioners would not soon be legally solved as promised, the lands in question would be invaded. Since several leaders who had directed the petitioners, had been assassinated,[c] it was also agreed that for each leader who in the future would fall, for vengeance, the life of a large landowner would be taken. The resolutions became known as the Acuerdo de Los Mochis, Agreement of Los Mochis. The press in Mexico gave very little attention to these facts, although Vincente Lombardo Toledano, Jacinto López and other national leaders spoke in the passive closing session in the stadium of Los Mochis. The UGOCM-affiliated peasants decided to wait until the end of the year to see if the government would accomplish its promises and/or fulfill the legitimate demands. When a solution to the problems was offered at the beginning of 1958, the agitation started again, in fulfillment of the Acuerdo de Los Mochis.

On 26 January 1958, a mass meeting of about 8,000 peasant representatives was held in Culiacan, later filing out through the main streets of the town in an orderly manner, making a powerful impression on local public opinion. Fourteen speakers explained the grievance of the peasants during the meeting and declared that the Agreement of Los Mochis, which provided for the occupation of lands held in circumvention of the national laws, would be accomplished. The hypoth-

---

[c]Francisco Solís and Maximiliano López were leaders assassinated in Sinaloa in the mid fifties.

esis was that the real owners of lands which were registered as small properties under false names, while forming part of latifundios as large as 22,000 hectares, would show up as soon as their lands would be symbolically occupied. The top leaders of the UGOCM had met with the governor and the Attorney-General of the state of Sinaloa, explaining that all legal means to obtain justice had been exhausted. Also, the military commander of the state was visited. The prudence with which the activities were prepared not only ensured a great deal of sympathy from the local population and adhesion of workers' unions in the regions but it also testified to the organizational discipline of the UGOCM.

On 10 February 1958, about 3,000 peasants symbolically occupied 20,000 hectares of irrigated land in the Culiacán valley in Sinaloa. In the cultivated parts of the claimed lands, occupation consisted of the planting of the national flag while the mass of the peasants were standing or sitting on the roads along these fields. A tactical aspect of the occupations was to start by occupying lands belonging to foreigners, in violation of the Constitution which prohibits foreigners from owning land within 50 kilometers of the sea-coast. Later, land belonging to Mexican citizens in tracts far above the legally allowed maximum were similarly occupied. When army units came to dissolve the sit-ins, the peasants left peacefully. They were intentionally unarmed. It should be noted that the army units behaved, under strict instructions, in a very disciplined and almost friendly way, using persuasion rather than force.

The peasants had the collaboration of the regional *Alianza de Camioneros de Carga* (Union of Truckers) to transport them quickly to other areas, where the lands under similar conditions were symbolically occupied. The unexpectedness of the moves was one of the reasons for their impact all over the region. The local newspapers noted that the top leaders of the UGOCM did not show themselves, but that the whole movement obviously was under the direction of the country's agitator No. 1, Jacinto López, Secretary-General of the UGOCM.

As a result, the Minister of Agriculture came to the region to promise and initiate a solution for the land tenure situation. He went personally to all the places where lands had been or were being occupied. When, on 15 March 1958, the process of giving possession of lands to the petitioners was effectively initiated by the Minister, Jacinto López sent a telegram with congratulations to the President and the agitation was suspended. Probably as a consequence of the warnings of the agreements of Los Mochis, no more efforts to assassinate peasant leaders had been made by the landlords.

This example of man-takes-control did not go unnoticed by Charles Erasmus, who was present in the area when some of these occurrences took place. However, apparently preoccupied to find examples of individual emulation, he seems to have overlooked the possibility that under certain circumstances of acute frustration, men can get together and try to take control through united or even collective action. The fact that he saw peasants who had invaded land, chased away by the army using tear gas, was mentioned, but not analyzed in his study. He noted the following about these events.

When I was there in 1958, the state administration was not favorably disposed toward expropriation tactics, and Jacinto Lopez, peasant leader who for many years has periodically led squatter invasions of private holdings, spent most of the year in jail, virtually a political prisoner.[28]

and . . .

At present, the organization attracting most attention in northwestern Mexico is the *Union General*, the farm labor branch of the Popular Socialist Party. Run locally by Jacinto Lopez, this labor union organizes landless peasants to invade private lands deemed by Lopez to be illegally large.[29]

Obviously, Erasmus did not draw any conclusions from these facts, or drew, unconsciously, the wrong conclusion (as the following excerpts show).

We find a situation in Sonora, much like that in Bolivia where a peasant population has been provided with opportunities for advancement but has persisted in clinging to older, more primitive patterns of consumption.

and . . .

His expectations are too low to motivate him to look around. Frequently, when I asked peasants if they would not like to have refrigerators and gas stoves like the people in the towns, they replied that the would, of course, but that poor people like them could never expect to have such things.[30]

Erasmus' preoccupations with refrigerators shows in an interesting way his own ethnocentrism.[31] In fact, in one of the best-organized affiliates of the UGOCM in the area, one of the few remaining collective *ejidos* (land reform settlements) created in the thirties, almost all members have a refrigerator in their homes. The leader of the group, a socialist, had tried to maintain a certain equality among the members and when the progress of the *ejido* made this possible, he stimulated all to improve their living conditions in more or less similar ways, and organized the wholesale purchase of some expensive consumer goods. Erasmus noticed the success of this collective as an exception to the rule. It should be noted that most of the collectives in the area were purposely undermined or destroyed by the Mexican government as part of its campaign to foster middle-class farmers. Quechehueca survived in spite of tremendous odds, including the assassination of one leader and several attempts on Arana.[32]

Repression as a Cause for 'Resistance to Change'

Although Foster and Erasmus consciously or unconsciously deemphasized the repression and struggle that bring perspective into the resistance to change of the peasant communities they studied, they were aware of some of the dynamic forces operating in relation to the syndromes they described. Foster at some points indicates the valid reasons the peasants have for their attitude.

The behavior of a peasant villager, however stubborn and unreasoned it may seem to an outsider, is the product of centuries of experience. It is an effective protective device in a relatively unchanging world. It is less effective in a rapidly industrializing world, and ultimately it becomes a hindrance. But the peasant is pragmatic; he is not going to discard the clothing that has served him well until he is convinced that he will profit by so doing. He sees that the future holds new things, but he remembers the past: 'Our lives are oppressed by many fears. We fear the rent collector, we fear the police watchman, we fear everyone who looks as though he might claim some authority over us, we fear our creditors, we fear our patrons, we fear too much rain, we fear locusts, we fear thieves, we fear the evil spirits which threaten our children and our animals, and we fear the strength of our neighbour.'[33]

In addition to the oppressive fears, the outside repressive forces were noted by Foster.

The truncated political nature of peasant societies, with real power lying outside the community, seems effectively to discourage local assumption and exercise of power, except as an agent of these outside forces. By the very nature of peasant society seen as a structural part of a larger society, local development of leadership which might make possible cooperation is effectively prevented by the rulers of the political unit of which a particular peasant community is an element, who see such action as a potential to themselves.[34]

However, Foster did not clearly see the possibility that among the peasants the awareness of their enemies could become a starting point for effective organization, as occurred in the agrarian movements in some places in the area he studied. Similarly, Erasmus made some observations regarding the awareness the peasants have about their repressive conditions, but again, without drawing any significant conclusions. In a recent study he noted that the peasants perceived the development agencies in the north of Mexico, particularly the credit bank for agrarian reform beneficiaries as a "heartless" and impersonal *patron*, a good reason for their distrust.[35] He also made an interesting observation which tends to confirm the idea that the *encogido* syndrome and peasant submissiveness is determined more by social conditions, the culture of repression, than by inherent characteristics. He observed this fact when, on several occasions, he watched the change in behavior and mood of a local peasant family in the presence of a higher status person.

The easy-going good-natured behavior of the adults becomes suddenly very tense and rigid, so that they appear almost hostile rather than uneasy. Under these conditions, the young children, too, become tense and frightened. They sense immediately the discomfort of the adults, and sometimes, the very young will even start to cry at this sudden transformation in their parents' behavior.[36]

Erasmus also observed how between 1948 and 1958 the peasants had transformed from *encogido* (timid and withdrawn) to *entrón*, more aggressive and inclined to make contacts. During his second stay (1958), Erasmus found the peasants more willing to give information and much less evasive than ten years before.[37] An explanation for this change in attitude is the much more frequent contact between the local indigenous peasants and peasants who immigrated from other areas, as well as the fact that the indigenous as well as mestizo peasants increasingly participated in the peasant unions. In common actions such as symbolical occupations of estates or mass demonstrations in the towns of Los Mochis or Ciudad Obregon, they are able to gain a feeling of strength and self-confidence, particularly where these activities were a direct response to the land tenure illegalities and other factors which were the cause of considerable distrust among the peasants. Erasmus, however, did not describe and analyze the implications of such developments, the obstacles they encountered, or their internal dynamics.

It seems that Banfield, Foster and Erasmus, although aware of some of the wider and political implications of the resistance to change of the peasants, limited themselves to the introduction of concepts (amoral familism, the image of the limited good and encogido syndrome respectively) which only describe or qualify the behavior of the peasants, but do not clearly indicate and explain the motivations behind it. Banfield[d] noted this limitation in his Chapter 5 when he made the following remarks

A very simple hypothesis will make intelligible all of the behavior about which questions have been raised and will enable an observer to predict how the montegranesi will act in concrete circumstances.

and . . .

The coincidence of facts and theory does not 'prove' the theory. However, it does show that the theory will explain (in the sense of making intelligible and

---

[d]A certain confusion may be noted in Banfield's book, with regard to the factors which are the cause of amoral familism. In the Introduction to his book, he stated: "This inability to concert action beyond the immediate family arises from an ethos—that of 'amoral familism'—which has been produced by three factors acting in combination: a high death rate, certain land tenure conditions, and the absence of the institution of the extended family."[39] Towards the end of the book, he said: "The mechanism which produces the ethos of amoral familism is undoubtedly complex, consisting of many elements in a mutually reinforcing relation. The dreadful poverty of the region and the degraded status of those who do manual labor, matters which were discussed in Chapters 3 and 4, are surely of very great importance in forming it; they are structural factors, so to speak, in the system of causes. If we turn now to other elements in the system, it is not to depreciate the importance of them."[40] He then dedicated some pages to the fear of premature death, the absence of the extended family system, and the insecurity of land tenure. Some of these factors were described as related to "feudalism," and thus seemed to be at least partly determined by the predominant social structure in Southern Italy.[41]

predictable) much behavior without being contradicted by any of the facts at hand.[38]

Also, Foster was aware of the limitations of his terminology.

At no point has an informant even remotely suggested that this is his vision of his universe. Yet each Tzintzunteno organizes his fashion entirely rational when it is viewed as a function of this principle which he cannot enunciate.[42]

In a similar way, Galjart, when explaining the term patronic syndrome, indicated

I do not suggest that I know the cause of the interrelation between the elements of the syndrome: I cannot even demonstrate that the elements are interrelated. The syndrome is an abstract construction, a generalization deduced from the observation of concrete acts, which clarifies the apprehension, and hence facilitates the observation, of certain categories of behavior. The Brazilian farm operators in the project behave as if they hold the values and attitudes subsumed under the term patronic syndrome, and it is only in this sense that their behavior will be explained.[43]

The various concepts used for resistance to change among peasants, seem, upon closer scrutiny, to apply to peasant behavior and make that behavior predictable, as long as the whole culture of repression in which the peasants live, is taken as a constant and static factor. If one looks at the repression as a dynamic factor, as something imposed upon the peasantry, but not an inherent characteristic of his life, one could state that the resistance to change of the peasantry is a reaction to and conditioned by the resistance to change of those who have power over the peasants, the landed elite.

Unfortunately, very little study has been made of the attitudes and mentality of this elite which is the basic cause of peasant distrust. Tentatively, one could say that the concept image of the limited good applies at least as well to the landed elite as to the peasantry. Erasmus made an interesting observation in this respect.

In the classic, exploitative model of peasantry where the ecotype is static, landowners and serfs are indeed very much like antagonists in a zero-sum game, since there are few inputs into the system and rewards are in very limited supply. Any increase in the well-being of the peasant must be at the expense of the leisure class which clearly recognizes this fact as it zealously guards its prerogatives. Among the peasants themselves in this classic situation, there was probably not as much need to apply invidious sanctions since the ruling class saw to it that there was very little mobility.[44]

This limited good image among landlords seems to explain the considerable resistance to change of the landed elites in most Latin American countries and the tremendous fear that by making concessions they may lose all privileges and pre-rogatives. Galjart also noted this mentality among the rural elite when he indi-cated that only exceptionally have the local elites understood that even a smaller portion of the cake could mean more cakes, if only the size of the cake increased enough.[45]

The authors dealt with in this chapter, and also Galjart, seem to take for granted the continuity of the present system and strongly emphasize that efforts to introduce change, moderate changes of the usual community development type, will generally have little chance for success. It seems that the pessimistic theories of Banfield, Foster, and Erasmus are a reaction to the naive optimism which has existed behind community development activities for many years. They all, at some stage in their work, express their disappointment in com-munity development. Along these lines, Foster wrote the following.

It is difficult for me to understand why, in the face of visible evidence to the contrary, so much work in community development and related programs is based on the starry-eyed assumption that there is something "naturally" cooper-ative about peasants. It is just not so, and there are good reasons in addition to suspicion based on economic scarcity.[46]

Erasmus in particular is strongly disappointed in "Community Development" (with capital letters).[e] He dedicated a strongly polemical article to denounce the failure of community development and the naiveté of those who continue to believe in its possibilities. He finds most community development projects that he knows through personal observation useless, utopian and anachronistic be-cause they try to stimulate voluntary cooperation among people in a paternal-istic way, and thus basically try to keep the people down. The examples he gives may not all be typical for community development as understood for example by the United Nations, but they are convincing. As the reason for the uselessness of many community development efforts, Erasmus gives the *encogido* syndrome. He sees the community developers as do-gooders who protect the *encogido* peas-ants rather than stimulate the *entrón*, the more aggressive person, to individual emulation, higher consumption and social mobility, which is pictured as the solution of peasant backwardness. However, Erasmus[f] noticed in Bolivia an alternative way of development of the peasants occurred, namely through the peasant federation and agrarian reform.

[e]The fact that he uses capital letters for community development may indicate that he once saw it as a kind of religion himself, but once he discovered it to be a "God that failed" he turned bitterly against it. The sharply disdainful tone of his article may also be explained in this way.[47]

[f]It should be noted that this statement of Erasmus somewhat neutralizes his attack on com-munity developers for claiming intangible, rather than economically calculable successes. One of the objects of Erasmus' disdain is an article in the Saturday Review of Literature[49] which wrote about the Vicos project: "Its people still live in adobe huts. They have no bathrooms. Their drinking water is impure. Their food is primitive. They weave their own clothes and wear them Indian style. 'But we didn't set out to change these people outside' Professor Holmberg says. 'We weren't putting on a show. We wanted to change them inside, where it matters.' "

The elimination of feudal labor practices, the formation of peasant syndicates, and the redistribution of land titles, all brought about by the agrarian reform, have permanently changed the self-image of the peasant. The *patrón* is no longer a symbol of invincible authority. While many peasants I interviewed did not feel they were eating or living better than before the reform, they felt that they now had more freedom and dignity.[48]

Erasmus did not emphasize that the agrarian reform in Bolivia was to a large extent the result of a strongly organized united peasant struggle, opposing the violence of the landowners, particularly in the Cochabamba area, as will be shown later. Perhaps this fact did not fit his preference for individual emulation above solidarian or collective action, although he applauds the peasant federation as it exists in Bolivia and Venezuela. Not, however, the socialist unions in Sonora, Mexico. As has been illustrated above and in some footnotes, this is not the only contradiction existing in Erasmus' views regarding rural development.

As noted before, Banfield, too, had doubts regarding the effectiveness of community development in a traditional society. He only sensed that other possibilities existed, at least in theory.

La miseria, it seems safe to conclude, arises as much or more from social as from biological deprivations. This being the case, there is no reason to expect that a moderate increase in income (if by some miracle that could be brought about) would make the atmosphere of the village less heavy with melancholy. On the contary, unless there were accompanying *changes in social structure and culture*, increasing incomes would probably bring with them increasing discontent. (italics added)[50]

Surprisingly enough, his recommendation is betting on the strong even more than in Erasmus' case: "The upper class should be encouraged to take the leadership in local affairs.[51]

Rather than looking for the reason of the evil in the approach of community development as it is generally taken, they appear to blame the peasant mentality for their lack of success. They give very little attention to the resistance to change of the rural elite as the fundamental cause nor to the possibility that the peasants can be mobilized under circumstances where the influence of the culture of repression has disappeared. They also neglected to look into the possibility of united peasant struggle to overthrow the repressive traditional system. (The statements of Erasmus regarding the Bolivian peasant federation and a few isolated observations by Foster indicate that they must have had *some* notion of the possibilities for united peasant action, but either they did not interpret this carefully or they neglected it.)

Overcoming 'Resistance to Change': The Vicos Experiment

What happens when radical change is promoted in a traditional community in which the culture of repression existed in a strong form (in fact: where the idea culture of repression found its origin), can be seen from the experiment carried out by Allan Holmberg and his team of Cornell University in the exhacienda Vicos in Peru. This is probably the best known example of a scientifically controlled experiment in radical social change.

Vicos, a typical Peruvian hacienda with about 300 Quechua-speaking Indian families, attached to the land (but owning none of it), was taken over by the Cornell University study-group in 1952. At that time, "standards of living were at a bare minimum. Health and nutritional levels were extremely low. Educational facilities were almost completely lacking. Cooperation within the community was the exception rather than the rule, and resistance to the outside world was high. Attitudes towards life were static and pessimistic."[52] The purpose of the experiment was that of "developing within the community independent and dynamic problem-solving and decision-making organizations which could gradually assume the responsibilities of leadership in public affairs in a rational and humane manner and along democratic lines."[53] The traditional obligations of the hacienda system were abolished immediately and a new relationship on the principles of friendship and respect for the human dignity of the peasants was created. The inhabitants were also helped with an attractive credit system to improve their agriculture.

Between 1952 and 1957, the management of the hacienda was transferred gradually to the indigenous peasants. The more respected peasants were carefully selected and trained in shouldering responsibility and settling conflicts. Decisions made by this group of leaders were discussed by the community as a whole. At the same time, improvements in health and education were introduced and local people were made responsible for such activities. The groups, organized to this effect, gradually learned to assume greater responsibilities so that in 1957, the management of the whole hacienda could practically be given to an elected body of local leaders.

This case can be considered as an example of a slowly executed agrarian reform. The results were striking. Production of potatoes doubled between 1957 (when everything was still managed under the old system) and 1958, with only a third of the labor force working on this crop. Production per man thus went up 600 percent.

From these findings in the Vicos project, Holmberg made the following conclusion.

While it is dangerous to draw general conclusions from a single instance of this kind, particularly from a single instance of this kind, particularly one in which many intervening variables were obviously involved, nevertheless, the data from Vicos are not without theoretical significance. They tend to confirm a hypothesis long ago expressed by Marx, namely that the alienation of people from control over the means of production retards social and economic development.[54]

The effects of the Vicos experiment are well summarized by Harold Lasswell.

Among the inhabitants of Vicos generations of oppression had created profound scepticism regarding the motives of an outsider, and particularly of the *patrón*. Hence, the strategy of rapid intervention, and the dramatic abolition of old abuses at the very beginning of Cornell's intervention. The new program was launched in a setting of surprise, incredulity, gratitude and hope.[55]

That this drastic change of social climate in one place had a strong appeal in the surrounding region and led to unrest and awakening among the peasants and resistance from the side of the landlords who feared to lose their age-old privileges, has been indicated by several anthropologists who participated in Cornell's experiment.[56] The shooting of three peasants, mentioned above, was a direct result of this resistance by the landowners.

A few important issues become clear from the effects of the Vicos experiment. One is that the strongest and most violent resistance to change comes from the traditionally wealthy, privileged and educated landlords rather than from the traditionally poor peasants. The other is that the best way to bring about dynamic change is to start with it in a spectacular and rapid way, abolishing the repressive atmosphere completely and dramatically,[g] replacing it by one based on confidence in which self-confidence can grow. Only a dramatic change gives the peasants incentives to give up their distrust and resistance to change. Peasant distrust appears to be a healthy reaction of normal people to a pathological social climate rather than an almost pathological mental state as it is sometimes pictured. And upon closer scrutiny, distrust can become a starting point for strong movements against this pathological situation.

Most community and rural development projects do not fulfill the conditions of radical and overall change which facilitates the mobilization of people, as happened on a small scale in Vicos. On the contrary, community development workers have usually emphasized continuity and compromise between the different, even opposing forces in the community. It is thus understandable that repressed people have generally reacted negatively to community development efforts, a thing strongly observed and emphasized by the authors dealing with the implica-

---

[g]A similar observation has been made for peasants in other regions of the world.

As long as the social order of peasantry seems to make ends meet (which is not the same as to give satisfaction, far less gratification), every social attitude is jealously preserved. Since the explanation of a particular phenomenon is possible only by reference to the entire order of phenomena in which it occurs, and since this is quite different from the relevance of a particular phenomenon for a particular problem, no one knows how important the single phenomenon is for the whole order. Neither can anyone measure the relevance of any phenomenon compared with that of any other. It follows that either the entire order of phenomena is religiously preserved as a whole, or it is all thrown overboard. This inability to examine individual aspects explains why peasantry resists so long the adoption of single ideas, and why, when relative deprivation and tension pile up, wholesale change is demanded without thought of the consequences.[57]

tions of resistance to change. Looking at this situation more carefully, one can see that in most cases—particularly those that inspired Foster, Banfield, and Erasmus—the resistance to change basically means resistance to piecemeal change, or resistance to change which is not really change. Community development has for many years taken as a frame of reference the idea of the harmonious traditional community where people have a natural inclination towards co-operation. A decade ago, the official United Nations statement regarding community development indicated: "These programs are usually concerned with local communities because of the fact that the people living together in a locality have many and varied interests in common."[58]

'Resistance to Change' as a Positive Force

A new interpretation of the possibilities for work at the community level is gradually winning ground. In a recent evaluation by United Nations of accomplishments and drafting of a future policy, it was emphasized that the idea of harmonious communities has often proved to be false, since most communities are ridden by factional or other forms of internal struggle and conflict of interests. Suggestions are made to evaluate these conflicts realistically and to utilize these forces constructively. Thus, this new UN document points out the following.

While the soundness of the strategy incorporated in community development has generally been accepted, this is not true for its conceptual components. As most of the concepts and 'principles' associated with community development were formulated—largely by 'western' specialists—at a time when systematic knowledge about rural societies in developing countries and the process of development had not sufficiently advanced, some of them were rooted in somewhat unrealistic assumptions and incorporated a utopian view of traditional rural communities. They were stated as if they had universal validity regardless of the context in which they were applied. For instance, the organic concept of rural communities implicit in efforts towards involvement of the whole community, or the establishment of local councils, assumed that there was no element of conflict emerging out of the compatibility of interests latent in any social system. The concept of "felt-needs" underestimated the determining effect of socioeconomic conditions on the needs felt and assumed that there was an identity between the felt needs of a traditional rural community and the needs of a society as a whole aspiring to enter the modern industrial era. Emphasis on the initiative and self-help could lead to development without significant structural changes in the rural economy and the power complex, such as through land reform, and without substantial external assistance to build adequate rural infrastructure.[59]

This document—with the usual prudence of a UN statement—also noted that the consensus built around traditional means may have development-impeding rather than development-promoting consequences, and that overemphasis on traditional concensus may block the development of innovation. In a traditional society, the dominant groups in the community have means to control those individuals who threaten the existing order. Therefore, it is important to consider weakening of traditional solidarity as

. . . a necessary cost that has to be paid for development. A more effective strategy than that of community consensus might be to identify creatively deviant individuals, help them to cultivate leadership qualities, and create new groups and organizations around them. Such a strategy would initially weaken the community consensus, but when the process of development is sufficiently advanced a new consensus may emerge around more development-oriented values and individuals.[60]

In cases where the social structure and climate are adverse to modernization and development, conflict may thus have a more positive quality as an innovating force than consensus based on traditions or adaptations in the status quo. The forces operating in the conflict situation which exists in rigidly traditional rural areas may be channelled constructively and become an asset for change and development. The cohesiveness and solidarity of the peasants, shown in distrust and resistance can be a positive force, facilitating active participation as a group in development efforts in their own interest.

We have seen already that much resistance to change of the peasants can be interpreted as resistance to piecemeal or basically useless change. Rather than a nuisance for developers, this counterpoint element can become a positive force. Although subordination generally implies a certain cohesion among the repressed, this cohesion is weak as long as the repressed have no common goal. Once they detect a common enemy or a negative reference group cohesion becomes strong. The awareness of this possibility is a crucial factor in the organization of groups that oppose or even combat the traditional system, as was demonstrated by the work in Partinico, described above. Once the need to rally the peasants in opposition to an overwhelmingly powerful establishment is recognized, the phenomena described in this chapter, summarized under the term resistance to change of the peasants, become positive and useful qualities. The image of the limited good as well as the encogido syndrome can be seen as ways through which peasants maintain among each other a minimum of solidarity, which only needs to be mobilized under proper conditions in order to become a dynamic factor. A new interpretation can now be given to some of the aspects of distrust described above.

It could be seen in the San Luis project (El Salvador) that the possibility to say no and to refuse quietly to participate in efforts the benefit of which is doubtful, is often the only means the peasants have to defend, or better, not to risk, their interests. Too many cases in the past have shown the peasants that participation in things proposed by nonpeasants are of little or no benefit to them, but rather to those who are already better off. Distrust and refusal to participate in things the consequences of which are not very clear, often appears to be pragmatic and wise response under the circumstances of rural life.

Not only distrust of outsiders and development agents can be seen as a means of defense of the peasants' common interests, but also the distrust which exists in the interpersonal relations between the peasants can be seen in this way.

There appear to be two positive factors in the whole syndrome of apathy, distrust, envy and other aspects of the image of limited good. One factor is the need for sharing the poverty in a more or less egalitarian way, which can be seen as a sign of solidarity among equally underprivileged people. The other factor is the importance of conserving for the community outstanding, not to say charismatic, leadership. The ideal leader is a kind of person whom the peasant villagers see as the only one capable of overcoming their traditional inability to organize and execute long-term efforts. One way to keep potential leaders within the community as promoters of group solidarity is to discourage able individuals from standing out and becoming strong on their own account. This fear of losing able group elements may prevent potential leaders from taking initiative in an individualist way. In cases, however, where local potential leaders take initiatives to defend the collective interest, the traditional communities will follow and applaud their action.

The difficulty of retraining good leaders for the community living under the impact of repressive circumstances was noted even by George Foster, who indicated that peasant societies under threatened circumstances have two alternatives: maximum cooperation and sometimes communism, or, on the other side, extreme individualism.[61] The fact that many communities appear to take the individualist approach is due to the difficulty in promoting cooperation without good leadership.

The mutual distrust existing among peasants can be explained by their frustration in facing the overwhelming obstacles presented by the status quo. It may be seen as potential aggression which is turned inward. Channelling this potential aggression outward in a constructive way through able leadership against those outside forces of power which prevent real change in the communities generally brings about forms of group-cohesiveness and cooperation which have not been expected. In the situation in which most peasants live, it seems that the need for strong solidarity and togetherness, facing the overpowering odds of landowner control, is very strong. It appears only logical that any capable individual who tries to escape individually from the general situation is discouraged among his peers. It may be only partly a conscious attitude of the peasants, but in some cases, they are well aware of the fact that the establishment they live under tries to buy off any person capable of leading resistance against it.[h] Many cases are known where peasants who were outstanding in bringing about solidarity and resistance against the rural elite were offered individual ways of upward social

---

[h]Statements of peasants in San Luis (El Salvador) and Partinico (Sicily).

mobility and even the facility to become part of the elite themselves. The life-history of Mexico's agrarian leader Zapata, to be dealt with later, is an outstanding case. As soon as his movement was so strong that it had influence at the national level, he was offered an estate for himself. Zapata refused the offer, but many other leaders have betrayed their adherents and accepted entrance into the elite. It seems sound practice for peasants to try to close their ranks as long as they are in their present unfavorable position.

The whole problem of distrust and its functions has been summarized by Wertheim as follows.

In our counterpoint concept, this very distrust may, in certain circumstances, be seen as a rational defense mechanism of those who have, from the point of view of their value system, valid reasons for distrusting those in power. Such a distrust may, for the time being, protect those who are only passive objects of an official policy of intrusions into the basis of their existence. They may, in this way, slowly develop a more active type of mutual solidarity which will enable them, later on, to participate in the 'modernization' process on their own terms. This might even, sometimes, forbode revolt for the future. But even then, their behavior is no anomie, and not dysfunctional if looked at from within a different system of values.[62]

That the possibility of organized peasant action and even revolt in Latin America is not remote can be seen from several cases where effective movements were created that achieved considerable changes to the benefit of the peasants. In the next chapter, the most important movements that have occurred in Latin America will be described.

4

Some Large-Scale Peasant Organization: Their Origins and Their Effects in Mexico and Bolivia

It has been demonstrated by empirical case studies that the organization of the peasants in favor of development is very possible if such organizations channel their activities towards radical changes in the traditional rural power structure as a condition for further development. To organize against the prevailing culture of repression seems the most feasible way to bring peasants into united action for their own benefit. Counterpoint elements existing in the traditional system, expressed in distrust and resentment, can be utilized to rally people in the struggle to defend their legitimate interests. This is possible not only on a small scale, but can also be organized on a regional or national level. Although until today relatively few experiences exist in this field, several large-scale peasant organizations that have developed in Latin America prove that this is possible. A careful study of the few important movements, generally related to the land reform problem, will be undertaken in this and the following chapters.

In order to gain insights into the possibilities for peasant organizations are kept in mind when describing the existing cases. The possible answers to these questions will be dealt with in Chapter 6, where attention is focused on the common factors of the peasant organizations. The issues raised in these descriptive chapters are more or less the following.

1. the conditions that were favorable to the formation of a peasant organization, such as geographical factors, specific conflict situations, availability of leadership, outside influences, opposing forces;
2. the actual process of formation of the organization taking place in stages such as the creation of awareness of a problem, the appearance of strong leaders, support from outsiders in the spread of the organization, stimulation from above;
3. the demands of the organization—generally land reform—and the means to pressure in favor of those demands;
4. the achievements of the organizations and the ways in which they became part of the existing institutional structure. After discussing these factors from past or present experiences of peasant organizations, we will take a look at the prospects for peasant organization in Latin America in general.

When dealing with different peasant movements, we could accept Landsberger's definition: "any collective reaction by rural cultivators to their low status."[1] A peasant organization is a movement that has taken some kind of organizational structure in order to be more effective. Not all peasant movements have such a structure. *Jacqueries* and other mob reactions of poor peasants protesting against their conditions are generally unstructured, but the movements discussed below were all structured and organized to some extent. Since the most spectacular and successful peasant movements in Mexico and Bolivia related to overall national revolutions and resulted in considerable change in the rural power structure, these movements will be dealt with first and most extensively in this chapter. In Chapter 5, some less important but large-scale movements, more or less effectively organized, will be described.

The Mexican Agrarian Movement

In this section, a description will be given of the peasant guerrillas headed by Emiliano Zapata in the state of Morelos and their struggle for the restitution of lands that had been taken away from them. This movement grew from a village committee defending communal rights into a large-scale organization strong enough to have a considerable impact in the Mexican Revolution of 1910 and to achieve land reform legislation. It had to continue the armed struggle to achieve the implementation of this legislation. After Zapata's death in 1919, the agrarian struggle went on in Mexico until president Cardenas started in 1934 a large-scale program of land distribution, supported in this effort by the organized and armed peasants. After his term was over in 1940, the peasant organizations which had become part of the official government party, were made virtually ineffective because the leadership was taken over or influenced by elements of the traditional or new landowning elite. On some occasions, the agrarian struggle flared up again where independent peasant organizations had a chance to develop. The ups and downs of the agrarian movement in Mexico are described in the light of the questions mentioned above.[2]

1910-1919

The Mexican Revolution which began in 1910 and in which the armed peasantry played a crucial role, should be seen against the background of the usurpations by large haciendas of communal lands which took place in the second half of the nineteenth century and was briefly described in Chapter 1. Many indigenous communities tried in vain to retain or recover their communal lands from which they had been deprived under the legislation which favored private property. Particularly in the densely populated state of Morelos, the sugar estates expanded at the cost of the communities. The peasants' homes and crops were destroyed to obtain land for sugar cultivation. The peasants affected were forced to work on the estates.

Emiliano Zapata, the son of a small farmer who lost his land in this way, became one of the most outstanding peasant leaders in the area. At the age of thirty, he was elected president of the committee of his village, Anenecuilco, which was trying to discover its lost lands. This occurred shortly after Zapata had returned from compulsory military service and work with a *hacendado* in México City, duties which had been imposed upon him as a kind of punishment for his rebellious attitude. During this period, Zapata had gained experience and insights which would serve him as a village leader.

Because of his able leadership, three other villages with similar problems formed a committee together with Anenecuilco. These villages, led by Zapata, hired a lawyer to defend their rights in the court against the claims of the large haciendas. After years of tedious legal struggle proved to be fruitless, the peasants started to look for other means. Finally, they decided to occupy the disputed lands, but—it should be emphasized—only after all legal means had failed. The fear created by the first rumors of national revolt, initiated at that time by Francisco Madero in the north of Mexico, prevented the local authorities from taking action against Zapata and his neighbors in their extralegal activities.

Medero had started a movement which was supported by many land-hungry peasant groups against the reelection of Porfirio Díaz to the presidency. The *Plan de San Luis Potosí*, which was the basic declaration of the opposition against Porfirio Díaz, contained a phrase referring to the seizure of the indigenous people's lands: "those who acquired land in so immoral fashion, or their heirs, will be required to restore them to their original owners paying them moreover an indemnity for the damage suffered."[3] After Zapata became acquainted with this revolutionary *Plan de San Luis Potosí*, he and other local leaders organized three guerrilla groups of altogether 70 men to support Madero. After two other leaders had been killed by government troops, Zapata was chosen as commander. Weapons were found in the local haciendas. After one month, the group had grown to about a thousand men. Zapata refused to accept money which was offered to bribe him and calm down his movement. Similar peasant guerilla groups were operating in other parts of the country. Under pressure of the various rebel armies, President Díaz left the country on 26 May 1911.

The land restitution promised by the *Plan de San Luis Potosí*, however, encountered opposition. During his first meeting with the new national leader, Francisco Madero, Zapata reminded the President of the land reform promises. In response, Zapata was offered an estate. Zapata refused the bribe. It seemed that even if Madero himself might be willing to execute the *Plan de San Luis Potosí*, with regard to land restitution (for which he had received massive peasant support), the execution would be difficult because he was surrounded by many men who belonged to the former government, the military and to the landholding families. They boycotted such a program.[4]

On 20 August 1911, a massive demonstration of 30,000 persons in Mexico City, near the Chapultepec Palace, in favor of Madero and Zapata and against the military and the hacendados, requesting the withdrawal of the army from Morelos, did not dissuade the landholding groups from continuing their efforts to crush the peasant movement. Zapata considered his cause betrayed. After escaping from an attempt of the army to capture him in Morelos, Zapata rose again in arms, and soon surprised everybody with the strength of his movement, threatening even the capital.

The way Zapata's troops operated can be compared with the modern guerrilla techniques. Whenever a strong army group came close to the guerrillas, they disappeared, either by hiding or by merging with the local population. They had no uniforms and were merely armed peasants, which made it difficult to spot them. At moments that the federal armies did not expect an attack, they suddenly appeared and struck. Whenever a town was taken by Zapata's peasant troops, all the records of landownership were purposely destroyed. Practically all the lands of the state of Morelos, fifty-three haciendas, farms and ranches, were given to the peasants. This explains the strong support which the Zapata troops received locally wherever they appeared and also the strong opposition from the ruling groups in Mexico City. The armed peasants defended the lands which they had obtained when the federal forces came to throw them out.

The rebel groups were not organized in a single army, but in dispersed groups, which were ready to be called upon at any moment and were, in the meantime, cultivating the land they had obtained. By that time, Zapata had about 12,000 men while in the country as a whole there were 150,000 men in the different armies and rebel groups. Zapata's army was probably the largest single military unit, but it was very mobile because of its guerrilla approach. This army was sometimes operated as a whole, such as during the raid (of 12,000 men) on the rich mines of Hidalgo state, demonstrating to the government that it could not even protect the cities within less than a hundred miles from the capital. It sometimes operated in 200 small bands spread over different areas. These bands consisted of 30 to 200 men, led by the most energetic *guerrillero*. Some men were on foot, others on horseback. Zapata himself often disappeared for days when he went out to inspect the various scattered groups.

Because of Zapata's insistence on the realization of the *Plan de San Luis Potosí*, the hacendados of Mexico tried several times to assassinate him and financed a press campaign describing his movement as bandolerism, banditry. Zapata and his collaborators recognized as the most effective defense against the accusation of banditry a positive statement clarifying to the world that the peasant movement really stood for social justice. Such a declaration was especially needed because the government itself had been unwilling to fulfil the condition under which the Zapatistas would have given up armed resistance, namely to issue an agrarian reform law as a follow-up of the *Plan de San Luis Potosí*. The new policy statement was drafted in Villa de Ayala. After the idea to launch such a plan developed, the peasant generals (including one protestant minister) and other villagers present contributed to the document. The local school teacher, Otilio E. Montaño, wrote this all down in a notebook. Based on suggestions from the peasants, Zapata and Otilio Montaño drafted what became known as the *Plan de Ayala*. The final text was signed in Villa de Ayala on November 22, 1911, and soon after that it was ratified by all the peasant guerrilla leaders in the mountain camp of Ayoxustla. A local priest made the first typewritten copies.

The *Plan de Ayala* proclaimed that the people should take immediate possession of the lands from which they had been illegally deprived and for which they still could show title. Those who would have difficulty proving their case could receive lands from the expropriation of one-third of all the hacienda lands. The lands of those hacendados who offered opposition against these measures would be nationalized. Although many lands had been taken by the villages, the first restitution of lands which had officially written evidence based on the *Plan de Ayala*, was in Ixcamilpa, state of Puebla, April 30, 1912.

There was a strong reaction from the side of the hacendados who at a meeting of the Mexican Agricultural Chamber decided to form groups of volunteers to combat the peasants. The official armed forces started to deport whole villages in order to suppress the movement.

In 1915, a new government under Carranza, in order to weaken and win to its cause the peasant revolutionary forces which practically controlled Mexico City, published in Veracruz a Decree (January 6, 1915) which incorporated the main points of Zapata's program and which is generally considered to be the formal starting point of the Mexican land reform. This measure, together with the creation of batallions of urban workers which helped the Carranza government to combat the peasant armies, weakened the peasant resistance. However, since no real effect was given to the new reform decree, the movement led by Zapata only withdrew from the capital, but retained military control in a large part of the states of Morelos, Guerrero and Puebla. In those areas, a land distribution program was carried out according to the rules of the *Plan de Ayala*, with the help of a group of students of the National School of Agriculture.

Due partly to the continuous pressure of Zapata's troops and to the action of the revolutionary generals in other parts of the country, the ideas of the *Plan de Ayala* were later integrated into the Mexican Constitution (art. 27) of 1917.[5] In spite of this official acceptance, however, effective redistribution of lands took place only in those areas where the peasants were well organized and had some kind of bargaining power, or were armed such as in Morelos. After 1917, the persecution of the peasant guerrillas became increasingly intensive. In 1919, Zapata was assassinated by an army officer who had been able to integrate himself into the peasant movement for that purpose. The movement subsequently disintegrated, but more than half of the haciendas in the state of Morelos remained in the possession of the peasants, a situation which was legalized during the following years.[6]

Tannenbaum summarized Zapata's movement as follows.

In those years, the only government in Morelos, and later in large parts of the states of Guerrero, Puebla, Mexico, Tlaxcala and even the federal district, was in the hands of Zapata and his men. He had at times an army of forty thousand. They knew the mountains, the *barrancas*, and they were fighting not a war but a revolution. It was an army without a commissary; it lived on the land. It was an army without an encampment; when a battle was to be fought the soldiers gathered in response to a call, when a battle was over the soldiers went back to their villages, hid their rifles, and turned to tilling the soil. A federal column could find no soldiers to fight, only unarmed peasants who humbly worked the land. When a campaign was on, the soldiers of Zapata would change every three months, some going home, others joining the army. So it went for nine years.

The federal government, whether under Madero or Huerta or Carranza, was equally bitter against Zapata, and spread ruin among his followers. It became a war of extermination. The federal army, realizing that it was fighting a whole population, began to destroy that population. Villages were systematically burned. Fruit trees and crops were uprooted, women and children were concentrated in camps; it was war without quarter. In those nine years, it is estimated that one-third of the population of the state of Morelos was destroyed. During those years, Zapata ruled and governed this war-ridden country without difficulty; was obeyed affectionately and implicitly like an old Aztec King, was a ruler of men. During those years, there was a heavy price upon his head, and yet, never in all of that time was he betrayed by his own people, never did one of his men attempt to bring himself to power and riches. That shows something of the quality of the unity that a social movement can develop among the Mexican Indian.[7]

1919-1940

After 1919, the opposition of the hacendados against agrarian reform took increasingly violent forms. In many areas, they formed the so-called white guards, bands of armed men who defended the landowners' interests by intimidating or terrorizing the peasants who organized the agrarian committees provided for by the law. The agrarian law stipulated that villagers, in order to obtain land from the haciendas, had to form a so-called executive agrarian committee to send a petition to the competent reform agency. Initially, only peasants who were not attached to a hacienda and lived in villages or hamlets, rather than on a hacienda, could petition for land in the area close to their village.

In some of the more densely populated and urbanized states of Mexico, such as Veracruz and Michoacán, the peasants organized themselves against these violent activities. In Veracruz, Ursulo Galván, a peasant's son who had become a labor agitator, organized the peasants into agrarian committees especially those who tried to petition for land according to law. These committees were brought together in 1923 into the Liga de Comunidades Agrarias del Estado de Veracruz (League of Agrarian Communities of the State of Veracruz). Whereas the governor of Veracruz supported the movement, the military commander of the state was on the side of the landowners. Army units and small bands armed by the landowners terrorized the peasantry in the places where the movement started to grow and several local leaders were assassinated. When a military coup to overthrow the national government was staged in 1923, with support of the army units in Veracruz, the peasants of the Liga were given arms and organized into a battalion. They effectively helped to defend the government against the generals who started the coup.

In the state of Michoacán, a similar movement headed by Primo Tapia developed in the early twenties, as described above.[8]

In 1926, the peasant leagues of Veracruz, Michoacán and other states that had witnessed similar movements formed the National Peasant League, which was supported by some politicians on the national level. In that period, many local or regional peasant organizations made their appearance directed by politicians looking for peasant support as a means of becoming important at the national political scene. Some land was distributed by state governors and many promises were made in an effort to win the peasants' vote or armed support in the political arena. This continued until 1934 when Lázaro Cárdenas became President supported by several peasant organizations. At the 1934 Convention of the National Revolutionary Party, where Cárdenas was nominated as presidential candidate, peasant representatives, particularly Graciano Sánchez, managed to introduce changes into the government program for the next six years and this meant an acceleration of the slow-moving agrarian reform process. These measures included speeding up of the land distribution; the creation of an independent Agrarian Department in charge of the reform; participation of peasant representatives in the state agrarian commissions which advised on petitions; and provisions that resident workers of haciendas could benefit from agrarian reform.

During the years when most land was distributed, such as the period of 1924-1930 and particularly 1934-1940, peasant organizations were able to support their demands effectively. It was in those periods that the government had to rely heavily on the organized and armed peasantry for its defense against several military coups staged by conservative forces opposed to the moderate but firmly reform-oriented authorities. That the need for armed peasant support for the stability of government was not exaggerated can be concluded from the fact that the New York Times reported 53 battles between agrarianists and their opponents during the first eighteen months of Cárdenas' government.[9] Several landowners hoped to avoid the distribution of their lands by burning down the villages in which the potential petitioners lived. According to the law, lands of estates within a radius of seven kilometres around a village could be expropriated to the benefit of that village. Several estates tried to take away the legal basis for a petition by making a village disappear or move elsewhere.

During Cárdenas' regime as well as during those of his predecessors, people who started to organize peasants to make a petition according to the law ran the risk of being assassinated by men hired by the landowners. Even government officials ran this risk. In the first years of Cárdenas' government, 2,000 people were reported murdered for such reasons in Veracruz alone. During three critical months of 1936, 500 people were killed in various states.[10]

Responding to a strong need, a Presidential Agreement of 10 July 1935 proposed the formation of peasant leagues, such as had existed in some parts of the country before, in all the states of the republic and the joining of these leagues into a national peasant federation—*Confederación Nacional Campesina* (CNC). This organization had as one of its main purposes the unification of all peasants into solid support for the government, which was chronically in danger of being overthrown by conservative interests. The CNC membership consisted mainly of the representatives of the beneficiaries of the reform and of the executive agrarian committees which were petitioning for land. The beneficiaries had received land in the form of an ejido. The land was collective property of the village as a whole, but it could be divided among the villagers for individual cultivation, or be used collectively. Every three years, the beneficiaries had to elect a representative body, the *comisariado ejidal*, as a kind of governing board, which also represented the peasants in the CNC and the Ligas at the state level.

It took three years of organizational work before all the states were represented at a national constituent congress of the CNC in Mexico City in 1938. It has been noted that this was due to the resistance of the rural elite to the establishment of local organizations.[11] In the CNC, practically all local, regional and national peasant organizations that existed before, were brought together, to strengthen themselves, and act as a counterweight against the strongly organized labor movement. *Ligas* which had been in existence for many years (such as those of the states of Veracruz, Michoacan and Tamaulipas) formed part of CNC as well as the new *Ligas* which had been formed as part of the campaign to create the CNC between 1935 and 1938 in the states where there was no such organization. In some areas, the separation of peasant organizations from workers organizations (such as in the Comarca Lagunera) brought certain difficulties. However, on the whole a strong and united body emerged.

One of the objectives of the formation of the CNC was to organize the peasants for participation in the national political party, the Party of the Mexican Revolution (PRM) which would support the government.[12] The official party had before consisted mainly of government officials who were more or less obliged to join. Cárdenas gave the party a solid mass basis by integrating into it the labor movement, the peasant movement and other groups of the population. This happened in a period when the nation was strongly rallied behind the president because of the crucial issue of the oil expropriation.[a] Cárdenas as a national leader had considerable charismatic qualities, but through the reshaping of the national political party, he tried to institutionalize this charisma and transform it into party charisma.

---

[a]In 1938, after serious labor conflicts which could apparently not be solved, Cárdenas nationalized the foreign oil companies operating in Mexico.

It is probable that political participation, through the National Peasant Confederation (CNC) together with the fact that the peasants were armed, were conditions for the vigorous land distribution program that took place during the years of Cárdenas' presidency. It is probably the combination of distribution of the land, political organization, and the possibility of armed defense by the peasants that in those years laid the foundation for the political stability Mexico has enjoyed since 1940. According to statistics supplied at the end of the Cárdenas' regime, a rural militia created by the decree of January 1, 1936, contained 60,000 men in 1940, all with arms and almost half of them with horses. They were organized into about 70 battalions and 75 cavalry regiments, directed by more than 400 chiefs and officers under 9 generals. The function of the rural militia was the organization and control of armed peasant defense.[13] Legal provisions for the distribution of arms to the peasants had already existed since 1926 when the white guards of the landlords were particularly active in trying to frighten the peasants from petitioning for land as the law stipulated.[14]

At times, the government seemed to have more confidence in the peasant militia than in the regular army. This militia defended the rights of the peasant class, and on several was used to safeguard the national government from severe threats of being overthrown by conservative forces.

It is difficult to say whether the existence of the armed peasant reserve was the reason why a certain peace began to prevail in the country. However, the coincidence between the progress of pacification in the country and the official support of the peasant reserve was striking. Particularly, the psychological effect on the peasants of legally possessing arms for the defense of their rights should not be underestimated. It helped to overcome the fear of the landowners and their allies.

The speed and determination with which agrarian reform measures were carried out under Cárdenas with the whole-hearted participation of representative peasant organizations, created a climate of popular mobilization and enthusiasm. There is evidence that changes occurred in the mentality of the population that could be seen as a kind of collective development fever which was a great asset to extra and voluntary effort.[15]

1940 - present

After 1940, the mobilizing spirit which had inspired the participants in and beneficiaries of the new institutions gradually disappeared. Not only had Cárdenas' charismatic leadership ended, but the official political party, which had carried part of the charisma, soon came under influence of sectors of the middle class that did not see the need to continue the vigorous measures initiated by Cárdenas.

The traditional landholding groups were able to reestablish themselves in new forms, through cooperation of the government technicians by bribery or other means. And through the dishonesty of various government agencies dealing with the ejidos, many peasant leaders were unable to resist the temptations of corruption. There is very little evidence that the CNC as an organization has been able to resist this tendency.

Soon political sectors within the official structure emerged which increasingly neutralized the impact of the peasant sector. Since many members of the growing middle sector were inclined to be favorable to the conservative forces (such as the Partido de Acción National or the fascist-oriented Sinarquistas), the government party (PRM) had to increase its appeal for those classes. For this reason, the so-called popular sector in the PRM was officially created in September 1942 under the name of Confederación Nacional de Organizaciones Populares (CNOP). The CNOP derives its power mainly from its largest constituent organization, the federal civil service unions, (about 250,000 members), the National Cooperative Federation (about 250,000 members), and the small agricultural proprietors, Confederación Nacional de la Pequena Propiedad Agrícola (claiming 750,000 members).[16]

It should be noted that the category of small proprietors included the former large landlords who had lost land in the agrarian reform but who were able to retain for themselves a maximum of 300 hectares of irrigated land (if cultivated with cash crops). It has been observed that the CNOP was dominated by those who were not interested in or opposed to agrarian reform.[17]

One of the main reasons for the limited effectiveness of the agrarian reform after 1940 is the fact that the large landholders were able to conserve or regain considerable strength. Those who were affected by the agrarian reform were generally allowed to choose for themselves the best lands, and their influence in the local power structure was modified, but neither broken nor drastically changed through the appearance of the *comisariado ejidal.* Since government credit facilities were not sufficient to satisfy the needs of the ejidatarios (members of *ejidos*), they were dependent on local money-lenders, generally directly or indirectly related to the landholders. At the same time, the commercial infrastructure remained in the hands of the rural elite. After 1940, it was not difficult for these groups to gain considerable influence *within* the political system of Mexico, after their violent and open resistance against it was practically broken during the Cárdenas years. The acceptance, since 1943, of the small proprietors, within the structure of the official party as part of the middle sector, the CNOP, opened a wide field for political strife in rural areas. The struggle between groups representing opposing class interests, was now transferred into the official party.

Thus, one observer noted that the principal source of rural factional strife was the tactics employed by many of Mexico's remaining landholders to defend their interests. They had given up open opposition to the agrarian program in favor of infiltration of the new system to change it from within.[18] One case study showed that the descendant of a traditionally powerful family, which had lost part of its local domination through the effects of the Revolution, gained back control of a community by joining the official party. He became the secretary-general of the municipal committee, and made friends with the high political officials through invitations for parties and dinners.[19]

In the village described by Oscar Lewis, the descendants of the old revolutionary elite returned to the municipality after the turmoil of the revolution was over. This initiated a period of factional struggle which cost many lives over the years.[20] In the case studied by Friedrich, as mentioned above, the old elite never left the municipality and opposed land reform until the agrarian faction became sufficiently strong to obtain land. However, the struggle for control of the municipality continued. In addition to intrigue and the managing of groups and people, partly through the official party, violence has been an important method by which political control has been exercised at the municipal level.[21]

Another case study in the state of Hidalgo reported that the *hacendado* tried to make a deal with the representatives of the petitioning agrarian committee of the nearby village in order to keep for himself more land than he was entitled to. He helped the agrarian committee inflate the number of petitioners so that they could claim land from other surrounding haciendas, rather than from his own. Some special land was reserved as part of the deal for the first president of the ejido commisariat. This man soon became the most powerful person in the ejido, a typical *cacique*,[22] cultivating much more land than was legally allowed.[b]

In most such cases the CNC did not strongly defend the peasantry against the privileged interests. A great deal depended on the local leadership. It frequently happened that at the municipal level (Comité Regional) of the CNC "small proprietors" or even hacendados, have been able to reach positions of power within the organization. It happened more frequently, however, that local peasant leaders attracted by the desire for power and the symbols of social status, have been coopted by the rural "elite."[23]

One factor which seems to facilitate potentially corruptive influences is the fact that the municipal government and the municipal levels of the official organizations depend on the higher levels for financial support which, however, is very limited. As Gonzalez Casanova has indicated: "The municipality fre-

---

[b]Padgett gave the following explanation.

"Cacique" in Mexican political usage originally meant simply chief, and its first major political connotation stemmed from the fact that the Spanish conquerors found it easier to keep a people subjugated as long as the chiefs were cooperative. Chiefs were thus given special favors in return for keeping the people pacified. Later on, the term *cacique* came to be applied to any person who could build a following sufficient in his local community to provide the influence necessary to keep the people there from demanding rights from higher government authorities. The *cacique* not only keeps order in the local area but is the one person who has contact in any meaningful way with the officials at higher levels. He becomes known as a spokesman for his area and frequently receives money from his own constituents as a reward for bringing certain problems to the attention of higher authorities. There are thousands of these persons throughout the country, and, as Mexican commentators point out, there are caciques of caciques, i.e., bigger chiefs over smaller ones. These are people who contact their government.[24]

quently lacks the power to execute minimal acts of government."[25] The municipalities all over the country receive altogether 3 percent of the governmental budget.[26] The effect of this is that the holders of local wealth, the merchants and small proprietors, can—often effectively—try to gain control of the local official power structure.

Since the CNC became increasingly a tool of authorities at the service of the middle sectors . . . "the militancy and determination of the CNC as a channel for effectively presenting the demand of the peasants seemed to me more lacking every year."[27] An indication of the dependence of the CNC and its branches upon the political system as a whole is its system of finance. It was practically impossible to obtain sufficiently reliable data on this topic, but it is known that various regional and state-level leaders of the CNC are at least part-time on the payroll of government agencies such as the agrarian credit bank, the BNCE (Banco Nacional de Crédito Ejidal). Whether this facilitates or complicates the bargaining function to obtain credit in due time and under favorable conditions for the member groups, is difficult to say. The almost universal complaints about the poor functioning and corruption of the BNCE's agencies at all levels may indicate that the peasant's interests and demands are not always served in the best possible way.

The structure of the CNC and its place within the overall political system with its stress on the centralization of power at the higher levels gives the impression that its present role in agrarian reform and other fields is mainly to keep the peasantry in line with the overall system.[c]

Many of the ascendant officials of the CNC at the regional, state or national level seem to fit the description, given by Eric Wolf, about the ways new power-holders utilized political manipulation after the Revolution. Since political advantages were necessary in order to obtain economic advantages, alliances between political and economic powerseekers came into being at all levels of society. This happened mainly within the structure of the official party through "judicious manipulation of social ties." A politician must have "the ability to adopt the proper patterns of public behavior. . . . He must learn to operate in an arena of continuously changing friendships and alliances, which form and dissolve with the appearance of new economic or political opportunities."[29] Those persons able to operate both in terms of community-oriented and nation-

---

[c]Manzanilla Schaffer has written the following passage.

Debido a sus limitaciones económicas la Confederación Nacional Campesina, organización a la que pertenecemos, se ha visto imposibilidata para intervenir en la organización social de los núcleos de población en la preparación de organizadores y administradores dentro de los ejides y communidades y en la orientación agraria de estos agrupamientos. Su labor se ha reducido al control político y la representación del campesinado, funciones que son muy importantes; pero que no agotan las grandes posibilidades de acción que dicha confederación posee. No pasamos per alto la importante función que ha desarrollade en la organización económica de los campesinos por ramas de la producción, labor que debe continuar con el máximo esfuerzo.[28]

oriented expectations then tend to be singled out for climbing the political ladder. They become the economic and political brokers of nation-community relations.[30] The tasks of mediation are generally fulfilled at the lowest levels by the most able—or shrewdest—peasant leaders, and higher up by urban people (often lawyers) with political ambitions who see in the role of mediator in the CNC a chance to build a career.

The national, state and regional leaders all have to mediate in a wide range of operations, such as obtaining credit, or withholding it as a sanction, and mediating between local rival leaders, giving letters of recommendation to a widow who is despoiled of her husband's land by the *comisariado ejidal*, or bribing or threatening a leader who tends to work outside the system, by joining an independent federation.

The successful mediators are those who find the right balance between being acceptable to the membership by doing something for them, while at the same time not asking too much at the higher levels. Since fulfilling the task of political mediator is one of the means of social mobility in Mexico, a great deal of competition, and skill is needed for the task. One has to outdo others at the local level in being benevolent with limited means to gain the greatest following.

This system of intermediaries[d] has been described as a continuation of the method traditionally employed by the underprivileged groups to get certain benefits or express their demands. While the overwhelming influence of regional and state *caudillos* in Mexican politics was more or less effectively halted or eliminated in the thirties,[32] the reform measures which transformed the rural power structure in that period were later counterbalanced by a return to personalism and clientelism in the official relations within the PRI (Partido Revolutionario Institucional, the new name given to the official party in 1946).

The system of intermediaries can be seen as a way through which the traditional rural elite has been able to maintain or recover considerable control. Especially after 1940, the selection and consequent election of regional and state level political leaders depended to a large extent on the groups who had financial power and social influence.

It might be expected that the development of peasant organizations, devoted to the solution of rural problems, as well as expressing rural opinion on national issues, would gradually produce political leaders of rural background. But no such tendency has been discerned in the 30-odd years of the P.R.I.'s existence, and the Peasants' Confederation has, with no important exception, accepted leadership of middle- and upper-class origin.[33]

In summarizing, it can be said that the traditional patrons in many areas in Mexico, who had lost their land and power to a new and more participatory

---

[d]Several terms are used for intermediatires: "padrinos," "valedores," "tatas," "compadritos," "coyotes," "influyentes," to which could be added the "abogaditos" of the CNC.[31]

clienteles, the agraristas, were able to regain a power position within the new system. Although the new patronage system of the official political party had been highly participatory during a number of years, particularly during the government of Cárdenas, the old patrons managed a comeback, in alliance with the new ones who were to some extent corrupted.

Even in those areas where the old hacienda system was most effectively eliminated, such as in parts of the state of Morelos, the new partronage system became less participatory over the years, under influences working at the national level, so that in the end, many aspects of the traditional and coercive patronage system reappeared.

This can be seen for example in a village in Morelos studied by a team headed by Erich Fromm. The leadership formed part of the new patronage system which integrates the village with the official bureaucracy. The successful village leaders were those who were skilled petitioners or intermediaries, who "... exercise the obsequious cultivations of those above them."[34] The practice of petitioning for an improvement of a school, a road, a basketball court, depends on attracting the appropriate outsider, state-level official of some agency, or an influential politician, and inviting him to a banquet, flattering him and appealing to his ability to be a benevolent patron to the village. This is not always successful. It is mainly the ambitious aspiring politician, who still needs the support of the ejido representatives at the regional committee level who will keep his promises.[35]

However, most politicians, once they have become powerful through fulfilling a brokerage function for the peasants, forget their former supporters and can become a patron in the traditional sense, who is in a position to use coercion rather than favors to keep people in line. In the village studied by Fromm and his team, the beneficiaries of the land reform later suffered new forms of bondage. According to the law, they only received credit to cultivate one-third of their plots with sugar cane to supply the nearby government managed sugarmill (officially, this was cooperative, but in fact, it was run by the BNCE). This was disadvantageous for the peasants who could earn much more by cultivating rice, if they could receive credit to do so.[36] The peasants therefore complained that the government agency in charge was like the former hacendados to them. The social climate in the area was strongly authoritarian. (In view of the frustrating situation of the peasantry in this area which had actively participated in the Zapata movement but which had undergone only a limited improvement, it is understandable that there was a great deal of alcoholism and violent behavior.)[37]

It is also understandable that in this area the radical peasant leader Ruben Jaramillo was able to gather a considerable following because he was less corruptible than the other local leaders and often protested against the official policies and their executors. Because he became a threat to the political status quo in the area he was assassinated by army elements in 1963.

It could be expected that, since the patronage system, which resulted from the Revolution, did not satisfy the peasants needs, new and more representative or participatory clienteles would develop to compete with the postrevolutionary official system. When in 1946, the Partido de la Revolución Mexicana was transformed into the *Partido Revolucionaria Institucional* (PRI) as a confirmation of the increasing support for and from the middle sectors, some labor and peasant groups started to look for other ways of expressing and transmitting demands. *The Confederación de Trabajadores de México* (CTM) virtually obliged its members to vote for the PRI in spite of the presence of many dissidents in its ranks, and expelled various prominent leaders when they insisted on the freedom to participate and vote for the more radically oriented *Partido Popular* (founded in 1948). The expelled leaders, Vicente Lombardo Toledano and Jacinto López, then founded an independent labor and peasant union, *Unión General de Campesinos y Obreros de México* (UGOCM). Although at its Constituent Congress, 20-22, June 1949, President Alemán was represented by his Minister of the Interior, Ruíz Cortinez, the UGOCM was never legally recognized as a collective bargaining partner by the Labour Ministry. The consequence of this was that labor unions dissociated themselves from UGOCM little by little and that it soon had almost only peasant organizations as affiliates.

The UGOCM can thus be considered to be a group which was expelled from the CTM, and its main strongholds among peasants were in areas such as the Comarca Lagunera and Sonora, where peasants had a direct or indirect relation with the CTM for many years. It was in those areas that the UGOCM found its strength and deployed radical activities after the legal approach had failed. Judith Adler's summary is apt.

The UGOCM asserted its power capability in a series of land invasions in 1958. As a result of the invasions, the organization was quickly recognized as a legitimate broker on behalf of peasants, not only in the Northwest, but in at least 15 other Mexican states throughout the Republic. And despite the fact that the UGOCM is not officially registered by the Ministry of the Interior, its political bargaining power is so strong as a result of its continued threat to carry out land invasions, that it operates far more effectively in many areas, without any legal status, than the CNC itself.[38]

The UGOCM was constantly under pressure from the CNC and other official political institutions. Some of its leaders at the local or regional level were assassinated.[39] Others were threatened, and again others were brought under the temptation of lucrative political jobs, if they were willing to bring their group into the official organizations. A great deal of factional strife at the village or municipality level occurred as a result of the appearance of this independent and more participatory clientele of the UGOCM. Local leaders and *caciques* tried to avoid or boycott the elections which are to be held periodically in the *ejidos* to renew the leadership. Intimidation and violence were used in this effort. The arbitrariness of local leaders in the country became so alarming that the central government had to intervene. One of the activities during the first three years of the López Mateos government (1958-1964) was to renew the membership of 17,000 *Comisariados Ejidales* and *Consejos de Vigilancia*, "as the most appropriate way to strengthen the democracy in the ejidos and to avoid the caciquismo."[40]

The fact that, according to the Agrarian Code, employees of the Agrarian Department or the Ministry of Agriculture can exercise influence in the election, integration and replacement of a comisariado ejidal, has frequently resulted in the election of commissariats without taking into account—or even in opposition to—the opinions of the ejidatarios. This was a source of many conflicts that led at times to situations where people were ambushed or had to be accompanied by soldiers for their own protection.[41]

Because of the strong interrelationship between the behavior at the village level and the political system in the country as a whole, it is difficult to give the official peasant organizations the function they potentially have, to foster popular participation in change and development. The need for a revision of the trends which developed since 1940 has been emphasized even in official statements, and seems to be increasingly urgent as shown by the rise of unrest in several areas in Mexico. Although the facts were generally not known beyond a small local circle, some cases of peasant protest and subsequent repression became known through the national press. Among these is the assassination of the peasant leader, Ruben Jaramillo, and his family in 1962 in the state of Morelos, about 100 miles from Mexico City.[42] One of the more recent events of this type was the massacre of about 25 peasants in Acapulco.[43] One former president of the PRI recently observed, in an interview with the New York Times: "The public is being 'chloroformed' to hide from it the true state of the country. To talk about poverty is 'officially forbidden.' The peasants have no representative organizations or leaders and the press confines itself to praise the Government."[44]

Only because of the competition of the independent peasant organizations, the CNC in Mexico in the early sixties had to step up its efforts in favor of the peasants on a few occasions for fear of losing its influence.[e] This happened par-

---

[e]In February 1968, a cleaning up of the state and regional levels of the CNC was announced by its Secretary General;[45] several years before, President López Matéos had made a speech, denouncing the corruption of "false revolutionary leaders."

El gobierno de la República será inflexible contra quienes no siendo sujetos de derecho agrario, sobre todo si se trata de funcionarios y empleados desleales, pretendan posesionarse de terrenos ejidales, por sí o por interpósitas personas, cualquiera que sea la forma o argucia de que se valgan, y contra las autoridades ejidales que resulten complices. Igualmente seguirá procediéndose contra los que defrauden y exploten a los ejidatarios especialmente en materia de créditos, compra venta de semilla, fertilizantes y equipos agrícolas. . . . Cuando en días pasados censuré a los simuladores de la Revolución, comprendí a los que hacen demagogía agraria para enriquecerse a costa de los campesinos; a los que por satisfacer intereses personales abusan a la buena fe de los ejidatarios con promesas y proyectos irrealizables o contrarios a la ley; a los functionarios que engañan con dotaciones improcedentes o en sitios inaccesibles o absolutamente estériles; a los falsos revolucionarios que aconsejan procedimientos reprobables y a los que siembran rencores y pugnas en las comunidades.[46]

ticularly after 1963 when the Central Campesina Independiente (CCI) was created and endorsed by expresident Cárdenas. Through cooptation of one wing of this group and repressive measures against the more radical wing (led by members of the Communist party), the overall system maintained control. However, discontent among the peasantry may become so strong that nonstructured forms of pressure are used again to express demands and protest. In the course of 1968, some guerilla groups supported by peasants operated in the states of Chihuahua and Guerrero.

In spite of the considerable economic progress of Mexico and the large-scale land distribution that took place over the last fifty years, at present there are in absolute numbers more landless peasants in Mexico than when the Revolution started.

Table 4-1
Occupation Structure

	1930	%	1960	%
Those who work in agriculture	3,626,000		6,144,000	
Landless Peasants	2,479,000	68%	3,300,000	54%
Ejidatarios	536,000	15%	1,500,000	25%
Nonejidal owners	609,000	17%	1,300,000	21%

Source: C.I.D.A. – Centro de Investigaciones Agrarias

From 1940 onward, government programs related to agricultural development benefited mainly the growing sector of middle farmers and agricultural entrepreneurs. The existing structure of peasant organizations was utilized to keep the peasants in line with these policies. It should be noted that the CNC consisted mainly of *ejidatarios*, those who had benefited at least to some extent from land distribution, and that the three million landless peasants have no representation. Many of the latter category are the workers for the middle farmers. Rodolfo Stavenhagen noted recently that the standard of living of the agricultural workers is very low, and that in violation of the Federal Labor Law, most employers do not provide housing, schools and medical facilities.[47]

A recent investigation by COTPAL of the income distribution in Mexico indicated that in spite of the impressive economic performance by the Mexican economy, strong evidence exists that there is ". . . a further widening of the relative disparity in incomes received by well-to-do segments of the population and backward economic groups."[48] This implies that while Mexico's development as a whole is considerable, the pattern of income distribution continues to be to the disadvantage of the lower income groups, and is becoming even worse. As the COTPAL report indicated, this is especially the case with the families who depend on agriculture for their living. They form the lowest level of poverty of the poorer third of the Mexican population. COTPAL noted that ". . . the total share of the total incomes received by the 30 percent of individuals in the lowest income brackets declined from 13 percent of total wages and salary in 1950 to 8 percent in 1956 and 6 percent in 1964-1965." Gonzalez Casanova shows data which indicate that the real agricultural minimum wage declined 45 percent between 1938 and 1960, while productivity went up 100 percent. The degree of exploitation of agricultural labor thus increased by 134 percent.[49]

It is clear that the progress of the national bourgeoisie[50] or middle sectors and, on the other hand, the marginal participation in development of the majority of the peasantry, creates a situation that is explosive. The Mexican Revolution has gone only half way. It eliminated the traditional power structure to make place for a more dynamic one, with help from the peasantry. However, it did not give full participation and benefit to the peasants after they were sufficiently underorganized control to be manipulated, and forms of internal colonialism are maintained or even extended in many of the rural areas. Foreign influence on this process has been limited but seems to be increasing.[51]

The Agrarian Movement in Bolivia

As was briefly indicated in Chapter 1, in Bolivia many peasant uprisings and agrarian protest movements had occurred in the nineteenth and the beginning of the twentieth century, all of which were repressed. The traditional hacienda system maintained itself while the culture of repression prevailed. Only after the Chaco War in the early thirties shook up the whole social structure of the country did a modern type of peasant syndicates become effective in some areas such as in parts of the Cochabamba valley. The growth of these syndicates and the ups and downs of the chances for peasant organization and agrarian reform over the years will be described. After the Revolution of 1952 which brought a government to power favorable to peasant demands, the peasant movement grew rapidly and could only be channelled and controlled by promoting a radical land reform program. After the demand for land was fulfilled, the peasant organizations became part of the political structure supporting moderate governments.

The Formation of the Peasant
Syndicates

The Chaco War, fought in 1932-1935 between Bolivia and Paraguay over a large border area, disturbed the status quo of the semifeudal and castelike social relationships. The fact that Bolivia was defeated made many people aware of the weakness of the traditional social system. The participation of many Indians among the 100,000 Bolivians who served in the army and supply lines, and the propaganda directed towards the Indian soldiers to stimulate them, caused a new consciousness among the indigenous people about their relations to the white who often depended on them in critical situations.[52]

In 1936, the first rural syndicate was formed in Ucureña close to Cochabamba, in the latifundio Santa Clara. A school was also created. Parts of the latifundio, belonging to a monastery, had been leased to a local landholder who exploited the peasants, tied to the land, in an abusive way. This abusiveness caused discontent, particularly after the combatants of the Chaco War had returned. One of the additional reasons why a union could be formed more easily in the Santa Clara estate (and also at more or less the same time in the Vacas estate in the province of Arani) than elsewhere was the fact that there was not one traditional landlord to whom the peasants were tied, but rather a group of owners. There was a less personal relationship between the peasants and the *patron*.[53]

Another facilitating factor was that even before the Chaco War, the monastery had sold a few plots to small peasants called *piqueros*, who through the purchase of this land became independent. This sale was frowned upon by the large landowners of the area. One of the landlords was particularly abusive.

For example, he had removed *colonos* from their usufruct plots on several occasions and brought in other campesinos who were more willing to cooperate. During the Chaco War, he had usurped the usufruct plots from the wives of some enlisted *colonos* because the men were away and were not working for the *hacienda*.[54]

The local peasants, in order to free themselves from the feudal obligations of service, got together under the leadership of the Delgadillo brothers to form a syndicate to lease the land themselves from the Santa Clara monastery. They received help from a school teacher, from students of Cochabamba and from Eduardo Arze Loureiro, the son of a landowner who was amenable to new ideas. He was helpful in the tedious legal procedures to obtain the lease for the union. However, the new arrangement worked for a few years only. In 1939, a small group of landowners got together to destroy the nascent syndicate and remove the threat to the customary pattern of landlord rule. With help from the government, they prevailed upon the Santa Clara convent to sell the land to them so that they could abandon the legal arrangement made by the union and its helpers. They cleared the land and destroyed the houses of the peasants (who had been living there for generations) under the pretext of rationalizing the cultivation. Those peasants who did not want to work again for the *hacienda* were driven from the land. Twelve peasant leaders were confined to an isolated area of the country in 1940.[55]

Of the consequences it has been said: This attack upon the syndicate members did more than anything else to unify the Indian population and awaken it to political life. Treatment which had hitherto been endured as acts against individual peasants was now recognized for what it was, a concentrated attack by landowners upon the whole group of campesinos.[56]

In the difficult period during and after 1940, the syndicate became increasingly dependent on the leadership of the local school director Juan Guerra, who became a member of the Leftist Revolutionary Party (PIR). With assistance from various intellectuals of the town of Cochabamba, Guerra helped the peasants purchase some parts of the estate, although for a price higher than landowners would have paid. About 200 peasants thus became the owners of one-hectare plots and gained independence from the *patron*. Guerra also helped peasants of surrounding estates to channel their complaints to the authorities about abuses by the landlords. The union spread its influence and, in turn, helped in the founding of various smaller schools related to the *nucleo escolar* (central school) in Ucureña. In 1946, there were 41 such schools with 62 teachers and 2,100 pupils in the area. Towards the end of 1946, Ucureña was chosen as one of the rural education centers to be assisted by the Servicio Cooperativo Interamericano de Education (SCIDE), a joint American-Bolivian fundamental education agency.

The syndicate regained its strength and developed further under the able leadership of José Rojas. The following passage describes him.

A native of Ucureña who had been driven from the latifundium on which his father had been a *colono*, Rojas escaped to Argentina only to return secretly to Ucureña later in the 1940s. There he worked as a laborer while he assisted in organizing the campesinos. Rojas affected to speak no Spanish but was an eloquent orator in Quechua. Deeply impressed by the platform of the Marxist PIR, he soon became a forceful and determined leader of the campesinos.[57]

Around 1940, various new political parties had been formed in exile. Among these was the Partido de Izquierda Revolucionario (PIR, Party of the Revolutionary Left), founded in 1940 under the leadership of the sociologist José Antonio Arze (who called himself an independent Marxist), while the Partido Obrero Revolucionario (POR, Revolutionary Workers Party), of Trotskyite orientation, became influential in those years through Juan Lechín, the leader of the Miners' Federation. The Movimiento Nacionalista Revolucionario (MNR), founded by a group of intellectuals headed by Víctor Paz Estenssoro, was a mixture of liberal intellectuals and young army officers who were dissatisfied with the mishandling of the Chaco War. It was later joined by tin miners and groups of the much-divided PIR. When the government of Enrique Peñaranda, after having declared war on the Axis powers, was overthrown in 1943, Major Gualberto Villarroel became president. He took several leaders of the MNR into his government, while repressing both the traditional and the Marxist parties.

During the government of Villarroel which came to power on December 20 1943, and in which Paz Estenssoro participated, several occurrences contributed to the increasing awareness and organization of the peasantry.[58] In August 1944, Paz Estenssoro and Walter Guevara presented to the National Convention a proposal for a moderate agrarian program. Opposition from the majority in the convention controlled by the powerful organization of large landholders, the Sociedad Rural Boliviana, was strong enough to block acceptance of the proposal. But the Movimiento Nacionalista Revolucionario, led by Paz and Guevara, which defended the proposal, awakened the peasantry to the fact that they had allies. Land reform became a cause to struggle for with more effective means than spontaneous uprisings.

Another event which seemed to confirm this tendency was the organization in the beginning of 1945 of the first Indian Congress, organized by the leader Luis Ramos Quevedo. The congress started on May 10, 1945, with approximately 1,000 delegates from all 98 provinces. The main points of the agenda were abolition of the unpaid personal services which peasants had to render to landlords; education; regulation of agricultural labor conditions and agrarian policy. No radical measures were proposed by the peasant delegates, but demands made were directed against the most abusive forms of servitude and lack of educational facilities. As a result of the Congress, government decrees were issued which abolished unpaid personal services and obliged the landlords to establish schools on the large haciendas. Land reform as such was not dealt with.

The opposition of the conservative forces against the new decrees and other proposed measures became increasingly strong. Little or no implementation was given to the decrees which were promulgated by the government as a result of the Indian Congress, particularly Decree 319 which abolished *pongueaje* and other forms of unpaid services to the landlords.

In the period around the Indian Congress, many of the spontaneous peasant movements and uprisings against the landholders, and also the struggles between indigenous communities over boundaries calmed down or even disappeared. The negative reaction of the landlords after the Indian Congress provoked the sit-down strikes ("huelga de brazos caídos") covering large areas in Tarija, Oruro and Potosí. These strikes implied a refusal to render the unpaid personal services, *defacto* fulfilling the decrees issued in May 1945. Indian peasant organizers, especially those who had experience as miners, travelled around in many areas to awaken the peasantry. Political organizers of the MNR also participated in this campaign. The press spread fear of the indigenous movements among the urban middleclass, exaggerating them in order to discredit the government which tolerated these movements. Altogether this counteraction led to the overthrow of the reformist government on July 21 1946, and the assassination of president Villarroel. All the measures decreed during the previous years were cancelled and the traditional situation was restored in the rural areas.

The peasant protest movements which occurred after 1946 as a reaction to the change of government were now met by armed force. Many peasant leaders, particularly those who had participated in the Indian Congress, were jailed. Revolts protesting the new tendencies started at the end of 1946. In Ayopaya, Cochabamba, several thousand peasants invaded large landholdings and assassinated a landlord who forcibly tried to reintroduce the feudal obligations. In Los Andes province of La Paz, similar protest actions took place after the landowners refused to negotiate the petitions. From then on, most of the peasant movements took on a violent character, and thus they shedded their former stance of nonviolence. Landlords' houses on estates and even some provincial capitals were threatened or effectively attacked. Miners had an important leadership function in the movements.[59]

The objectives of the movements at this stage went beyond mere changes in working conditions and included radical changes in the political and social structure of the country. The intransigence of the landowners had apparently provoked a strong awakening of the peasants. Workers from La Paz who were affiliated to the Federación Obrera Local, related to the MNR, helped to organize the peasant protest movements on the Altiplano. Several labor leaders active in this field were jailed.

The movements in various parts of the country were repressed by large-scale military intervention. A special rural police corps was created. About 250 peasant leaders were sent to a penal colony in Ichilo which was created in the jungle for this purpose. During the years of turmoil between 1946 and 1952, the MNR remained illegal and attempted several times to overthrow the regime. Then in the presidential elections of 1951, Paz Estenssoro won 45 percent of the vote. The military junta which took over in order to prevent the MNR from coming to power through legal means lasted only eleven months until General Antonio Seleme, chief of the *Carabineros*, or national military police, went over to the MNR. In April 1952, a violent revolution broke out with street fighting between the army on one side and the *carabineros* and armed workers on the other.

But from the beginning, most of the men and women who carried arms in the rebellion were civilians: miners, trade unionists, and other wage earners of the city, small shopkeepers and members of the middle class, all of them members of or sympathizers with an organized political party [the MNR]. When the fighting ended, it was this party, and not the defecting general who organized the new government.[60]

About two weeks later, Paz Estenssoro returned from Argentina and became president. Some estimates indicate that 3,000 people were killed in the turmoil.[61] In some of the areas close to La Paz, such as Achacalla and Patamanta, the peasants had joined the struggle of the other groups which brought about the revolution.[62]

Relatively soon after the new government had taken power, amnesty was given to the peasant leaders who were in concentration camps because they had participated in protest movements which occurred in different places between 1946 and 1952.

In the meantime, the MNR tried to get control of the growing peasant syndicate movement in the Cochabamba area by trying to replace José Rojas as head of the syndicate by a moderate leader. However, at a meeting in Cliza, the provincial capital, Rojas won and became the undisputed leader of the *Sindicato Campesino de Ucureña del Valle.* The Ucureña syndicate sent out many peasant leaders and MNR students from Cochabamba to the surrounding areas to create new syndicates and to carry the news of the revolution of April 1952.[63]

Immediately after the coming to power of the MNR on 12 April 1952, the Ministry of Peasant Affairs was created. It is curious that the formation of peasant unions was not officially included among the objectives of this Ministry, and neither was agrarian reform. However, these fields became its main occupation after considerable peasant pressure had occurred in favor of radical reform. This pressure was a reaction to the intransigence shown by the landlords after April 1952, particularly in the Cochabamba area.

When the Ucureña syndicate requested that holdings be returned to those peasants who had been driven from their land and the landowners refused, a general uprising was called in which the peasants of three provinces threatened to invade the town of Cliza and burn the houses of the local landowners. The subprefect of Cliza succeeded in pacifying the peasants, but once they were aware of their strength, acts of violence became more frequent. It is said that the incident which gave the movement a strong impetus occurred in Chilicchi, close to Cliza and Ucureña, when a landowner locked up a worker because he had not brought his tools with him when coming to work. The peasants organized a machete-waving demonstration to free their colleague. They became so threatening that the landowner fled, leaving everything behind. Such demonstrations occurred more and more frequently, the peasants taking over the lands immediately and transforming the hacienda houses into syndicate centers, schools or hospitals. The leaders were not able to restrain their followers.

After a few months, 1,200 syndicates were active in the department of Cochabamba with 200,000 members. This movement and the violence which accompanied it in some instances should be seen as a reaction to the efforts of the landed elite, particularly in Cochabamba, to organize an armed counter-revolution. The violence which occurred was, according to the reports of the ministry, due to the anxiety of the peasants to defend the new regime which promised them agrarian reform and the abolition of servitude.[64] There was no evidence of mob acts of vengeance for past abuses and injustices suffered, although in some of the scattered cases of looting of a hacienda house, revenge may have played a role. Given the desire of the peasants to undo ages of repression, it was difficult for the peasant leaders to check the movement and channel its energy in an orderly way.

The activities of the peasant syndicates, occupying haciendas and demonstrating in the towns, took place mainly during the first half of 1953. This movement strongly alarmed the landowners, many of whom fled to the cities leaving house and land to the peasants who armed themselves with the weapons they found in the haciendas. The effects were noted:

The uprising of the campesinos could not but arouse the national government to the necessity for drastic action. If far-reaching concessions could no longer control but only channel the emergence of the campesinos, they would at least demonstrate that the sympathies of the government were on the side of the now irresistible movement.[65]

The peasantry in most of the country remained initially distrustful after the change of government, because of their experiences with former revolutions and particularly with the severe repression which they had suffered since the fall of the Villarroel government. Only in the Cochabamba area were the peasants at that time relatively well organized, being independent and somewhat more radical than the MNR.

In order to gain the support of the peasantry as a whole, the new Ministry of Peasant Affairs started a campaign to organize the peasants all over the country into syndicates. An agreement between the government and the newly created Central Obrera Boliviana, in which Juan Lechin had great influence, arranged for many of the mine workers who had worked in unionization (most of whom were former peasants and spoke the indigenous language) to travel all over the country to help create the peasant syndicates. They prepared meetings and peasants of several communities and haciendas were called together by pututu (the traditional horn). Then a commission of the Ministry of Peasant Affairs came to institutionalize the new syndicates. Participants in this campaign testify about the enthusiasm with which the peasants, traditionally accustomed to gatherings of this kind dealing with community affairs, responded. In several areas, an indulgence in legalistic procedures was encountered. The peasant leaders were not content until their syndicates were recognized with all the signatures of local authorities and the Ministry of Peasant Affairs obtained.

The whole campaign culminated in the ceremony of the promulgation of the land reform Decree (Decreto Supremo No. 3464) on 2 August 1953 in Ucureña, where according to some sources, 200,000 peasants were present, one-third of them with their weapons.[66] The peasants from all over the country could see there with their own eyes how their colleagues in the Ucureña area and around had already effective control over the lands which they had seized from the latifundia.[67]

Since the government needed peasant support in defense against conservative forces attempting to overthrow it, the weapons of the dissolved army were given to newly formed peasant units. Also, the miners obtained an important share of the arms. The experience gained by peasants and miners during the Chaco War made the formation of these new defense units relatively easy. One objective was to impress the citizenry of the larger towns with the growing strength of the peasantry, as happened for example during a march of peasants through La Paz. Omasuyos province alone, which came marching from Achacachi, had 10,000 peasants. Similar regiments came from all over the country.[68]

The newly organized force had a chance to prove itself soon after the promulgation of the agrarian reform decree. On November 9, 1953, another coup and also an attempt to assassinate president Paz Estenssoro were staged. Cochabamba was practically controlled by the conservative forces, particularly the FSB (Falange Socialista Boliviana). The armed peasants came by the thousands to the city and after a battle of seven hours gained control.[69] The watchwords for the newly created organizations were

Take the political power, arm and organize in regiments and syndicates, abolish the *pongueaje* and all forms of servitude, take over the lands of the *haciendas*, drive the landowners away, establish that all work is paid.[70]

Only large properties which were run as efficient commercial farms rather than feudal estates were respected by the peasants in accordance with the reform decree. In those enterprises, wages were paid and there was no obligation to render feudal services.

Regarding the most important step, that of giving the land to the peasants, the Decree of August 1953 had provisions to give *de jure* recognition to the *de facto* changes which had taken place in many areas. Effective land redistribution spread all over the country with the help of the syndicates. Almost all latifundios were distributed to about 300,000 peasants in less than a year.

The Agrarian Reform Process

The Bolivian agrarian reform is not only different from the Mexican but in many respects contrary to it in its approach. In Mexico, only in critical stages, such as the initiation of the agrarian revolution in the period between 1910 and 1919, and in some particular instances later, *de facto* distribution of land preceded the completion of the legal procedure.

On the whole in Mexico, the process of *de facto* land distribution was even slower than the legal assignment of *ejido* lands, which as such could take several years. As a result, many peasant villages lived for years in insecurity and tension, since opposition of vested interests against land distribution generally did not stop until the land was effectively given over to the peasants in an official ceremony.

In Bolivia, the actual reform process was started before the law was promulgated, and once an appropriate law existed, the process of effective and legitimate taking possession of land by the peasants preceded the legal transfer of the title from the landowner to the reform beneficiaries.

Another contrast between the approach in the two countries is that in Mexico the main stress of the agrarian reform initially was to return the lands to the comunidades or to those peasants who had it in earlier years. Only from 1934 onwards were the *peones acasillados*, the peons who lived on and were tied to the haciendas, affected by possible land distribution. This was almost twenty years after the first agrarian law was promulgated. These *acasillados* on several occasions had been used by the landlords to combat groups of peasants who lawfully claimed land. The agrarian reform decree of 1953 in Bolivia also gave due satisfaction to the needs of the comunidades to recover their original lands, but it supported particularly the peasants who lived on the haciendas, tied to the land and obliged to serve the landlord. The break with the traditional system was much more drastic and immediate than in Mexico. This probably explains why the Bolivian reform did not provoke the violent struggle that swept Mexico for years. Landlord opposition in Bolivia was eliminated in a relatively short time by the organized and armed peasantry.

The difference between Mexico and Bolivia regarding the land reform may partly be due to the fact that in Mexico there was initially no united and organized group or party with a more or less specific purpose or ideology behind the revolution. The Mexican national party was formed a decade after the most severe revolutionary turmoil was over. In Bolivia, the revolutionary party, the MNR, had been struggling and winning support from urban labor and some peasant groups long before the Revolution of 1952 occurred.[71] It seems, however, that the radical peasant action in Cochabamba pushed the MNR beyond its original intentions regarding land reform.

Although within the MNR there were differences of opinion with regard to the question of how radical the agrarian reform should be, there was unanimity of opinion about the need for abolition of the feudal or semifeudal social structure prevailing in the rural areas. Moreover, the peasants had considerable influence and representation within the MNR, particularly in the local and regional party cells *(comandos)*, through which they could pressure for the acceptance of a more or less radical reform legislation. While the special commission, nominated in February 1953, to draft a land reform law proposal was working, the peasants by taking over haciendas in the Cochabamba valley and other areas where they were most strongly organized, pressured for a radical solution. Because of their influence within the Party and this direct action method, they obtained a law favorable to their demands in many respects.

In the Mexican Revolution, certain personalities in order to gain power initially promoted the land reform issue to rally the peasants behind them. But once they had achieved their goal, the land tenure problem was not given priority. It was only because of the insistent struggle of one leader, Zapata, and his group in an important area of Mexico, that the government had to promulgate reform legislation. Then, it took many years of hard struggle by the organized peasantry to bring about the application of the law.

While in Mexico, it took fifty years of ups and downs in agrarian reform to come to a stage where most of the land concerned had been distributed, in Bolivia, the latifundia system was *de facto* abolished in 1952-1953 in a sweeping campaign that probably lasted altogether less than a year.

Before the official promulgation of the agrarian reform decree, latifundia were taken over by the peasants in some areas such as the Cochabamba valley. Once the decree was issued, this procedure was legalized to some extent, and an accelerated taking over of latifundia was promoted by the government all over the country. This was made possible through Art. 78 of the land reform law.

Peasants who have been subject to a feudal work and exploitation system, in their capacity of servants, dependents, laborers, tenant-farmers, "agregados," outside workers etc., and who are over 18 years of age, married males over 14 years of age and widows with children who are minors *shall, upon proclamation of this Decree, be declared the owners of the parcels at present in their possession and cultivated by them until the National Agrarian Reform Service shall grant them all they are reasonably entitled to* in accordance with the definition of the small property or shall compensate them in the form of collective cultivation of lands enabling them to meet their family needs.[72]

Latifundia were abolished and divided among those who had worked on them. The parts already possessed by the peasants as *sayanas* in exchange for free labor on the owner's land would be theirs immediately and of the rest of the estate each would get a share. A parcel for collective use and for the school would be set apart. The unpaid labor obligations were abolished.

Edmundo Flores, at that time the United Nations advisor assisting the reform program noted

One should stress the importance of Article 78 to achieve rapidly the objectives of the agrarian reform. Without this automatic clause, the decree would have been another law, so common in the legislation of Latin America, which never has results because it lacks the political determination and the administrative and technical machinery for its application.[73]

While latifundia were no longer permitted, small and medium private properties and well-exploited agricultural enterprises would be respected by the law, and in most cases were in fact respected by the peasants. In estates where the relationships between the landlord and the peasants had been relatively cordial, arrangements could often be made to guarantee a continuation of the production of the estate for mutual benefit. Where the landlords had been abusive and tension existed between both parties, the landlord and his family generally left the estate out of fear of possible reprisals. In such cases, which were frequent in the Altiplano and Cochabamba area, the syndicate took over the estate. In cases where the landowner stayed on his property, he had to pay cash wages to the peasants who worked for him, or make some kind of sharecropping arrangement if no cash was available. This concerned only the part of the estate that the landlord cultivated for himself with peasant labor. At the same time, the landlord completely lost the ownership of the numerous plots of land which were formerly occupied by the peasants in exchange for labor services. Later, he would also lose that part of his latifundium which was in excess of a medium-sized farm as defined by the reform law. This was all part of the transformation of semifeudal landlords into medium-sized proprietors.

The application of the law took place with help from the syndicates that had been or were being formed in all parts of the country. Organizers from the Ministry of Peasant Affairs, many of whom were former miners, had been working all over the country since the early days of the Revolution to help organize peasant syndicates. In the local communities, syndicates were formed by gathering the peasants and electing in a meeting a secretary-general and other members of the directorate. They were sworn in immediately in the presence of a representative from the Ministry of Peasant Affairs. The minutes which were compiled gave immediate legal personality to the syndicate. The traditional experience of community meetings, reinvigorated in many areas during the earlier years of struggle and repression, was an asset in the rapid formation of syndicates in all the areas that were not too difficult to reach.

Although the peasant unionization drive had been going on for more than a year, official recognition to peasant unions was given only as part of the Agrarian Reform Decree of August 2, 1953 (Art. 132). This document briefly stipulated that peasant syndical organization be recognized as a means to defend the peasants' rights and to conserve social gains. The peasant union's function with relation to agrarian reform was mentioned but not specified in the decree.

The peasant syndicates in those areas where they did not yet exist when the Land Reform Decree was promulgated, were organized from above. July 15, 1953, the Confederación Nacional de Trabajadores Campesinos de Bolivia was founded with help of the Ministry of Peasant Affairs. The top leaders helped to form federations in the departments where they did not yet exist and the leaders of those federations in turn organized the centrals (centrales) and subcentrals in the provinces and smaller areas. The leaders of the centrals and subcentrals had an important function in organizing the local syndicates. As was revealed in some of the case studies carried out at the local level, there were generally some progressive leaders who tried to convince the more traditional ones that the formation of a union would be advantageous. They prepared the ground and it only needed the official visit of a provincial leader and an official of the Ministry of Peasant Affairs to actually formalize the formation of a syndicate. In other cases, the community was more apathetic and the commission which came to help organize a syndicate practically had to nominate its directorate.

In each province and department, mass meetings were held where hundreds or even thousands of delegates from the villages came together to found the provincial centrals and the departmental federations. After the promulgation of the reform decree, it was explained to the peasants in these mass meetings how to go about the land reform and to occupy immediately the latifundia, in expectation of the legal transfer of title which would be performed later in each case. People who participated in this campaign testified to the enthusiastic response of the peasantry and their ability to take their fate into their own hand. Since most landlords were afraid of reprisals and had fled to the city, the syndicates had to fill the vacuum that resulted in the local power structure. They took responsibility for the running of the part of the estate formerly managed by the landlord or his administrator. The whole process was accomplished in less than a year.

The Vice-President of Bolivia said in 1954:

Up to the present time, the liquidation of feudalism has been conducted like a short but effective trial. We believe this experience has hemispheric importance because of the contrast of methods it offers with other countries. In Bolivia, it has been carried out in all places legally and peacefully by the central government. . . . . . the achievements obtained in less than a year from the application of the Law of Agrarian Reform can be summarized as follows: all peasants who were under a colonization or patronal system are now free economically because they own the lots to which they were joined . . . [74]

The president of the National Agrarian Reform Council estimated in 1955 that 324,355 peasants had automatically benefited with 973,065 hectares of land that they had worked formerly in exchange for unpaid labor.[75] It was an automatic consequence of the law that a number of the leaders of the MNR Party lost their own or their family's land, such as President Paz Estenssoro and the Minister of Peasant Affairs, Ñuflo Chavez.[76] This made a big impression on many people.

The rate at which the program was applied prevented opposition from becoming violent or gaining strength. In the small urban centres, the peasant marches, often armed, convinced the merchants and other townsmen of the fact that power had effectively been taken over by the peasantry and its leaders. This fact was underlined by the distribution of arms, which had been taken from the old army, to a number of peasants in each village and the formation of peasant regiments. In order to impress public opinion, at the marches sometimes wooden imitation rifles were carried by those peasants who had not received or captured real ones.[f]

It gave the peasants for the first time some sense of security to be able to prevent a return of the landlords and of the climate of lawlessness which had prevailed. Very few acts of vengeance have been reported. The fact that there was little violence in the movement is all the more surprising seen in the light of the abuses suffered by the peasants before the Revolution. Up to 1952, for example, there existed the constitutional right of landlords to have sexual intercourse with any peasant girl on his estate before she married (derecho de pernada) and as late as 26 July 1953 a case was reported in Achacachi where the police chief ordered that peasants be shot because they had refused to greet their patrón.[77] It seems that in most cases the desire of the peasants for justice was

---

[f]The official institutionalization of the rural armed defense and security system was defined in Decree 03756 of June 10, 1954.

satisfied by the fact that the landlords disappeared from the scene, or that it could openly be shown that there were no more privileges, but that everybody was equal before the law.

The consolidation of a new political system after the 1952 Revolution eliminated the traditional domination of the rural areas by the landlords and a greater freedom of the peasantry resulted. Expressions of this freedom, in addition to the absence of landlord domination, were the disappearance of the designation Indian, replacing it with the term *campesino* (peasant), and the extension of the right to vote to illiterate people. Regarding the political voting, one observer made the following remark.

The last element of freedom must be qualified, recognizing that peasant votes are managed in blocks by federation leaders. Still, while the individual peasant may have little voice, the political position of the peasants as a whole is enhanced by even the managed vote.[78]

From 1952, the peasant organizations were closely related with the government as well as with the Movimiento Nacionalista Revolucionario, (MNR), the government party for many years. The Confederacion Nacional de Trabajadores Campesinos de Bolivia (CNTCB) was founded in La Paz in July of 1953 and its honorary president and vice-president were Víctor Paz Estenssoro and Hernán Siles Suazo, president and vice-president of the country. The first executive secretary of the CNTCB was the Minister of Peasant Affairs, Ñuflo Chavez Ortiz. Ties with the Ministry of Peasant Affairs have been strong. The main office of the CNTCB is in the Ministry building, and the national level leaders of the CNTCB and most of the departmental level leaders are paid by the Ministry.

The peasant unions also formed part of the Central Obrera Bolivia (COB), but its influence was relatively small in the COB structure. In the Delegate Assembly, the 83 member votes were divided as follows: 12 peasant votes, 38 workers votes, 21 middle-class votes, and 12 votes for the members of the executive committee of the COB.[79]

The exact quality of the relationship with the MNR party is unclear, particularly since 1964. The CNTCB has supported the government rather than the party in power, as long as the government did not antagonize the peasants' interests. Since practically all land available for the land reform program has been distributed and what remains to be done in over half of the cases is the granting of a legal title, peasants are more or less satisfied and will remain so as long as the new structure created in 1952 is not changed.

The main function of the peasant syndicates seems to be that of acting as agencies of local government. Many of the secondary functions of local government such as those of *corregidores* and subprefects were taken over by peasant union leaders.

In the functioning of the syndicate at the local level, the secretary-general elected by the assembly of peasant members has the most important role, replacing in many ways the functions formerly fulfilled by the landlord or his administrator. He represents the community and has a responsibility for its well-being. Some take this responsibility very seriously by visiting all the members periodically to see that everything is well and that people participate actively in the community life. He organizes community works, such as road improvement or school building, and settles disputes between members and their families, including marital problems and quarrels over the boundaries of plots. The second important person in the local syndicate hierarchy is the secretary of relations *(secretario de relaciones)* who accompanies the secretary-general on official visits and replaces him when he is away.

The secretary-general is generally the most experienced leader in the village but is not irreplaceable. Although many of the secretaries-general of the unions are to some extent paternalistic or authoritarian—in some cases they were called Don Secretario or Don General (Mr. Secretary-General)—they have to rule by community consensus and can be replaced as soon as they misuse their authority. Case studies in various areas of the country confirmed that the social climate in the syndicates at the community level is generally democratic and that the local leaders are under sufficient controls by the community members to check tendencies towards extreme authoritarianism, if that might occur.[80] General assemblies where community problems are discussed are held generally twice a month.

At the provincial, departmental or national level, leaders are not democratically elected but are designated by the central government. These are political posts to a large extent and the Ministry of Peasant Affairs, the Presidential Office and the leading national party have a strong influence. Since 1956, the peasants have had their own representation, which is part of the MNR party in the Chamber of Deputees and the Senate. A few peasant leaders have risen very high such as José Rojas, who became Minister of Peasant Affairs.

While most local leaders are peasants, the higher level positions do not require the leader to be a peasant himself. Several *vecinos* (townsmen) and urban labor leaders have taken posts in the provincial *centrales* or the departmental federations. The same applies to the leaders of the national confederation. A considerable number of peasant union leaders at the provincial, departmental and national level are former rural school teachers, many of whom seem to have had their education in the Warizata training school, close to Achacachi.

Financially, the CNTCB is dependent on the government. There is no system of quota collection from the membership. The top leaders of the Confederation receive a salary from the Ministry of Peasant Affairs, and from the office of the President. The same occurs with leaders of the federation of the department of La Paz. The interior departments of the country get financial support from the departmental prefect or the departmental agrarian reform offices. Congresses at various levels are generally subsidized by the government.

The leaders of the departmental federations and the national confederation generally establish themselves in the departmental capital or in La Paz. Their economic situation is much better than that of the lower level leaders. A tendency has been noted for some of the leaders at the departmental level to lose contact with the membership and become official bureaucrats.

The leaders of the CNTCB who form part of the Parliamentary Peasant Brigade run most risk of losing contact with the members, particularly where under the present situation (since 1964) several of them seem to have been handpicked by the government. Recent observers noted a decline in the activities of the agrarian syndicates at various levels since 1964. Provincial and cantonal concentrations and meetings were held less frequently, or were more or less paralyzed as a consequence of the presence of army units (it was noted that the strength of the army increased between 1964 and 1967 from 4,000 to 25,000).[81]

It is clear that the postreform political clientele system, more dynamic and much less rigid and coercive than the traditional system before 1952, implied considerable risks of authoritarianism and personalism. In 1959, the CNTCB's close link with the governing political party became a problem when the MNR suffered a top-level internal division. Walter Guevara created his own following against the leadership of Víctor Paz Estenssoro. Local-level leadership rivalries between the unions of Ucureña and nearby Cliza had existed since 1952. However, when in 1959 the Cliza leader, Veizaga, sided with Walter Guevara and José Rojas of Ucureña sided with Paz Estenssoro, the conflict became extremely acute, and resulted in street fights in Cliza where a considerable number of peasants were killed.[82] After the division in MNR, the struggle for peasant support intensified. Later, Juan Lechin organized a leftist party (Partido Revolucionario de la Izquirda Nacionalista), while General René Barrientos began to create a following for himself among the peasants. After the coup which overthrew the MNR government in November of 1964, General Barrientos was able to count on peasant support, particularly after a reshuffling of top leaders of the CNTCB.

In spite of the fact that the peasant unions at the base have little control over the top leadership of their organization, they have some influence through the threat of direct action and the channels of direct pressure created during the revolution. One reporter noted

Perhaps the most important political aspect of the *sindicatos* is the armed militias they support. In some particularly strong *sindicatos*, these exist as units of fully armed men, quartered in barracks, at the disposition of the group's officials. In less well-organized groups, they are composed of the members themselves, mobilized at need. The amount of force available in the *sindicatos* is large. In the Ucureña prototype, an armed force of 1,600 men is quartered permanently in the town, and a far greater supporting force is reported to be available from the leagues of the Cochabamba Valley on 48 hours' notice.[83]

It has also been observed: "In Chuquisaca, for example, one syndicate boss led armed peasants into the city of Sucre when he thought it necessary to remind the old aristocracy that it was no longer in power. And, when some syndicate officials were murdered near Monteagudo, armed syndicate militia converged on that area to apprehend the men responsible and to pillage their haciendas."[84] This force gives the peasants considerable potential political bargaining power. They had considerable self-confidence, particularly those of the more politicized areas around Cochabamba and Achacachi.

One observer noted that although urban Bolivians almost unanimously assume that the agrarian unions are manipulated by a few shrewd urban politicians, in part of the Yunga area, for example, this was not the case.

In fact, it is clear that campesinos realize the strength of their voice in dealing directly with politicians at the national level. Executive decisionmaking is so centralized that delegations from individual *sindicatos* or provincial federations often bypass local authorities and carry their appeals directly to cabinet officials or even the President. That is to say, they short-circuit official lines of communication. And they do this not with a hat-in-the-hand humility, as in the many paternalistic Latin regimes; on the contrary, they often demand schools, roads, potable water systems, and other benefits, and offer bloc-voting as a reward, or threaten to put up roadblocks if they don't get what they ask.[85]

The peasants, aware of their political bargaining power, are not passive. After a period in which the peasant syndicate leaders had enjoyed considerable influence and representation in local government in some provincial capitals in the years following 1964, local authorities were nominated who were known to be opposed to the peasants' interests. These facts made peasants in several areas distrustful. More representative leadership at the provincial or cantonal level was demanded. In some, generally quiet, zones such as Sucre, a considerable radicalization of the peasants took place. For example, in the town of Sucre, spontaneous peasant concentrations occurred when a mayor was nominated in 1967 who was considered an enemy of the peasantry. They threatened to stop food being brought to the market and to cut off the water supply and brought about the replacement of the new mayor. The conflict was mainly the result of the mayor's refusal to comply with peasant demands that he lower the market tax. In several of the traditionally radical places, such as Quillacollo, similar things happened, but there they were more to be expected.[86]

One of the main problems which keeps the peasants alert and prepared to defend their interests is the fact that although by mid-1954 practically all latifundio land had been taken over by the beneficiaries of the agrarian reform, the process of the distribution of property titles to these lands in the following years has been slow. By 1966, approximately 170,000 peasant families, only half of those who received land, had benefited from the title distribution. The other half had their cases still pending.

This insecurity of title possession was one argument used by parliamentary peasant representatives to defend the right of peasants to carry arms in Bolivia. As long as not all plots possessed by the peasants according to the agrarian reform law have been duly legalized as their property, the former landlords may try to reverse the process of land distribution.[87] In personal talks, some of these representatives confessed in 1966 that the lack of a stable government and subsequent doubts about its intentions (possibilities of an increase in illegitimacy) was reason enough for the peasants to keep their arms as a guarantee that their interests would not be impinged upon.[88]

This power capability made it possible on some occasions for local peasant unions to overrule the leaders at the top levels who had approved the introduction of a land tax for the small peasant owners in 1968. Opposition at the base against this measure was so strong that in Belen and in Achacachi the top leaders of the CNTCB and President Barrientos had to flee to avoid violence by a peasant assembly which the President had addressed to explain the need for the tax.

Compared with the situation before 1952, the peasants in Bolivia had on the whole benefited much more from land reform than those in Mexico. The great majority of the Bolivian peasants was transformed from semifeudal serfs into small proprietors. The improvement in the living conditions, particularly nourishment of the peasantry was so obvious that the average size of the army recruits increased notably in the years after the land distribution.[89] The peasants simply ate a good deal more, which is also one of the reasons for the temporary decrease in marketed agricultural produce, in the first postreform years. In spite of the radical changes in the rural areas, the fundamental problems of the Bolivian economy remained unsolved. These were, however, not so much in the agricultural sector but rather in mining, on which sector the country depended heavily. Although the major tin mines were nationalized after 1952, the dependence on foreign controlled markets remained the same or worsened, which prevented the country from making a complete change in its social structure.[90] While the mine workers unions continued to struggle for more radical and fundamental changes in Bolivian society, the peasant unions, after they had benefited from the land reform, were on some occasions utilized to appease or even combat the miners. This was particularly the case after 1964. Once the peasants have received land through agrarian reform, they seem to lose interest in promoting further revolutionary changes in society as a whole.

In summary, it could be said that in Mexico and Bolivia peasant organizations initially grew and became strong in a spontaneous way, uncontrolled by the government. Only later were they institutionalized as part of the national political system after this system had undergone considerable and drastic change. In both countries, the peasant organizations had a certain influence on the creation of a new political structure which arose after the revolutionary changes. The peasants initially won significant benefits, mainly land distribution. As a result, they were so indebted to the new system that they supported it in spite of the fact that the flow of further benefits was very small. They continued to live at the margin of society although somewhat better off than under the prerevolutionary situation.

The role of peasant organizations in the postreform situation in Mexico and Bolivia was limited. In neither of these countries did the peasants gain an influence in national policy making which corresponded to their numerical force.

Peasants and their organizations were helpful in bringing about a change in the traditional social structure, opening up possibilities for a more dynamic development of the country as a whole. However, after the transfer of most or part of the political power from the traditional elite into the hands of more dynamic groups (generally middle sector), the peasantry was neutralized as a political force. The potential for peasant mobilization after the reform was, on the whole, not realized, except in a few periods such as in Mexico under the Cárdenas regime. Rather, emphasis was placed on consolidation and institutionalization of the peasantry's role as political supporter of the new elites.

From the outset, the Mexican and Bolivian peasant organizations were strongly related to the agrarian reform process and were recognized or institutionalized by the agrarian reform laws. Membership became almost obligatory for those peasants who did not participate in the initial spontaneously growing organizations.

Other Peasant Organizations and Movements

The Mexican and Bolivian agrarian movements, described in Chapter 4, show particularly well what is possible in the formation of effective peasant organizations. Both movements grew from below and only after they gained strength on their own account did the government support and help extend the organizations. Both movements were quite successful in achieving large-scale land distribution. They were neutralized as part of a new establishment only after the original demands were largely fulfilled. In Chapter 6, we will try to draw some lessons from the Mexican and Bolivian experience. In order to give perspective to the generalized conclusions to be drawn from these more successful experiences, it will be useful to take into account the few other, less successful or less authentic movements that had occurred in Latin America. One of these is the peasant federation that has been functioning in Venezuela with ups and downs from about 1945 until the present. This federation was not a peasant movement that grew from below as a reaction to the culture of repression, but was organized from the outset by urban politicians. During and after ten years of repression, this organization became quite militant and achieved considerable gains such as land distribution to many peasant groups.

In the Peruvian highlands, particularly in the Convencion valley, a movement grew that could have followed the Bolivian pattern if the Peruvian government had not halted it by a localized land distribution or promises to that effect and large-scale army intervention. The movement did not reach national proportions, but the way it grew from below and particularly the methods of struggle it applied, such as the occupation of disputed lands, are important for the study of the possibilities of peasant organization in Latin America.

Another important movement that should be taken into account, although it was almost completely destroyed in 1964, is the formation of the Peasant Leagues in the northeast of Brazil. This movement grew from below, more or less along similar lines as other movements, but before it became a well-structured organization, it was crushed by the opposition of conservative forces. The same happened to a lesser extent with competing movements that were created by the Church in the same region to neutralize the influence of the leagues. The leagues of the northeast of Brazil are a particularly useful example of how a peasant movement can grow in a region where the traditional patronage system weighs heavily on the peasants.

In some countries, especially in Colombia and Guatemala, peasants have been in movement in more or less unstructured ways, resulting in considerable violence. These cases are important to show briefly that the violent reaction of the peasants is not so much an inherent characteristic of their movements, but a result of the fact that the landed elite makes orderly development of representative peasant interest groups impossible through the provocation of struggle between peasant groups or through repression. In Colombia, a great deal of violence broke out after a populist leader who could well have channelled peasant discontent in an organized fashion, was assassinated in 1948. In Guatemala, violence was used to undo the effects of the agrarian reform and peasant organizations drive that was introduced by a populist government in the early fifties.

Particularly when looking at the revolutionary potential of peasants (as will be done in Chapter 7), it is important to consider the reactions of the peasants in Columbia and Guatemala, although at present and for the time being, no organized or structured movements exist in those countries.

Venezuela: The Peasant Federation

Contrary to what happened in Mexico and Bolivia, in Venezuela, peasant organization was initiated and stimulated from above as part of the political system at the national level. The whole peasant movement was organized as an electoral clientele for the reformist Acción Democratica (AD) party, which through its political influence was able to utilize certain benefits to win adherence for the Federación Campesina de Venezuela (FCV) it created.[a]

From the outset and consciously, a political clientele was built up to compete with the existing traditional hacienda system. Although charismatic leadership played an important role, the new clientele was created through the granting of favors, which were at the disposal of the initiators of the organization because of their influence within the government.

During the government of Juan Gómez (1909-1935), the Venezuelan rural areas already showed a good deal of unrest. This can be seen as a reaction of frustration of the squatters on formerly virgin land *(conuqueros)* who were forced into peonage when large landholders in that period received property titles to thousands of hectares of such land. There was evidence in the 1930s of land invasions by peasants and the number of conflicts between *conuqueros* and sharecroppers, tenants and landowners over tenure conditions grew rapidly. A movement started among wage laborers toward a militant unionization and in several places scattered eruptions of violence were noted. Some of those actions were violently repressed. But an unintended consequence of the government's policy of repression was an increased potential for militant organized action by the peasants.[2]

The group of political leaders around Rómulo Betancourt, who had returned

---

[a]Powell indicated that such organization took place through a system of exchange of goods and services which was summarized in the phrase: "votes for agrarian reform benefits. . . ."[1]

to Venezuela after Gómez' death, saw in this potential a possibility for winning mass support for the political party which they were organizing, and which later became Acción Democrática. The formation of a national peasant organization was an important aspect of their campaign. Betancourt himself, according to many informants, played an active role in the establishment of peasant syndicates on a national scale. A liberal labor law, passed in 1936 by Gómez' successor, Gen. Elías López Contreras, made rural unionization legally possible, although the law had such strict operating requirements that, at times, more local unions lost their legal personality than were recognized. The increase of officially existing unions was thus rather slow. The number rose between 1936 and 1945 from 3 unions (with 482 members) to 77 (with 6.279 members).

Many difficulties were encountered in those years by the initiators and charismatic leaders, such as Ramón Quijada. Union activities were often considered illegal and politically subversive by local authorities and national guard commanders. They were often repressed. The men who led the movement during this period took great risks. As a result of their efforts, it could be claimed that in 1945 there existed 500 groups, with about 100,000 members.[3]

This strength was built up by about 200 professional organizers who were sent out to recruit local leaders who were able to mobilize the peasants effectively. Initially, this was done mainly in the areas of greatest population pressure and concentrated holdings—the state of Aragua and Carabobo—where great numbers of peasants came into conflict with the large landowners over tenancy or sharecropping conditions.[4] It was in those areas where the peasants were relatively advanced that pressures were most strongly manifested. The tenants and sharecroppers appeared to respond more vigorously to agitation than the squatters in more remote areas or the wage laborers on commercial farms. In areas ready for organization, local leaders were approached with offers to help organize the peasants into effective peasant unions related to the nationwide peasant and labor movement, which was part of the reform-oriented political movement of Rómulo Betancourt called Acción Democrática since 1941.

The peasant movement followed the pattern of the general Venezuelan labor movement. There was not, however, a monolithic control of the labor movement by Acción Democrática before 1945. According to an ILO Mission report, there were two factions in the movement which were, with help from the CTAL (Confederation of Latin American Workers), to which both factions were affiliated, brought together in August 1945.[5] When in October 1945, Rómulo Betancourt became President after a *coup d'état* organized jointly by his party and a group of dissident army officers, a crisis arose in the labor movement.

The new Workers' Federation found itself once more torn between the men who wished to give active and unreserved support to the new government and those who wished to adopt a benevolent but completely independent attitude. The latter were not opponents of the Democratic Action Party but they were suspicious because of the circumstances in which the *coup d'état* had been carried out. They considered that, at this time, the advances made by the military to the Democratic Action Party were evidence not of a sincere desire to establish a progressive social policy but, essentially, of a desire to obtain the support of a popular force which they lacked.[6]

This suspicion seemed to be reinforced when Betancourt initially suspended not only the constitutional rights but also the right to strike.

Strong impetus was given to the labor movement between 1945 and 1948 that benefited mainly the unions of Acción Democrática (AD) orientation. The mobilization of the voters behind the Acción Democrática proved to be successful, when in 1946 this party received 80 per cent of the popular vote. Under the AD government between 1945 and 1948, the number of legally recognized peasant unions increased from 77 to 515, with 43,302 members. In 1947 at the national level, the *Federación Campesina de Venezuela* was formed with Ramón Quijada as its first president.

In the years between 1945 and 1948, certain measures helped to strengthen the peasant union movement significantly. Through various decrees, arrangements were made to lease lands belonging to the government (such as those formerly owned by Gómez) and also privately owned land which was not actively farmed—and this was done under favorable conditions to peasant union members. Thus by the end of 1948, an estimated 125,000 hectares of land had been leased to approximately 73,000 members. In addition, through the Instituto Técnico de Immigración y Colonización (ITIC), large sums were made available to farm those leased lands. The credits were distributed locally by committees consisting of a representative from ITIC, a credit specialist and an official from the peasant syndicate, who had the responsibility of verifying the performance of the applicant in the tasks assigned in the technical farm plan drawn up by ITIC.

These arrangements gave great power, status and prestige to the local peasant union leaders. Recruited initially as social and opinion leaders in their rural communities, these people by virtue of their connections with the government, had been granted powerful instrumental attributes—as leaders in forming the syndicates, they could choose the peasants whom they desired as members. They also could petition the ITIC for land grants for members to farm and be in a position to influence the granting and control of the accompanying farm credits.

By 1948, the National Peasant Federation officially had 43,302 members, but in fact probably had many more, since 73,000 received certain benefits, such as better tenancy conditions and credit. It should be noted, however, that rural workers totalled around 600,000: 245,376 day laborers, 289,169 renters, sharecroppers and squatters and 125,509 unpaid family workers, according to the 1950 Census.[7]

In October 1948, an Agrarian Reform Law was promulgated which could have had significant effects if it had not been for the overthrow of the Acción Democrática government by Lt. Colonel Carlos Delgado and Lt. Col. Marcos

Pérez Jiménez, both of whom had helped to bring Betancourt to power, but who wanted to impose restraint on the Acción Democrática government.

In the years following 1948, the peasant and labor movement were again severely repressed. The executive committees of all the 515 peasant syndicates were dissolved. The report of the ILO Mission expressed criticism of the strong tie between the Venezuelan Confederation of Labour (CTV) and the Acción Democrática Party, to the detriment of the former's independence. However, it strongly condemned the dissolution of the labor movement by the military government after 1948 under the pretext that this movement was a political party organization.[b] The Agricultural workers' unions, although the most numerous of all the different kinds of unions existing, decreased more than the others as a consequence of the government policy.[9]

The effects of the initial steps of agrarian reform, made in the previous years, were mostly undone. A great part of the government land, which was being leased under favorable terms to members of the unions, was recaptured by the members of the Gómez family, sometimes "accompanied by cruelly treacherous treatment for the campesino occupants,"[10] and private lands for which reasonable leasing conditions had been obtained could again be used by the owners as they saw fit. Eviction of peasants from such lands, occasionally accompanied by violence, was not rare.[11]

The experience of repression, however, indirectly helped to strengthen the peasant movement so that it was able to develop stronger than ever when the years of dictatorship were over in 1958. Powell made the following notes.

The arrest, torture, imprisonment and exile of campesino movement leaders served to highlight the dedication and sacrifice with which such leaders were serving the peasantry, perhaps thereby entrenching the loyalty of that sector even more deeply. AD leaders were captured while distributing resistance literature, while organizing campesino clandestine groups, and in at least one case, while attempting an assassination of the Junta Militar. Such acts of bravery and courage were used by remaining campesino leaders as examples to maintain an intense respect and devotion on the part of the campesinos.[12]

Immediately after the fall of the Pérez Jiménez regime in 1958, the peasant unions of the FCV, which had led a clandestine life for about ten years, came into the open apparently stronger than ever. In the few areas where land had been taken from the peasants between 1948 and 1958, peasant unions simply recovered the lands. Competition for peasant support existed between various political groups and this resulted in the more radical groups, which most forcefully represented the peasants' demand for land, setting the tone. Because of fear of competition from Christian-Democrat and communist forces, Acción Democrática peasant groups began to take over lands claimed by their members.

---

[b]I.L.O. indicates that the Campesino Federation was singled out by the Minister of the Interior after 1948.[8]

Rómulo Betancourt, who became president again in 1958, condemned the invasions, branding them as violence and expressed the hope that the leaders of the Federación Campesina de Venezuela, at that time organizing a national peasant congress, would prove a moderating influence.[c] On June 2, 1959, the First Venezuelan Peasant Congress organized by the FCV accepted a resolution strongly demanding land reform legislation. It also decided on the active mobilization of the peasants all over the country to prepare the petitions for land. The pressure was so strong that in the first years of its operation the land reform agency (Instituto Agrario Nacional)—to get ahead of the invasions—gave land to 24,000 families, while it had planned to settle only 10,000. Only provisional titles were given out in that period and the distribution of the lands of a certain estate among the peasants was initially left to the union or committee which had presented the petition or had organized the occupation of the estate in question. These provisional titles consisted of *Actas de entrega* (bills of delivery) to the peasant committees or individuals.

The procedure for land distribution in Venezuela was relatively simple. The law (Art. 93) stipulated that individuals as well as groups could petition for land. As a first step, the peasants would have to form a Comité Campesino Provisional which would formulate the petition, including data about the peasant members and the lands petitioned for, and send it to the state level Delegation of the National Agrarian Institute. If the landlord was willing to sell his land to IAN, such would be arranged; if he was not willing and the petition was declared valid, after a certain period, the estate could be expropriated.

Once an estate was acquired by IAN and transferred to the peasant committee, an *asentamiento*, settlement, was formed. An Administrative Committee was elected to deal with IAN as representative of the peasants.

While most invasions took place in 1958 and 1959 immediately after Pérez Jiménez' fall, they continued to occur after the promulgation of the land reform law in 1960. The government had to find a way to deal with this. While in very few cases invasions were repressed or halted by public force, elsewhere they were channelled or avoided by a solution of the problem before the peasants had taken radical action. Some cases are known, such as the pilot project La Julia-Jobo Dulce, where the public forces were present when the invasion took place and watched that everything occurred in an orderly way. Opposition by the landowners was generally of limited scope. The change in the political climate in the country after the fall of the Pérez Jiménez regime and the strong public opinion in favor of radical changes in the rural areas, in addition to the sweeping action undertaken by the FCV peasant unions, made it clear to the landlords that opposition would be useless and that immediate sale of lands to IAN, rather than waiting for expropriation, would be inconvenient.

Only one-fourth of the private estates which were invaded were well culti-

[c]Carta a los Ministros de Relaciones Interiores y de la Agriculture y Cría, con Motivo de la Ocupación Violenta de Predios por Campesinos.[13]

vated. This indicates that invasions could often be seen as bringing into cultivation lands which were of little or no use to agricultural development. Particularly where lands were underused in the densely populated areas, the efforts of landless peasants to occupy those lands and bring them into intensive cultivation was understandable. The legislation emphasized the importance of the land's social function, and distribution through legal procedure was to be initiated. Conversations with peasant leaders who have actively participated in or organized invasions of underutilized lands confirm that this was an important motivation for action.[14]

According to studies made in 1966, of the 761 landholdings acquired by IAN for land distribution, about one-third, 256, had been invaded, mainly in the years 1959-1961. The invasions which took place in those years covered approximately 60 to 70 per cent of the landholdings acquired for reform in those years. They occurred mainly in the areas where urban influences were strongest, such as those states where more than two-thirds of the population lived in cities. Thus, 203 land invasions, almost 80 per cent of the total of 265, took place in the states of Aragua, Carabobo, Yaracuy, Trujillo and Zulia, where peasant unions were most strongly organized.[15] Half of the invasions took place before the official promulgation of the law and were influential in accelerating its acceptance.

In several instances, the frequency of which is difficult to estimate, the invasions were favored by the landholders because the sale of their land to the Instituto Agrario Nacional extracted good prices, particularly in areas close to the cities. Some landlords were so eager to get rid of their land that they helped stage an invasion (called autoinvasión) in order to gain priority from IAN. Thus, in the *asentamientos* La Unión, La Belén and Las Marios, the landowners made an agreement with the peasant union to pressure IAN for expropriation. These landholdings were in decay, coffee production was low and there were debts and mortgages. Expropriation and payment was in this case advantageous to the owner.

By 1961, leadership problems emerged within the FCV concerning what policy to follow. One of the issues was the speed of agrarian reform. Some leaders wanted to militate for a more rapid and drastic agrarian reform program. The idea of the main leader of the FCV, Ramón Quijada, expressed in an interview with a national newspaper, was that a radical agrarian reform should be carried out in four years, giving land to 87,500 families per year.[16] Others wanted to use more restraint in the demands and follow the increasingly moderate line, emphasizing consolidation and solution of the administrative problems of the agrarian reform program.[d]

At all levels where the *Federación Campesina de Venezuela* was active—the local unions, the state federations, and the national federation—a shift in leader-

[d]Lord noted that, e.g., for the year 1961, 90 per cent of the FCV's budget came from the Ministry of Labor, which is an indication of the organization's dependence on the government.[17]

ship was provoked. The more radical leadership elements were purged, particularly at the local level. Urban labor leaders were brought in to replace them. Ramón Quijada, the national president of the FCV, was replaced by Armando González, who followed a less radical line with regard to land reform.[18]

The change was related to lack of money to remunerate the landowners according to the legally established high rates. A decree was promulgated in 1962 that no more invaded lands would be used for land reform purposes, which practically brought an end to the invasions. After a purge of the leadership of the FCV at all levels, the moderation in the demand for land distribution was transmitted through the FCV to the peasantry, apparently with success. The most active and organized areas had been satisfied during the first years of the reform and the deemphasizing of the importance of accelerated land distribution did not encounter much opposition after the more radical leaders had been replaced. The FCV then became increasingly an instrument through which benefits such as credits, schools, roads and other facilities could be channelled to the peasant clientele in exchange for votes to the government parties. However, the votes of the peasants were obtained at a price which has decreased over the years. This was a consequence of the disappearance of the use of radical means of action by the peasants after the most militant groups were contented with effective agrarian reform. They now only demanded additional services.

In those syndicates where little unity and cohesion exist among the peasants, the risk of dissidence is so small that there is no need to channel any benefits. People will stay in line anyway as long as no new forms of repression arise. On the other hand, where unions are well organized and militant, only a constant flow of benefits ensures that the peasants support the overall system.[19]

Peruvian Highlands: The Peasant
Movement in La Convención and Other Areas

In many areas of Peru, there persists to this day the system of personal services as part of the peasants' obligations to the landlord.[20] Thus, in the valley of La Convencion and Lares, department of Cuzco, there were 174 haciendas with much idle land which was increasingly occupied by so-called *arrendires* in exchange for their labor. The *arrendire* is a peasant who, in exchange for a plot of virgin land, is obliged to work a number of days (5-15 per month) without remuneration on the land cultivated for the landlord. It often happens that the *arrendires* lease out part of their plot to an *allegado* who helps him fulfill the service to the landlord. The *allegado* in turn may have a *habilitado, agregado,* or *manipure,* a peon or manual laborer in his service. Although the Constitution of 1933 prohibits work without remuneration (Art. 55), such forms of servitude continued to be the case in La Convencion as well as in other areas. In the Convencion valley, there were about 4,000 *arrendires* in the area with 12,000 *allegados* and an unknown number of day laborers—altogether about 60,000 people.[21]

Still, in La Convención, the peasants were in a relatively favorable position compared with other areas. The valley forms part of the higher selva and most inhabitants came to the area during the last few decades as migrants or pioneers. They became *arrendires* on the large haciendas of mostly virgin lands but were able, after a number of years of work, to improve their income considerably by the cultivation of coffee and other tropical or subtropical cash crops. The obligations of *arrendires* to work a number of days per week on the owner's land became increasingly burdensome, especially when the *hacendados*, in view of the growing economic independence of their *arrendires*, started to increase their demands or tried to evict them.

By 1952, the peasants of one hacienda had already combined to hire a lawyer who could formulate a protest and represent them at the labor inspector's office. In the next few years, peasants of other haciendas followed this example and started to band together and organize unions. The protests were mainly concerned with the number of days worked for the landowner, the excessive working hours per day compared with the legally established working day and the free sale of crops without intervention of the *hacendado*.

In 1958, eight of these newly formed unions joined together in the *Federación Provincial de Campesinos de la Convención y Lares*. Some of the initial leaders were Protestant, and one of them, a lay leader for over a hundred protestant believers, was elected Secretary-General of the Federation (and later sent to prison, as a communist agitator).[22] Although initially lawyers of different political affiliations helped in representing the peasants in their protests, most assistance was given by the legal advisors of the *Federación de Trabajadores de Cuzco*, a militant communist-oriented organization. Since these lawyers took the trouble of moving from Cuzco into the valley, they became the recognized legal advisors and came to exert influence also on the strategy of the movement. Labor leaders from the town of Cuzco, who gained acceptance among the peasants because of their obvious Indian origin, also occasionally gave assistance.

Despite the outside advisory roles of the lawyers and various F.T.C. representatives to the valley, the major part of the organization and development, particularly during the early phase from 1952 to 1960, was primarily an autonomous development within the valley and constituted an unusual Latin American phenomenon of a rural labor union organizing itself from the bottom up—rather than being organized and directed from outside.[23]

The estate where the movement developed most strongly and where the conditions were particularly bad was Huadquiña, of which the haciendas Santa Rosa and Chaupimayo formed part. The entire property, one of several belonging to the same family, was over 100,000 hectares according to conservative estimates. What created most resentment and hostility among the peasants in Chaupimayo were the abuses of the landlord and the way he tried to show and confirm his overwhelming power, for example, by flogging peasants who were not servile enough.[24]

As a response to this situation, the peasant union was formed. Its secretary-general, Andrés Gonzalez, was originally from elsewhere in the area, but he had fled after a violent encounter with his landlord. When the union was formed in Huadquiña, a Ministerial Resolution prohibiting the *arrendires* and *allegados* from forming syndicates made it possible to declare the union illegal, consequently, the main leaders were jailed for two years. During this period, Andrés Gonzalez became acquainted with Hugo Blanco, an agronomist from Cuzco, who had been active before as a labor organizer and Trotzkyite political agitator and who was in prison for that reason. They became friends and González took Hugo Blanco as an *allegado* on his plot in Chaupimayo when they were set free after a hunger strike in 1959.

The union work was resumed and the first list of demands included

1. that the union be free to build a school and hire a teacher;
2. that the landlord give receipts for the days of unpaid work accomplished each month;
3. proper payment for improvements, such as coffee plants, if a peasant leaves or is evicted;
4. that the landlord let the peasants use some days of obligatory labor to build bridges across the streams;
5. that there should be a first aid box on the estate;
6. that clothes and utensils which the overseers had taken from the peasants be returned;
7. that the landlord supply the peasants with tools and food during days of unpaid work.[25]

The landlord's answer to these demands was an effort to evict the leaders. The peasants responded with a strike refusing to perform the unpaid work. When policemen came to dislodge the peasants, they found them prepared to defend their homes. This was the beginning of a large-scale movement.

Hugo Blanco soon became his union's representative to the local federation and helped in the formation of new syndicates in other places of the valley. He began to establish a name as an effective organizer. Care was taken that in the unions the *arrendires* as well as the *allegados* and the day laborers participated so as to avoid internal divisions. In 1960, strikes were organized in the haciendas Paccha Grande, Chaucamayo and Chaupimayo to demand better treatment and the end of abuses. The strike meant that the peasants refused to fulfil the days of unpaid work on the lands of the estate used by the landlord. This had the advantage of allowing them to work more on their own plot. For the landlords, this meant serious problems, particularly during the harvest periods. The tactics were successful and spread rapidly through the area, particularly during 1961 and 1962. Many more syndicates were formed and by the end of 1961, there were 42 unions on strike in La Convencion. Officially, it was difficult to do anything against the strike since the unpaid services were not allowed according to the Constitution. At the end of December 1961, a general strike on all haciendas was announced and had a great impact. As a result, the government of President Manuel Prado issued a decree on April 24, 1962 which abolished the obligations of unpaid labor in the area.

In the meantime, in 1961, the *Federación Departmental de Campesinos y Comunidades del Cuzco* had been formed with 214 sections, but a split soon occurred within the movement. Hugo Blanco and many of the newer unions wanted a radical land reform brought about, if necessary, by occupations of the haciendas, a tactic which could lead to violence if the landowners opposed. The older leaders were less ambitious in their requests. In the election for Secretary-General of the Federación Departamental, Blanco received a majority, but the leaders of some twenty peasant unions refused to follow him and walked out. It was in that period, mid 1962, that Blanco became known, in many newspapers, as a Castro-type guerrilla leader. The press magnified the reputation of Blanco to legendary proportions, and thus obscured the emergence of a strong movement based on concrete demands.

Hobsbawm, who visited the area in its turbulent period, indicated that Blanco encouraged in Chaupimayo—the estate where he lived—the building of a school, the hiring of a teacher by the union, the building of roads and similar community projects. A certain revolutionary exaltation existed in Chaupimayo: alcoholic drinks were forbidden and union meetings were held daily.[26] One way for the peasants to defend themselves against the arbitrary acts of the landlord, such as eviction, was to congregate in small hamlets instead of living in relative isolation all over the estate. In Chaupimayo, three such hamlets were formed. Another means to enhance the strength of the peasant groups were mass meetings in Quillabamba and Cuzco.

Chaupimayo also became the base at which several training courses gave instruction to 150 peasant leaders from all over the area about agrarian reform.[27] At a later stage, it seems that instruction in armed self defense formed part of these courses. The idea behind this was that the peasants needed to form small militia groups in order to protect themselves and their wives and daughters against despoliations and abuses of the landlords and to achieve effective political power. Contrary to the tactics of guerrilla groups which operated in some areas of Peru, these militia groups strongly emphasized self defense. It was stressed that this was only one aspect of the syndicate's activities, directed towards the elimination of the landlords' power. The publicity given to Blanco was partly caused by the fact that in May 1962 a group of Trotzkyite political activists had been captured who had robbed two banks and used part of the money to support the peasant movement in La Convencion. The relationship between Blanco's movement and those activities in Lima or elsewhere was probably a reason that an order for his arrest was issued mid 1962, which forced him to go into hiding in his area. Because of the protection given by the peasants, he was relatively safe there.

The peasant mobilization went on and became, partly as a result of the strong opposition of the landlords, more and more radical. The issuance of the decree abolishing unpaid labor in April 1962 was not sufficient to calm down the movement. The most radical policies promoted by Blanco among the unions were at that time the occupations of haciendas. Later, Blanco explained that this was to be part of an overall revolutionary strategy to win political power for the peasants and workers, beginning in the rural areas. A first stage of the strategy was a refusal to render the unpaid services or to pay the rent. The second stage was to start work on the idle lands of the hacienda. As planned, the third stage was to occupy those lands worked for the owner. Also his house and other establishments were to be put to collective use. If the landlord worked his property efficiently and had not committed abuses, his property would be respected.[28] Some landlords, such as the owner of the Huadquina estate, known for their abusiveness, were chased away and not allowed to return. The argument of the peasants was that they had long since paid with unremunerated work for the value of the land they now occupied. In some estates, the peasants built provisional huts to indicate that the land was now theirs.

The occupations were organized simultaneously in different places and carried out in a coordinated way so that an effective power would be developed in competition with that of the landlords. These occupations went on during several months of 1962, particularly in October. Many landlords left the area at that time. The peasants formed armed defense groups to defend the lands they had occupied or which they possessed but from which they were threatened to be evicted. That practically no violence or destruction was involved in such activities is, according to Hobsbawm,[29] surprising, when seen in the light of the treatment which the peasants generally had to suffer.

Shortly thereafter, some landlords tried to divide the peasant movement by creating free unions, and some repressive acts by the police against peasants caused the escalation of peasant resistance leading to considerable violence. Troops were moved into the area at that time. It is impossible to unravel the mutual accusations of provocation regarding the violent acts. The incidents culminated in a massacre in Chaullay, in which according to official sources five peasants were killed. According to eyewitnesses, scores of people fell. A few days later, in January 1963, hundreds of peasant leaders and lawyers in the area were taken captive. However, the occupations of lands could not be undone, and the only way to calm the movement appeared to be to legalize the new situation.

The military government which had overthrown the Prado regime in mid 1962, issued a special land reform decree for the valleys of Convencion and Lares (No. 14444 in March 1963) which recognized the *de facto* control by the *arrendires* of their holdings. They were under obligation to pay in twenty years to obtain a legal title. Priorities were established for expropriation: 1) the estates operated with the help of *arrendires* and *allegados*; 2) those which were not well farmed; and 3) those which constituted an excessive concentration of property.

Hugo Blanco was aware that the movement he led came to a climax too early and before other areas of Peru had been sufficiently organized to spread it all over the country as a revolutionary effort. This made it possible for the military government to check the revolt and keep it within the limits of the Convención area through land distribution and military action.[30] With the arrival in the area of many troops, the hiding of Hugo Blanco became increasingly difficult and he was captured in May 1963 and sent to prison in Arequipa. He was sentenced to 25 years in prison for the killing of three policemen in an encounter.

The agrarian movement continued to be strong and probably the instructions given by Blanco were even more faithfully followed since he was taken prisoner in a manner which made him appear a martyr. This was noted by an observer who visited the area in early 1964 and attended a peasant mass meeting in Quillabamba.[31]

All this happened while the legitimacy of the national government was severely in doubt because of a military take-over in the middle of 1962, after elections in which Haya de la Torre, the candidate not well seen by the military, had won the most votes. In early 1963, while the country was still under military rule, another presidential election campaign went on in Peru, in which the candidates made strong promises regarding land reform. One candidate, according to eye-witnesses, distributed small bags with earth among the peasants as an advance on the lands he would give after becoming president. This candidate, Belaunde Terry, won the elections and became president in mid 1963. It is obvious that a good deal of political agitation resulted from the promises made by those who later formed the government. Peasant pressure in Peru except for the Convencion valley was partly a result of the political competition during the election campaigns of 1962 and 1963. This pressure was not organized systematically into groups following national directives (as happened in Venezuela), but was mainly locally organized.

The CIDA study of Peru noted that by mid 1963, there were altogether about 300,000 peasants actively pressuring through invasions of lands for the reforms which had been promised by the various politicians in their campaigns. To a large extent, the politicians had responded to strongly felt needs and grievances existing among the peasants about their formerly communal lands which they had lost over the years, and which were either in litigation or under consideration for recovery by the peasant communities.[32] Only in a few areas, such as in the Central Highlands in the departments of Junín and Pasco, did peasant pressure appear to be sufficiently coordinated and organized to achieve a lasting impact similar to La Convención. It was in those areas that the land reform program was initiated and land was distributed. A great deal of less effectively organized activities took place in other areas in those years.

The large-scale movement in the Cerro de Pasco area in the Central Highlands grew between 1960 and 1964. The first invasion in that area occurred in May 1960 when 1,200 peasants of the *comunidad* San Antonio de Rancas occupied land of the hacienda Paria of the Cerro de Pasco Corporation. This invasion was triggered when the Cerro de Pasco Corporation closed its estate and started to drive off the cattle of the surrounding *comunidades* which had been grazing there. Many of the *comuneros* worked on the estate and it was a right of the workers of the estates to let their own cattle also graze on the estate's land. When the company wanted to extend its cattle operations, it fenced the lands and prohibited the peasants to use those rights. Their demands were not considered. The company did not even want to rent to the peasants the land they needed. Only after possibilities to come to a legal arrangement were exhausted, the *comuneros* decided to invade those lands of the estate to which they had old titles. Several hundred policemen moved in to dislodge the peasants who had entered the estate with women, children and cattle and had built about 50 symbolic dwellings. When the police wanted to lead away the leader *(personero)* of the *comunidad*, a fight broke out and three peasants, including the leader were killed.[33],[e]

The mayor of Cerro de Pasco, a leftist lawyer, tried to support the peasants and later helped to form a federation of those *comunidades* in the area which had the same problems, the *Federación de Comunidades de Pasco*. Thus they would be able to face the large landholders more effectively, and in an organized way. The experience of the Rancas *comunidad* served as a lesson. The next action promised to become large scale.

In the same area, another invasion was organized in January 1961 by one thousand *comuneros* and in November of the same year, the peasants of San Pedro de Yanahuanca invaded several estates. They brought with them thousands of head of cattle and started to build provisional dwellings. When the civil guards came to dislodge them, they defended themselves with stones, rifles and pistols and in the fight eight peasants were killed. In relation to the Yanahuanca incident, the CIDA report quoted from a Lima newspaper a denounciation by the *comuneros* to the President that nine of them, after the despoliation, were undressed and flogged in the hacienda. The peasant delegation who visited the President after the incident received a promise that medicines, clothing, tents and foodstuffs would be sent to those whose houses had been burned down. They complained that their cattle had been killed and their crops had been destroyed.[34]

During the invasions organized by the federation in the Cerro de Pasco area in March 1962, the peasants had formed an agrarian army of 2,000 men on foot and 1,500 on horseback to defend themselves. In another encounter with the armed police, eight peasants were killed and 23 wounded. A state of siege (mar-

[e]It should be noted that the Algolan estate and the estate belonging to the Cerro de Pasco Corporation, altogether over 600,000 hectares are spread over large area of the Cerro de Pasco province and other provinces of the departments of Junín and Pasco, with the town of Cerro de Pasco, where one of the most important mines of the Cerro de Pasco Corporation is located, as its main urban center.[33]

tial law) was declared in the region. In the town of Cerro de Pasco, meetings of more than four people were prohibited, and the streets were patrolled by the police. The miners and railway workers organized a sympathy strike in Cerro de Pasco on the day of the funeral of the victims. Later, in 1962 and early 1963, the peasant movements in Pasco and Junín apparently calmed down, since the second election campaign (a first one had taken place in early 1962) had evoked strong promises by practically all parties involved in the contest regarding a legally established land reform program that would give back the lands to the *comunidades*. Direct actions were apparently suspended in most areas where they had been taking place. Those *comunidades* that demanded restitution and had hopes that this would be done in 1963 said that they would resort to invasions if no solutions according to the law would be given soon. The slogan "land or death," "tierra o muerte," which was introduced in the Cuzco department shortly before, had also reached this region.

It was noted that the land tenure conditions in the Pasco and Junín departments were particularly bad in the sense that 72 families or entities possessed over 90 percent of the pasture and cultivable land, while the remaining 10 percent of the land belonged to a population of about 650,000. Some additional important factors about the Cerro de Pasco area which explain the strongly organized peasant movement that developed there are good communications; relative closeness to Lima, location on a highway to important frontier development areas in the *selva*; and 60 percent literacy. Thus, the region was under considerable modernizing influences.

Another factor which considerably enhanced the possibility for organized action among the peasants, particularly the *comuneros* in the Junín and Pasco departments, was the fact that many of them had worked for a number of years (often until they contracted silicosis) in the mines, and had syndical experience during those years. They had become politicized during that period and thus responded more readily to the possibilities that were apparently opened to them during the election campaigns.

Immediately after the new government of president Belaúnde Terry had taken office on July 28, 1963, a new wave of direct peasant action started. The first invasion was organized on July 30, 1963, in the Chinchausiri estate in San Pedro de Cajas, Junín. 3,500 *comuneros* peacefully entered the estate and occupied 8,000 of its 16,000 hectares. This part belonged to them according to old titles and had been in litigation since 1927. The house and cattle of the estate were not touched, and the peasants built 1,200 provisional dwellings on the occupied parts of the estate. The peasants were organized in groups of five and the cattle of the estate were taken care of by some groups. People had practically abandoned the town of San Pedro de Cajas and lived in the provisional dwellings. A few days after the initiation of the activities, approximately 8,000 people were involved, including women, children and old people.[35] It was part of the organized activities that the patron saint of the town was carried along to accompany the groups. A police service was organized among the peasants and alcohol was forbidden. ("With morals and without alcohol" was one of the slogans.) In a mass meeting with a commission of the government, the peasants, particularly the women, declared that they would not leave the lands which they had recovered through invasions, because the lawsuit over thirty years had not come to any decision.

Shortly after this on August 1, 1963, *comuneros* of Oyon occupied part of the Algolan estate in Cerro de Pasco province with 1,000 head of cattle. This was the first of a series of ten invasions covering 60,000 hectares of the 300,000 hectares estate of the Sociedad Agrícola Ganadera Algolan, S.A. Several haciendas, part of this estate, were occupied simultaneously by the peasant communities which had old titles. The federation supported their action.

The new government's reaction was favorable. After it had made an extensive study of 62 *comunidades* in the Central Highlands which had land tenure disputes with neighboring haciendas concerning altogether 512,000 hectares of pasture land, Supreme Decree No. 11 was issued on August 9, 1963, expropriating 78,000 hectares to be distributed among those *comunidades* after reimbursement to the owners. It was noted, however, that this Decree guaranteed the payment to landlords of lands the property of which was still in litigation and undefined.[36] Other invasions followed, particularly in the Department of Junín in the Central Highlands.

One official publication described how the peasants of the federated *comunidades* which had invaded lands in the Central Highlands were appeased when a delegation of the President and seven ministers went to Junín in September 1963 and distributed among the peasants truckloads of agricultural tools, beds, books, medicines, etc., altogether for the value of 3,000,000 soles. They obtained an agreement from the *comunidades* that they would withdraw and not invade any more lands.[37]

The movement created by the peasant federations in Cuzco, Pasco and Junín spread in late 1963 to other areas where local organizations and federations had been formed. During the following months, many invasions took place, sometimes accompanied by violent acts. Several parts of the country, particularly the coastal zone close to Lima, and the departments of Piura, in the North and Cuzco in the South became the scene of such activities.

When the Minister of the Interior had been severely criticized by representatives of the land-owning class for tolerating the invasions, the government's policy changed. At the end of 1963, a new minister had been appointed and the police forces started to repress the peasant movements. This policy resulted in considerable violence. In the densely populated Sicuani area in the department of Cuzco, the roads were blocked by the peasants to prevent the entrance of the police force. In the ensuing battle, 20 peasants were killed.

However, for the most part, the invasions were not violent in the sense that they led to intentional destruction of human life or goods. This was clear from an eyewitness report of one observer in the Cuzco area where the invasions had a wide impact.[38] This reporter indicated that generally the lives, houses and other belongings of the landlords were safe as long as negotiations were started and no efforts to dislodge the peasants or their cattle from the parts they had occupied were undertaken. One landlord who had killed seven peasants in an encounter, however, was not allowed to return to his estate.[39]

The organized invasions reached proportions, in some areas, that came close to what Bolivia had experienced in 1952–1953. Descriptions of the occurrences in those areas indicate that the patrons were practically obliged to come to an arrangement with the local organizations and federations. If this was done on a basis of mutual agreement and compromise, the landlords were generally respected.

However, after January 1964, the government did not tolerate or channel this process, as in Bolivia, but undertook efforts to repress it. A considerable army or police force was stationed in several of the urban centers in the agitated areas and the leaders of the organizations were captured and imprisoned.

In addition to this, the promulgation of the agrarian reform law on May 21, 1964, included a statement indicating that invaded lands would not be used for the reform program. This had the effect that many of the invaded estates were unoccupied.[40] In Cuzco alone, 104 of the 114 occupied estates were peacefully left by the peasants.[f] Another reason for the abandonment of invaded lands was that the most agitated regions, such as the departments of Pasco, Junín and Cuzco were immediately declared agrarian reform areas. A great number of technicians of the Oficina Nacional de Reforma Agraria (ONRA) were sent to establish themselves in those areas, giving the peasants the impression that a solution to their problem was close. The two huge estates where most of the invasions occurred, in the departments of Pasco and Junín, the Algolan estate and the Cerro de Pasco Corporation, soon became part of the agrarian reform program.

It was indicated by several local informants that the actual beginning of the reform project, the distribution of the plots to the *comunidades* for exploitation through communal enterprises, occurred in a period when a group of guerrillas, headed by Guillermo Lobatón, which formed part of a campaign started in early 1965 by leftists groups to overthrow the government by armed force, came close to the area.

It seems that there was no organizational relationship between the peasant invasions in the years 1960-1963 and the guerrilla groups that operated in Peru in 1965.[41] While in the Convención and Cerro de Pasco area, where strong peasant organizations existed, the pending implementation of agrarian reform was probably accelerated when guerrilla groups appeared close to those areas, else-

---

[f]The special provision in the Land Reform Bill (translation by USAID) was: "persons who instigate or foment or promote or execute acts of invasion or usurpation of lands owned by the State, Corporations or private persons, or execute acts disturbing possession, are thereby excluded from the benefits of the allotment of lands under the Agrarian Reform . . ."

where, in the Satipo region for example, peasant organizations were completely repressed because of the presence of guerrillas. The pretext used by the military authorities was that the local unions, affiliates of the moderate Christian-Democrat labor movement in Peru, had contacts with the guerrillas. One top leader was assassinated, another imprisoned and tortured, and several hamlets of organized squatters, disputing lands with large landowners, were destroyed.[42] The relationship between the guerrillas and the peasant organizations remains unclear. For example, the guerrilla group headed by Luis de la Puente Uceda which operated in the Convención area in 1965 apparently did not find much response among the peasants. (This guerrilla leader had originally adhered and defended a moderate agrarian reform program without the APRA party, but after the alliance of APRA with the party of the conservative general Odría, he became more radical.)

Some of the divergencies between guerrilla groups and the peasant movement led by Hugo Blanco came out in a statement by de la Puente.[g]

... there are Trotskyists such as the Frente Izquierdista Revoluncionario, formerly led by Hugo Blanco, who uphold the thesis of dual power, with peasant organizations taking over, one by one, the functions of the oligarchic power, spreading and developing in provincial departmental, regional federations, and finally attaining control of a gigantic peasant and popular movement. This movement, following a process of growing radicalization, would undertake the creation of its own armed militia and would culminate in the seizure of power as an essentially mass phenomenon.

De la Puente noted however, that this system did not function as an insurrectional scheme.

The dual power scheme had to be discarded owing to the failure of Hugo Blanco, who, in spite of having developed an interesting process of mass organization and struggle, was not able to survive the first assaults of the repressive forces.[43]

The guerrilla forces were all repressed in 1965 by the armed forces. The peasant movement in La Convención and Pasco and Junín as such survived and—temporarily it seems—withdrew into nonpolitical activities related with the agrarian reform program carried out in the area.

The Northeast of Brazil: Peasant Leagues and Competing Organizations

The growth between 1955 and 1964 of the Ligas Camponeses in the northeast of Brazil, mainly in the states of Pernambuco and Paraiba, should be seen as a con-

---

[g]No data are available regarding an interview that took place between de la Puente and Hugo Blanco before the latter was imprisoned.

sequence of the overall situation in which the peasantry in these areas lived. It should be noted that the area where the activities of the leagues were mainly concentrated was relatively close to Recife, the state capital, with good communications. Because of the low sugar prices during the thirties, several sugar plantations *(engenhos)* in this area had been rented out by the owners, who lived in the city, to peasants who cultivated fruits and cereals to supply the city. In cases where the landowner cultivated part of his estate himself, generally through an administrator, his tenants had to render free services, called *cambao* or *condiçao*, or to work for wages lower than the prevailing rate. When sugar prices went up again during and after World War II, landlords tried to evict the peasants from the plots they cultivated and to transform the estate again into a sugar plantation. The peasants lived in great insecurity and paid (in money, kind and/or services) a rent which was per year almost half the commercial value of the plot of land. It was in one of these *engenhos* that the Ligas Camponeses (Peasant Leagues) found their origin.[44]

Peasant leagues had existed in Brazil for a good number of years. The first leagues were formed in the forties by the communist party in several parts of the country. One of the participants in this campaign was José dos Prazeres who was a peasant's son who had worked on the land in his youth but later went to work in town and managed to become literate. He became involved in the anarcho-sindicalist labor movement and tried to go as a volunteer to support the peasants in the Mexican revolution of 1910. He landed in jail however, before the recruiting ship had left Recife. He later worked as a tram conductor and became a member of the Communist Party. As such, he participated in this party's campaign to organize peasant leagues after 1945. When, in 1947, this party was outlawed, the leagues which had been formed were practically all destroyed by police repression, except the one in Iputinga, on the outskirts of Recife. Prazeres left the Communist Party and started to dedicate himself again to peasant organization. In 1955, when in the *engenho* Galileia in the municipality of Vitória de Santo Antao, where he worked, he helped to found the *Sociedade Agricole e Pecuaria dos Plantadores de Pernambuco* (SAPPP).[45]

The main purpose of the Sociedade was to establish through contributions in cash or in kind a small fund which could be used to help the peasants to avoid eviction because of failure to pay their debts to the landlord. The rent which the peasants had to pay was extravagantly high, about 6,000 Cr. per hectare per year. While the value of the land was 10,000 to 15,000 cruzeiros per hectare. This meant that in about two years of rent payment, the owner received as much as the value of the rented land. In Galileia, this situation applied to about 150 families who rented altogether about 500 hectares.

One of the ideas of the initiator of the newly created sociedad in the *engenho* Galileia was to collect money to be able to buy the land from the owner and avoid in the future the extravagant rents and the danger of being evicted, if they were not able to pay the full amount of rent. In order to avoid the repression

which the former leagues had encountered, the purpose of the new society included a range of civic activities, including the cooperative buying of coffins, and
the owner of the *engenho* was chosen as honorary president. Apparently under
pressure of his son and other landowners in the area, the owner soon resigned,
however, and the society started to encounter serious difficulties. Prazeres then
looked for support among urban professionals and political figures of different
tendencies. This was particularly needed when the son of the landlord, who
usually lived in Recife, wanted to evict the peasants who were forming the association, and use the land which they had been cultivating for years, for cattle-
breeding, so as to get rid of the problem. The peasants had been working those
lands for over 15 years. When the landlord's son went ahead with his intentions
to evict the peasants, the new association looked for help from Francisco Julião
de Paula, a lawyer in Recife and state deputy for the small Socialist Party. The
leaders of the society then succeeded in making the owner bring a suit for eviction against them in the courts.

Julião helped the society to gain legal status in January 1955 as a civil association with mutual benefit purposes, with headquarters in Recife and several municipal branches or delegations. Such branches had been formed in Tamatamirin
and in Surubim. Soon the groups were called leagues. The society was registered
as a civil association and not as a labor union, because the problems which the
peasants had to face were generally related to the contractual conditions of land
tenure, which fall under the civil code rather than labor legislation.

As part of the campaign to make the leagues known and respected, mass
meetings or marches were held at times in Recife. In 1955, 3,000 peasants
marched to the Legislative Assembly when a session on land reform was going
on. On the first of May 1956, 600 peasants met in Recife with workers and
demonstrated together.

It should be noted that Francisco Julião was from a landholders family himself, his father owning a relatively small estate of 280 hectares in Bom Jardin,
managed by one of Julião's six brothers. 40 workers were employed on this
estate.[g] Among the first leagues was the one formed in Bom Jardin (in the estate
of Julião's brother) which was at that time the only estate where meetings could
be held and which became a center of agitation in the area. On other private
properties, meetings were forbidden and had to be held secretly. At that time,
there was a great deal of agitation against the leagues. Talk about agrarian reform

[g]This information, supplied independently by several persons involved in the leagues, including Julião, contradicts the polemical article by Leeds, "Brazil and the Myth of Francisco
Julião," in which he suggests that Julião was just another landlord and political boss, who
tried to organize the peasants into a political clientele (separated from his own latifundium)
for his political career. It is not conducive to better understanding to put a movement as the
peasant leagues which agitated with considerable effect for radical change in the rural social
structure in the northeast (and at the same time promoted the political careers of a number
of collaborators) under the same label as the political manipulations by those who only
want to maintain the status quo.[46]

was branded as subversive and when at times public meetings were held in the towns, police loudspeakers said that "the strike was invented by Lenin and improved by Stalin."[47] On one occasion in 1956, Julião was taken captive.

One way to protect the leagues, which initially led an almost clandestine life, was the frequent visit of state deputies who with their parliamentary immunity and status could prevent police attacks. The urban supporters of the society formed a steering council which could defend it at the level of the state capital. For that purpose, the society had been conceived as a regional organization covering the whole state of Pernambuco with local base organizations or nuclei. Having a seat in the state capital and a group of supporters to defend it at that level was a guarantee of survival for the peasant organization as a whole. From a legal point of view, it was also an advantage to have a regional organization legally recognized and registered. Local nuclei could then be created which obtained legal status without delay. This method of creating a regional organization with increasing local nuclei rather than that of creating local organizations and bringing them together into a federation, proved to be a great asset. It was the reverse of tactics which had formerly been applied with little success.[48]

The movement benefited considerably from the wide publicity given to the problems of the northeast of Brazil at the Congress for the Salvation of the Northeast which was held August 20-27, 1955, in Recife. There were 1,600 delegates from the nine states of the northeast, representing all strata of society, labor unions, educational institutions, government, business, industry and also peasants. Representatives of the leagues participated, particularly in the 200 member committee on land problems. The backward agrarian situation prevailing in the northeast was criticized and a declaration in favor of agrarian reform adopted. This Congress and some similar meetings in the following years led to the creation of a Committee for the Development of the Northeast out of which SUDENE (Superintendencia de Desenvolvimiento do Nord-este) grew.

In September 1955, the leagues demonstrated their existence by attending the First Congress of Peasants of Pernambuco, organized with the support of FAO president Josue de Castro. José dos Prazeres was elected president of the SAPPP, the society to which all leagues officially belonged. The congress ended with a mass demonstration of several thousand peasants through the streets of Recife, which made a deep impression on urban public opinion, and gave the peasants, possibly for the first time, a sense of their power.

Through such activities, the leagues emerged from the isolation in which the landowners of the area tried to keep them. The commercial and industrial groups which, allied with representatives of workers and peasants had promoted the Congress for the Salvation of the Northeast soon gained a victory in the elections, and obtained for the first time a mayor for Recife who was not the representative of the conservative landowners' interests. The landed interests quickly started a campaign against this new alliance, by promoting a tax reform which could be harmful to small commerce and industry. This provoked a stronger unity in favor of reforms. During the struggle between the opposing interest groups, the peasant leagues suffered considerably, particularly in the beginning of 1956. Many peasant and labor leaders were imprisoned. Later during the year and again in the beginning of 1957, a general strike took place which was supported by the peasant leagues and helped to increase political awareness among the agricultural workers and peasants.

In 1958, a state governor was elected who was an industrialist and the candidate of the alliance of interests opposing the traditional landed elite. The repressive climate which had existed particularly in the rural areas changed and it was under those circumstances, in 1959, that the peasant league of Galileia, still litigating with the landowner in the courts, was able to obtain the distribution of the land of the estate. This happened after huge peasant demonstrations in the streets and even in the legislative assembly of Pernambuco, exerted pressure for the approval of the expropriation of the estate as proposed by the socialist deputy Carlos Luis de Andrade.

The leagues gained considerable prestige through this victory, although the peasants of Galileia lost their interest in the agrarian struggle after their own success. Other leagues became the center of the movement. Several leaders of the leagues had a chance to visit Cuba in 1959 and 1960 and thus became acquainted with a radical agrarian reform. During those years, the movement spread through the states of Pernambuco (altogether in 26 municipalities), Paraiba and even beyond. The mutual help of experienced peasant organizers such as José dos Prazeres and urban political and labor leaders led to an effective agitation and formation strategy.

The strategy used in the formation of the peasant leagues included the following points:[49]

A great flexibility of structure. Since the Liga was legally a civil association, once a Liga existed at the state level, in each community or municipality, a delegação could be founded. The word "delegação" was used on purpose, because it was the same as the word for local police station, and it would help to overcome the tremendous fear the peasants have for the police, once they had their own delegação. In order to form a local nucleus, or delegação, it was sufficient that a group of thirty or forty people gave their approval of the statutes of the Liga (at the central level) and elected a board.

Choice of people not totally impoverished. The policy of starting to work with small farmers, tenants, sharecroppers and in general with those peasants who have a stronger economic base than the agricultural wage workers. The last category had very little means to support the movement and had nothing to fall back upon when there was need to resist. Since many agricultural workers were seasonal, they could not be counted upon in the building up of a locally well-established organization. The workers could join and strengthen the movement, but a firm base should be given by those who had at least a guaranteed subsistence.

Before the passage of new labor legislation in 1963, a small peasant-farmer within the context of the civil law had a stronger position than the agricultural worker had under the labor law. Sanctions against tenants or sharecroppers were difficult. If they refused to leave the land when such was indicated to them by the landowners (as frequently happened), the legally protected waiting time while an eviction suit was going on at the court was no loss to the peasant-farmers. They continued cultivating their plots, and thus could continue litigating in the court for years until they had won their case. In the time before the 1963 labor legislation agricultural workers below the subsistence level soon found it difficult to keep up a strike.

Identification with attitudes of peasants. The technique of winning the peasants for the Ligas was based on the highest possible degree of identification with their mentality so as to win their confidence. This was done mainly through struggling on their side to win cases against the pressures of the landowners. In the process of identification and winning of confidence, the well-known *violeiros*, popular and peasant poets and singers, played an important role. Later, during the struggle which kept on for years and with the intimate contact needed to wield the support from the communities, a strong solidarity grew.

Publicity. Especially cases in which the landowners violently and illegally opposed organization, such as the assassination of the peasant leader of Sapé, João Pedro Teixeira (see below), gave the movement a strong impetus. In a later stage, the Ligas had their own weekly paper. Urban supporters including lawyers, workers and students helped to spread the leagues. They often tried to find popular leaders in a local community and found out what were the strongly felt grievances. Many of the initiators of local branches of the Ligas were peasants who had got in touch with the already existing leagues and their leaders.

Soon the movement spread beyond the state of Pernambuco. The leagues were brought to the state of Paraiba in 1959 by João Pedro Teixeira, a peasant of Sapé, who had spent some time in Pernambuco. In 1963, the league in Sapé had about 10,000 members. Sapé had in common with the area of Vitoria de Santo Antao, where the first league had been formed, that the majority of the peasants, rural wage workers generally, had a plot for subsistence. The town of Sapé had good communications with the capital of Paraiba, Joao Pessoa.

The first activities of this league were to claim indemnification in the courts in cases where peasants had been evicted. It was in this stage that landowners started to prohibit the peasants who rented a plot from planting fruit trees or other permanent crops. Also, the repair of the houses inhabited by the peasants was prohibited in some cases. The initial leader João Pedro Teixeira was assassinated in April 1962 by henchmen of the landlord when he protested against eviction without proper compensation for the improvements he had made. This happened when the estate had changed ownership, and the new owner wanted to get rid of him.[50] One of the most difficult obstacles in the formation of the Ligas was the threat of assassination of leaders, particularly since on several occasions this threat was executed. Traditionally, the landlords had private policemen, so-called *capangas*, in their service to do these jobs.

However, with the slowly increasing strength of the movement, the peasants started to fight back and at times *capangas* or even landlords were killed in such acts.[51]

The impact of the agitation and growth of the peasant leagues became particularly visible during the First National Congress of Peasants and Agricultural Workers in Belo Horizonte, 15-17 November 1961. In this congress, several agricultural workers organizations participated which had been founded in the meantime in other parts of the country. The most important ones were the Union of Agricultural Workers of Brazil (ULTAB), with headquarters in Sao Paolo and the Movement of Peasants without Land (MASTER) of Rio Grande do Sul. The President of the Republic and many high authorities, including the members of the National Agrarian Reform Commission, were present. There was a strong delegation from the peasant leagues which made a tremendous impact by their radical demand for land. While most organizations present had a moderate reform program, the vociferous way the peasants of the northeast, the poorest looking delegation in the congress, demanded radical reform won over the congress.[52]

The movement started to gain support from more important urban circles. Several informants indicated that the campaign of the formation of leagues and, e.g., the periodical Liga, which appeared in Rio de Janeiro and propagandized the work of the leagues and the need for agrarian reform at the national level, was financed partly by industrialists of Sao Paolo. These groups had an interest in agrarian reform, because a more equal distribution of income in the rural areas would considerably increase the market possibilities for industrial products. Meanwhile, other groups became fearful of the Liga's growing strength.

Already prior to the congress of Belo Horizonte, the Catholic Church in the northeast had started to organize peasant unions in order to counteract the increasing and radicalizing influence of the peasant leagues.[53] In 1960, in the state of Rio Grande do Norte Bishop Eugenio Sales of Natal started a program to supplement the community development activities of the Rural Assistance Service with a rural unionization movement, led by Julieta Calazans, a social worker. It was stressed that the unions were professional and not political organizations, and a moderate and conciliatory approach was emphasized.

In 1963 a Federation of Rural Unions was formed and legally recognized. Later that year the First Brazilian Convention of Rural Unions was held in Natal with delegates from 17 states. At that time, the movement claimed about 50,000 members in 43 unions, 17 of which were legally recognized.[54] The unions tended to emphasize the finding of a compromise with the landlords regarding the compensation for improvements (in cases of eviction of tenants) and similar problems. Only if that was impossible, was help sought at the labor courts. The need for cooperatives was stressed.

An important element in the unionization campaign in Rio Grande de Norte was the so-called conscientization. This was done through the Basic Education Movement, MEB, promoted by the General Assembly of Bishops since 1962. Radio schools were used, with assistance of local promoters, to bring to the peasants awareness of the need to change the paternalistic social structure. In many different forms, MEB tried to introduce new ideas.[i] One of the methods used in MEB was a form of literacy teaching which helped people at the same time to become aware of their social situation and the need to change it. This method is named after its inventor and promoter Paolo Freire.[56]

The difference between the peasant unions in Rio Grande do Norte and the peasant leagues comes out in the statement of one union leader.

Our union works against the communist. The peasant leagues wanted to take from those who have in order to give to those with nothing. We don't want anything from anybody, but only our rights, a proper indemnification, and not the land of the patron.

In spite of this the landlords considered the church-sponsored unions as "communists."[57]

The example of Rio Grande do Norte was to be followed in 1961, in Pernambuco, where the leagues were strong. The archbishop of Recife appointed four priests to become union organizers. Among these were Father Paolo Crespo of the town of Jaboatao, an important urban center close to Recife and Father Antonio Melo in the town of Cabo. A catholic rural youth movement played an important role.[58] A group of parish priests from all over Pernambuco came together and in August 1961 SORPE (Rural Orientation Service for Pernambuco) was founded. In the whole of Brazil, since rural labor legislation was initiated in 1903, only five syndicates had been officially recognized. In 1963, however, 22 newly formed unions assisted by SORPE were recognized. In March 1963, a new Rural Labor Statute facilitated the formation of unions. Then, many of the peasant leagues transformed themselves into unions. The leagues often won the respect of the peasants because they took the initiative at strikes while the church unions had signed an agreement with the landlords. The landlords themselves, by breaking their promises to the church unions but yielding to the threats of violence by the leagues, indirectly helped the leagues.

---

[h]For example, in mathematics courses, the following problem was used: "In one place 270 people live. There exists a school for only 70 persons. How many persons in that place cannot go to school?" or "The family of Mr. Joaquim cannot nourish itself well because his salary is unjust. He earns 350 Cruzeiros per day. What is his salary per month?" or "In one place live 550 inhabitants. 415 will vote consciously and the others will sell their votes. How many people sell their liberty?" or "In one municipality live 5,200 workers, 4,150 of those workers want to struggle for a different kind of society and form a syndicate. How many workers in that municipality did not unite?"[55]

[i]For example, in mathematics courses, the following problem was used: "In one place 270

Competition for the leadership became more severe as more church groups, political groups, government agencies and other interests tried to become involved in the movement to create peasant organizations. The Rural Labor Statute provided that rural unionization fell under the terms of the Consolidation of the Labor Law of 1943. This implied that in one municipality there could exist only one peasant union. A consequence of this was that within a municipality the competing factions had to fight the struggle for control within the only existing union. The formation of rival unions in the same municipality was legally impossible, which resulted in struggle in various municipalities.[59]

The church unions also formed a federation, which in its policy has tended towards a conciliatory attitude towards the landlords with stress on social harmony and avoidance of conflicts.[60] This comes out well in the description of local activities given by one observer.[61]

In June 1963, shortly after the promulgation of the Rural Labor Statute, the Ministry of Labour and SUPRA (the institute designated to be in charge of agrarian reform) jointly started a peasant unionization campaign. Its main promoter, Father Francisco Lage Pessoa, stressed that President Goulart needed the organized peasantry to obtain a majority in parliament.[62] For that reason, the organization started in the more densely populated areas close to the cities, where important sectors of the electorate lived. In about half a year, 2,000 unions were created with each between 50 (the legal minimum) and 3,000 members. Students, often radical catholics of Acciao Popular, helped in the campaign. It became clear that the peasants had picked up the idea of land reform. In most places, the proposals for moderate improvements brought forward by the organizers were overruled by the peasants demanding land.

In the northeast, unions were formed where they previously did not exist, causing the peasant leagues to lose some of their impact. At times, they worked with the syndicates, e.g., in the organization of the massive strike of 200,000 peasant workers in November 1963, which brought to the peasants all the benefits required by law, such as legally established minimum wage and working hours.j

These continued efforts gave additional strength to the movement, but with the coup d'état of April 1964, the whole situation was reversed and repression started. Leaders were imprisoned and tortured and the government interfered with many unions including those of the church.k[64] Most of the gains of the unions, such as minimum wages and working hours, were undone.

---

jAccording to Celso Furtado, the sugar estate owners could afford to agree relatively easily because the sugar prices on the international market had increased considerably.[63]

kOne of the tortured leaders was the head of the 30,000 member union of Palmares, Gregorio Bezerra, a communist peasant leader highly esteemed even by his opponents. He was a sugarcane worker and an army sergeant and was elected to the National Assembly in 1945, but not allowed to take his seat. Bezerra was liberated from prison in 1969 with 14 other people in exchange for the kidnapped United States Ambassador.[64]

Colombia: A Case of Illegitimacy
and Violence

As we saw from the cases of Mexico, Bolivia and also Venezuela, there is a close relationship between the existence of strong peasant organizations and agrarian reform. In Colombia, agrarian reform legislation has been related to unstructured peasant movements that were a reaction to the illegal practices, intransigence and violent actions of the landed elite.[65] As yet, there are practically no structured organizations of peasants in Colombia. The study of the spontaneous movements gives some insights into the possibilities for peasant organization.

In the twenties and thirties, the land tenure issue came up partly as a result of the introduction of banana—and particularly coffee plantations in some areas—which led to the proletarization of many peasants. Experienced peasant leaders such as Juan de la Cruz Varela and urban organizers started an effective agrarian movement, particularly in the Sumapaz area, not far from Bogotá. An important issue that radicalized the peasants in some places, such as Viotá, was the demand of the coffee workers to have the right to cultivate coffee on the small plots which they were allowed to use for their subsistence. The landlords were afraid that this right would lead to greater independence of the peasants and refused. This problem forcefully awakened the peasants to the land tenure issue.

It was not only in the areas of the coffee estates that resistance to gradual change of the landowners created opposition among the peasants. In several neighboring regions, the landlords aggressively tried to assert their real or alleged property rights. This was most frequently done by evicting tenants or squatters with support of the police or the armed forces. Many local battles resulted. This happened particularly in those areas which became more accessible through road building and where—at the cost of the taxpayer—the value of landed property increased. This kind of activity had been taking place particularly in Tolima, Cundinamarca and the Cauca valley which later became the principal scene of guerrilla and *bandolero* activities summarized under the name, la violencia. But Guzman noted that the peasants do not talk about the violence, but about the first and second war they were engaged in between 1947 and 1958.[66]

In an official investigation of the problem of boundaries and properties, it was noted that surprisingly large extensions of land were in the hands of private persons who had taken it from the national domain without legal titles.[67] In the departments of Cundinamarca and Tolima alone, authorizations to start lawsuits against such persons covered about 500,000 hectares. Partly as a reaction to the growing peasant unrest in some of those areas and the fact that the liberal government tried to gain control over them, Law 200 regarding agrarian reform was promulgated in 1936.[68]

This law provided that private lands which were not cultivated by their owners for more than ten years would return to public property. The law had

enhanced the hopes of the peasants to get land, since certain guarantees were
included for squatters who had worked certain lands for two years or more.
However, a result of the law was that many peasants were evicted from the plots
they had cultivated (with or without compensation for the improvements they
had made). Many landlords believing that tenants or sharecroppers would claim
the rights guaranteed in that law, tried even more to get rid of them.

The complications of the law, and the way it was often interpreted by the
landlords, had a strongly frustrating effect on the peasants. Invasions became
more frequent and their legitimacy was always debatable.

It increasingly occurred, however, that peasant activities in defense of their
interests were branded as violence and then taken as a pretext for violent intervention of the police, army or the private bands of the landowners. The land
tenure problems became part of a conflict between the Liberal Party and Conservative Party that flared up in 1947, but extended rapidly after the assassination of the Liberal presidential candidate with leftist tendencies, Jorge Eliecer
Gaitán, on April 1, 1948, in Bogotá.

The violent activities occurred particularly in those regions where most injustices had been committed by landowners with help from the police, army of
their own hands and where as a result a climate of lawlessness prevailed.

Another issue which continued to cause violent reaction was the despoliation
of indigenous groups by the landholders, provoking efforts to recover lost lands.
This happened for example in Chaparral, department of Tolima, where two haciendas which had been indigenous *resguardos* before, were invaded in 1938. The
peasants on such occasions expressed the belief that they were acting in accordance with the law.[69] The despoliation of indigenous groups continued. In
1949, the Troche Indians in the Marquetalia area were forced to sell their lands.
It was in this area and in the region of Viotá, where the peasants had strong
organizations that self-defense regions were established in those years. Later,
some of these areas became internationally famous as independent republics.

In most areas of Colombia, violence raged in a very disorderly way at times
taking the forms of mere banditry. In some periods, it grew into a civil war between the opposing Liberal and Conservative parties that used the more or less
ignorant peasantry to fight out their party conflict. Altogether, in a little over
ten years, 200,000 to 300,000 people were killed, but little or no concrete benefits were gained for the peasantry.[70]

An interesting explanation of *la violencia* was given by the sociologist Father
Camilo Torres R.[71] The lack of social mobility, and an increasing awareness of
this lack among the rural population, created frustration and latent aggression,
which at a certain stage became manifest because no constructive ways to overcome this situation were opened. One of the results of the whole experience of
la violencia was a break in the status quo, in the sense that peasants became
conscious of their power and lost a great part of their habitual feeling of inferiority.[72] The peasants also lost respect for the traditional and rigid social structure,

and a greater class consciousness or group solidarity has resulted,[73] similar to the effects provoked by the Chaco War in Bolivia.

Already during the years of strife in a few areas, the political parties which were initially responsible for the violence started to lose control over the peasantry which began to become aware that its own interests were different from that of any of the two parties. Later, when the leadership of the guerrilla groups as in the Llano, fell into the hands of leaders of peasant background rather than party politicians and the first programs were elaborated which proposed land reform (the laws of the Llano of 11 Sept. 1952 and of 18 June 1953), the Liberal and Conservative parties both felt simultaneously threatened and began to look for a coalition.[74] The new government that then came to power under General Rojas Pinilla tried to appease the peasantry with promises for amnesty and land reform. However, conservative opposition against possible execution of these promises caused the violent struggle in the rural areas to flare up again after a short period of tranquillity.

The Conservative party adherents in southern Tolima, the Cauca valley and the department of Caldas, started again to terrorize small towns to oppose and provoke difficulties for the Rojas Pinilla government. After a massacre of peasants at the end of 1954, the communist-led groups in Sumapaz, headed by the peasant leader Juan de la Cruz Varela, took again to guerrilla activities. In April 1955, the government sent 10,000 to 15,000 soldiers to Sumapaz with planes and tanks and broke the communist defense line. Thousands of peasants fled to more isolated regions. Then, in the south of Tolima, the Liberal-oriented peasants influenced by the communist groups took up arms until the defense zone was taken by assault by the army. The groups in the Llanos declared solidarity with the peasants of Sumapaz and Tolima in February 1957. In the 1955-57 period, the struggle was more limited to certain specific areas than in the earlier periods and apparently became a confrontation between thousands of peasants and the army. Although it was generally in rhetorical terms, the peasants' proclamations in this period spoke of revolution and agrarian reform.[75] Hobsbawm remarked

Of course, the *violencia* is often revolutionary and class conscious in a more obvious sense, especially in recent years, when the armed men, deprived of the justification of fighting for the two big parties, have increasingly tended to see themselves as champions for the poor.[76]

As a result of the large-scale military actions and the ouster of the Rojas Pinilla government replaced by the Liberal-Conservative coalition, the struggle in the rural areas diminished in 1958 and afterwards. The need for important reforms in the agrarian structure, however, was forcefully brought to the attention of the nation.

As was noted before, one important result of the violence which swept the rural areas was that the government promulgated in December 1961, agrarian reform legislation (Law 135) and created an agency to apply the law, the Colombian Land Reform Institute (INCORA). The first project initiated by INCORA was in one of the most violence-ridden areas—Cunday, department of Tolima. In that area, large coffee plantations and other estates had been neglected for years because of the violent activities.

The few land reform projects which were initiated by INCORA during the following years generally coincided with areas where trouble existed, mainly in the form of land invasions. In some villages, the local priest, impressed by the blatant injustices suffered by the peasants, helped them to organize occupations of idle or disputed lands. Sometimes, this was done in order to keep the peasants from joining more radical movements. The activities of these priests were often coordinated with that of the *Federacion Agraria Nacional* (FANAL), created by Conservative party groups with help from the Church in 1946. FANAL has only a small minority of the Colombian peasantry in its ranks (at present 10,000 of 1.5 million) but has gained some publicity because of its support of various land occupations which then led to effective intervention of INCORA. One of the moral advisors of FANAL wrote a leaflet to justify the occupation of idle privately owned lands by peasants in need.[77]

Looking at the rural struggle in Colombia in terms of patronage, it seems that the competition between the Liberal and the Conservative clienteles burst into open conflict between the Liberal clientele (headed by Gaitán) started to pressure in favor of radical reform of the traditional system as a whole. During the struggle that resulted, the peasants became more conscious as a class, opposing the traditional patrons, whether they be Liberal or Conservative. That the peasants' consciousness had been heightened was realized by the latter who united in order to bring an end to the struggle and appease the peasants, both through minor reforms and armed force. This repression was relatively successful, but since later only very few effective reform measures have been carried out, discontent will probably rise. Under proper guidance, this discontent might well be channelled into a strong movement in favor of radical change or even overall revolution if no other ways of solving the existing conflicts are open. How frustration of orderly and legalized ways of radical agrarian change leads to an increasing potential for violent peasant action is shown by the developments during the last decades in Guatemala.

Guatemala: Reform and Counterreform

Guatemala has in common with Venezuela that peasant organization and agrarian reform were introduced from above by a reformist or populist government. When the reform started to become effective, the government was overthrown by outside intervention and a counterreform movement was initiated to reestablish the culture of repression. From the Guatemalan case, it becomes clear that frustrated reform efforts have a radicalizing effect on the traditional and repressed peasants. For an assessment of the organizational potential of peasants in Latin America, the Guatemalan case is an important example.

When in 1944 after many years of repressive dictatorship, the populist Juan José Arévalo came to power, labor unions, collective bargaining, minimum hours and similar measures were allowed and promoted. The process of formation of peasant organizations was begun after the reform of the Labour Code in July 1948, which recognized for the first time the right of peasants to form unions. In August 1948, there were only 13 legally recognized agricultural labor unions comprised of 4,000 members (not counting the two unions of the United Fruit Company, formed in 1944). Previously, the main legal obstacle had been the old Labor Law that stipulated that unions could be formed only in estates with more than 500 workers. In 1949, there were 46 recognized unions with altogether 10,000 or 12,000 members, but many more were in the process of obtaining legal recognition.

Urban labor groups were the main promoters of the campaign to organize the peasants. Organization began and was most effective in the areas with better communications and where modernizing influences were stronger. This was in the areas close to Guatemala City and Esquintla. One factor favorable to the organizability of rural workers in those areas was the frustrating effect of the presence of the United Fruit Company establishment.[78]

In 1950, the National Peasant Federation of Guatemala, the CNCG, was founded with Leonardo Castillo Flores, an exteacher who became union organizer, and Amor Velasco de León, an agricultural worker with experience in Mexico, as main leaders. Some 200 delegates representing 4 regional federations and 25 peasant unions participated in the founding of the CNCG.[79] There was friction with communist-oriented urban labor organizations because the Partido Accion Revolucionaria (PAR), one of the main forces in the government coalition, supported the initial efforts of CNCG.[80]

The movement grew rapidly under the presidency of Arevalo's successor, Jacobo Arbenz, elected in 1951, and had, according to calculations by Nathan Whetten, in 1954, 1,500 active unions with 180,000-190,000 members.[81] This was accomplished in spite of the fact that on the one hand some communist groups competed, and on the other hand, certain Catholic priests tried to stop the peasants from joining by labeling the movement as "communist."[82]

To support the agrarian reform law in May-June 1952, various peasant rallies were held in Guatemala City to pressure the Congress into action as well as to give the thousands of peasants brought in from the countryside a sense of participation in the making of the legislation which was to govern them.[83] Provisions for participation of peasant organizations in the execution of the land reform were included.

The agrarian reform law (Ley de Reforma Agraria, Decreto numéro 900) promulgated on June 17, 1952, was designed to liquidate idle latifundia property and to abolish all types of servitude.[l] It provided for the expropriation of privately owned land which was not cultivated by the owner or on his behalf. No private land which was farmed by the owner or under his supervision was to be taken, and properties of less than 2 caballerías (90 hectares) would be respected, whether cultivated or not.[m]

In some areas, the local affiliates of the CNCG anticipated the promulgation of the reform law by publishing lists of landholders they considered to be eligible for expropriation. When the law was issued, they began to measure off these same lands. Because of the opposition of the landlords to the law, on occasions leading to violence, an amendment was included shortly after its promulgation punishing them with total expropriation without any indemnification. Although there was some unrest in certain areas, on the whole, the reform process went with considerable speed and order.[85]

CIDA has indicated that about 100,000 peasants benefited from the reform in 18 months. It has also noted that between January 1953 and June 1954, a little over 600,000 hectares were expropriated.[86] This land represented 16 percent of the country's total idle lands in private hands which could be available for cultivation. Production of foodstuffs went up considerably in 1953-54.[87]

The social impact of the reforms has been observed by anthropologists who studied the indigenous population of Guatemala. Thus, Richard Adams made the following remark.

Among its effects, the Arbenz period destroyed any remnant of mutual interest between farm laborers and farm owners. The paternalism of the earlier pattern persists today mainly in the written provisions of the labor code. The farm labor groups are now acutely aware that a new type of relationship is possible between themselves and the cosmopolite local upper and middle classes.[88]

Adams also indicated that unions and other mass organizations helped to overcome paternalism by creating an atmosphere that allowed more initiative on the part of the peasants, especially the indigenous peasants.[89] However, the fact that 83,000 hectares of unused land of the United Fruit Company were expropriated[n] (with reimbursement only for the declared tax value of the land), created an international problem which contributed to the overthrow of the Arbenz government through outside intervention.

In June 1954, after another government had taken over, Decree 31 was issued

[l]The first article of the *Ley de Reforma Agraria* del 17 Junio de 1952 (Decreto 900) is: "La Reforma Agraria de la Revolucion de octubre tiene por objeto liquidar la propieded feudal en el campo y las relaciones de producción que la originan para desarrollar la forma de explotación y metodos capitalistas de producción en la agricultura y preparar el camino para la industrializacion de Guatemala."

[m]Paredes Moreira indicated that the Guatemalan land reform law of 1952 had certain similarities to the Italian one. It had an outspoken capitalist orientation, and would not touch lands that were properly cultivated.[84]

[n]CIDA noted that the UFCO cultivated only 15% of its lands.

that made it possible for the landowners to reclaim lands which had been expropriated. CIDA observed that Decree 31 in reality represented the legal justification of the acts carried out by the landlords who, upon the fall of the Arbenz regime, began the *de facto* recovery of the lands which they had lost. In the legal revision of the expropriations, made possible by the new decree, the great majority of cases were decided in favor of the landlords. The peasants who had received land through the reform program were displaced, at times by force, or fled, causing considerable unrest in the rural areas. Although the government urged the landlords in several statements not to take vengeance on the peasants who benefited from the land reform, a good deal of violence occurred.[91] The General Confederation of Labor compiled a list of 217 cases of assassinations of peasants which occurred during the first few weeks after the take-over.[92] Since these and similar events occurred, violence has prevailed in several regions of Guatemala up to this day.[93]

Shortly after the change of regimes, interviews were held with a sample of about 250 peasants from among the thousands arrested and jailed for supporting the Arbenz government. The sample was taken from the 1,500 to 2,000 people confined in the city jails of Guatemala City.[94] After discussing the variety of answers and their significance, Newbold gave the following explanation.

It cannot be concluded from the answers discussed above that the population of the sample has been heavily politically indoctrinated with communist-line ideas. There is evidence, however, that certain ideas which were sponsored by the post-Ubico regimes [1944-1954] did receive considerable acceptance. Specifically, these were the ideas that a democratic government is selected by the people, that there should be a distribution of land among those who do not have it, and that there should be laws controlling working conditions.[95]

He went on to make several conclusions.

The sample, which we have assumed was receptive to agitation of the Arbenz regime was older than was anticipated, was economically somewhat better off than had was anticipated, and was surprisingly active in religious affairs. . . . An awakening of profound import did take place for many of the members of this sample, but it was not what usually has come under the rubric of "ideological." It could better be called a "sociological awakening," for it amounted to a realization that certain of the previously accepted roles and statuses in the social system were no longer bounded by the same rules, and that new channels were suddenly opened for the expression of and satisfaction of needs. The heretofore established series of relationships between political leader and countryman, between employer and laborer, between Indian and Ladino, were not suddenly changed, but it abruptly became possible to introduce some change into them. This was a sociological alteration of first importance, and it was to a few of the ramifications of this that they awakened.[96]

6

Some Important Factors Regarding the Formation of Peasant Organizations

In the first three chapters of this book, it was demonstrated with considerable empirical evidence that distrust and resistance to change of peasants, as it exists all over Latin America, as such is not a hindrance to the creation of effective representative peasant organizations. On the contrary, distrust and resistance to change are quite suitable to be utilized as a starting point for strong peasant interest groups, if these groups are directed towards forms of change that are radical enough to satisfy the basic peasant demands. In general, this implies that these interest groups are formed in opposition to or in conflict with the vested interests of the large estate owners. Since in most of Latin America, the traditional hacienda system and the culture of repression accompanying it are maintained up to the present, a general climate prevails that is potentially favorable to the formation of radical peasant organizations. In the present situation, it is not difficult to find a negative reference group to rally the peasants effectively into their own interest groups. That on the whole, relatively few such peasant interest groups have been formed in Latin America is due to the lack of a number of factors that altogether seem to be crucial for the creation of such organizations. This topic will be dealt with in the present chapter.

The few effective and large-scale peasant movements that occurred in Latin America have a number of common factors that seem to show what is needed as a condition for the formation of a successful peasant organization. 1. In addition to the overall organizability of peasants implied in their resistance to the culture of repression, there are a number of specific frustrating conditions that are favorable to the actual initiation of a peasant protest action. Contact with urban and other modernizing forces comes out as a crucial factor in this organizability. 2. In the actual process, an important first step is the creation of awareness among the peasants of their basic interests and grievances, and of the possibility that united action can be undertaken to defend those interests—even if this implies a conflict with the traditional landed elite. 3. In order to bring the peasants into active struggle for their interests, the availability of strong or charismatic local leaders is crucial. Such leaders have to be able to fulfill certain roles, such as inspiring confidence and courage, that make it easier for the peasants to withdraw from and even oppose the influence of the traditional patronage of their landlords. 4. Support from educated urban allies who can help in the building up of a well-structured large-scale organization is another crucial factor for success. Peasants' organizations generally become effective only when they cover at least a whole geographic region. 5. In the dynamics of the formation of a peasant organization, the kind of demands and the means used to pressure for their fulfillment are very important. In general, one can note an escalation of demands as well as the means of pressure. This is a result of the intransigence and sometimes violent opposition of the landlords. While initiating with concrete and minor issues and using strictly institutionalized ways of demanding, peasant organizations have seen themselves obliged, in order to reach their legitimate goals, to rely on more and more radical approaches. These often include forms of civil disobedience and sometimes even violence. Since the land reform issue is generally the main reason for peasant discontent, peaceful occupations of unused or badly used parts of large estates has been an important means in the peasant struggle, to which considerable attention has to be given.

In this chapter we discuss these factors which are important for the formation of peasant organizations. Chapter 7 will be dedicated to a look at the prospects for peasant organization in Latin America, and to the revolutionary potential of the peasantry.

Some Common Factors as Conditions for Effective Peasant Organizations

The few important peasant organizations which grew in Latin America and which were described above have some factors in common which should be highlighted.

It is clear from a comparison of the various organized movements that they all occurred in areas where modernizing influences of some kind had entered. The striking fact about these influences, however, was that they brought frustration to the majority of the peasants rather than improvement, or left them at the margin of the benefits of development. The expansion of the sugar estates at the cost of the lands and the independence of the communal farmers in the state of Morelos, Mexico, where Zapata operated is a clear case in point. The local population was practically forced to find a living as workers on the sugar hacienda lands which formerly belonged to them.

In Ucureña, Cochabamba, peasants who through organized effort had achieved some degree of liberation from traditional feudal obligations were forced back into the old system which had become increasingly burdensome. They were thrown off the land they had rented together. It also frequently happened in that area that once a certain independence was achieved by a few peasants through buying a small plot, the others, attracted by this example, were punished or frustrated when organizing to obtain the same.

In la Convención (Peru), the increasing economic progress of the local peasants leading to greater independence from the large landowners, provoked the latter into blocking that progress and to return to the earlier situation of imposed dependency. In the northeast of Brazil, the Ligas Camponeses found their origin on an estate which demanded extravagant rents and tried to evict the peasants when they started to organize to buy the land. In the state of Michoacán in Mexico, it was the resistance of the landed elite to the execution of the agrarian reform law that provoked the peasants in the early twenties to build a militant organization. In Sonora, in northwest Mexico, it was the refusal to let the peasant participate or benefit in regional development according to existing laws that provoked the peasants to build up strong bargaining groups, not afraid of radical activities.

The most strongly modernizing influence in Bolivia was undoubtedly the Chaco War which took thousands of peasants from their more or less isolated villages into the army and gave them a view of other possibilities of life. The first leaders in Ucureña were excombatants. In Mexico, the years of armed struggle which was part of the Revolution had in part a similar effect; it enhanced the organizability of the peasants in many initially isolated areas which were touched by the struggle. Isolation and lack of perspective were broken in many regions of Mexico during the years of turmoil, so that the movements, once they were initiated, spread rapidly.

Also, the experience of severe repression after a period of hope and initial change in both countries seems to have enhanced the willingness of the peasants to undertake drastic action to defend their interests: in Bolivia, the period of military regime between 1946-1952, and in Mexico, the restoration of the power of the military and old elite shortly after the success of the 1910 revolution.

Another characteristic that the regions, where the movements described above took place, have in common is their good accessibility and communication with urban centers. The state of Morelos is at less than a hundred kilometers from Mexico City and an important supply area for that city. The Cochabamba valley where the Ucureña syndicate had its origin is closely linked to the town of Cochabama and is one of the most productive agricultural regions of Bolivia. The Convencion valley was undergoing a boom in coffee production and had good communications with the urban center of Cuzco. In the areas in the northeast of Brazil where the Ligas Camponeses started, the influence of Recife is very important. An excellent road network linked the rural areas with this city, and agriculture is comparatively highly developed. All these regions can be seen as relatively better-off compared with the national average. There was, however, acute frustration or a good deal of relative deprivation among the peasantry of those areas. The regions in question were generally densely populated.

The peasants who participated in the initiation of the movements were not the poorest and most destitute. In the state of Morelos, it was those who were proletarianized after having lived as independent small peasants belonging to comunidades who were the initiators of the movement. In the Cochabamba valley, the movement was initiated by landless peasants who aspired to become independent farmers, like some of their better-off neighbors, but who saw their efforts frustrated. Also, the *arrendires* in La Convención were small farmers who saw the possibility of becoming independent. They were better off than most of the peasants living on estates in the Peruvian highlands. The peasants in the northeast of Brazil had experienced some improvement or were somewhat above the subsistence level. They all had relatively frequent urban contact of some kind.

Another important factor which these movements had in common was that the initial leaders, although of peasant origin, had some kind of urban or modernizing (e.g., travel) experience. Zapata was in the army and worked some time in Mexico City. José Rojas spent various years in Argentina. Rojas had, to a certain degree, some syndical organization experience in an urban environment before he became a peasant leader. In Morelos, many peasants worked as wage-paid agricultural workers, a kind of rural proletariat, on the sugar plantations or in the mills. In the Cochabama area, a number of peasants had worked at some stage in their life in the mines, or had relatives working there. Also in La Convención and the northeast of Brazil, the initial leaders were mirgrants or had worked in urban centers. José dos Prazeres had many years experience as a labor organizer and had participated in political movements. Among the leaders of the Federacion Campesina of Venezuela, there were many union organizers and even local merchants.

It has been noted by several observers that the peasants in many areas, in spite of considerable differentiation according to relative well-being or social status within the community, all have the same feeling of social distance regarding the large landowner, a uniting factor which generally seems to be stronger than inner divisions among them.[1]

There is great differentiation within the peasantry, ranging from landless rural proletariat to indigenous comuneros, but it seems that effective organization is possible among all these types once the condition of frustration or deprivation exists. The only groups that appear difficult to organize are the most destitute peasants who live on the margin of subsistence, are highly dependent on their patron, and live in isolated conditions or as migrant workers. It seems that such peasants only join organized movements when their lot becomes unbearable and for some reason, an unorganized violent explosion results. There is evidence that the migrant peasant workers who ... "harvest coffee in Caldas, cotton in Tolima, and tea in César ... " were the most apt to be recruited for violent movements. They have no roots and no organizations to defend their interests. It seems that these peasants have played an important role in the period during which severe violence swept the rural areas of Colombia.[2]

There appear to be some gradual differences in organizability. From various outstanding examples, it appears that tenants or sharecroppers, who have a certain independence and manage their own plots, are relatively more apt to feel frustration and to take the initiative to organize than other types of landless peasants. Despoliation of land cultivated for many years without reimbursement for the improvements made, insecurity of tenure related to the arbitrary attitude of the landowners, and high rents as such, often seem to be major causes for frustration. Many such tenants have the feeling that the relatively large share of the produce or the cash which goes to the landowner is an unjustifiable expenditure. The more alert ones are well aware that the result of their toil is being conspicuously wasted in the cities in luxurious housing and other status symbols. These views contribute to the feeling of frustration which the more independent and somewhat educated peasants have. One expression of the revolution of rising expectations and of relative deprivation is a statement by a group of Ecuadorian Indians who came to the capital.

We are tired of living as animals in the mountains. We want to have the same homes, the same cars, the same job opportunities which you people have here in the cities. And if these opportunities are not given to us peacefully, we will all descend from the mountains and claim them by force.[3]

The present tendency in development policies in several countries, which apparently stress middle-class emulation through conspicuous consumption, is a factor that tends to enhance the relative deprivation and thus the organizability of the majority of the peasants who stay on the periphery of these developments. In this respect, the fact that in several countries the production or sale of luxury automobiles far exceeds that of tractors or small trucks, is interpreted by some peasant leaders as relevant to the matter.

In addition to the modernizing influences and urban experiences of the initial leaders, the areas where peasant movements began were influenced by what could be called rural promoters. Although there were no community development programs as such, there were certain modernizing agents working in the areas. Zapata received a great deal of help from the school teacher of his village, Otilio Montaño, and later from the lawyer, Antonio Diaz Soto y Gama.

The syndicate of Ucureña was strongly supported by the school teachers and was at one stage even led by the director of the school. The construction and maintenance of schools was in turn a main objective of the growing syndicates. This mutual collaboration was so effective that the local school system was chosen as a demonstration project by a community development agency. Also, students and intellectuals of nearby Cochabamba gave support to the unions at various stages. The fact that some sons of landowners for personal or ideological reasons align themselves with the peasantry against their own class is not rare. Arze Loureiro in Cochabamba and Juliao in Pernambuco are cases in point.

The different movements were able to achieve nationwide impact because of their alliance with a political movement at the national level which needed peasant support. Zapata's peasant guerrillas supported the new government of Madero in return for promises of agrarian reform. The Ucureña movement got a chance to fully develop and influence national policy after a revolutionary movement, with which it had relations and which was led by middle-class intellectuals and workers, had overthrown the old regime and dissolved the army. Since both national revolutionary movements had more or less of a middle-class orientation, continuous peasant pressure was needed in order to obtain the acceptance and the beginning of the implementation of an effective agrarian reform program. This only happened after the peasants, through armed or nonviolent occupation of estates in large territories, had shown that they were determined to struggle for their demands.

The peasant federation in Venezuela was almost completely organized by national and local political leaders of Accion Democratica. In the Convención valley, there was considerable support from lawyers of the communist labor unions of Cuzco and later from the Trotzkyite movement, mainly through the person of Hugo Blanco. In the state of Pernambuco in the northeast of Brazil, the main urban supporters were politicians of one of the radical tendencies, including Juliao, who was a socialist deputee.

These political allies had generally a radicalizing influence, but it seems that it was particularly the intransigence and violent reaction of the large landholders that acted as a stimulus to the radicalization of the peasant movements. The insistent and often violent opposition to demands such as the sale of lands for which too high rents were paid, the restitution of usurped lands or the acceptance of a proper land reform legislation, provoked these peasant groups towards greater cohesiveness and drastic actions. These actions at times went as far beyond the orderly legal practices as did the activities of the landowners. One could almost say that the main opponents of peasant movements aided them by obliging them to unite and harness their forces.

It was clear in several cases that although a need for vengeance was strongly present among the peasants, this was generally not expressed in destructive ways. In the Cochabamba area and La Convención as well as in the state of Morelos, the leaders saw to it that constructive measures were taken in addition to the elimination of the traditional system. Particularly in Bolivia where the agrarian revolution was accompanied by little violence, some landlords who had not been abusive and cultivated their lands well, were respected and not subjected to the reform measures as were their more abusive colleagues.

A great variety of tactics was used by landlords against the incipient movements. Intimidation, isolation, corruption, or elimination of leaders or potential leaders of peasant movements appeared to be most frequent. Emiliano Zapata was drafted into the army even before his efforts to rally the peasants of his area became effective. After the movement had become strong and contributed to the Mexican Revolution, he was offered an estate for his services if he would give up further efforts to struggle for a real agrarian reform. Because he did not give in, he was assassinated in 1919. José Rojas in Bolivia was persecuted for several years, and after the 1952 Revolution, the moderate leaders of the winning party, Movimiento Nacionalista Revolucionario (MNR), tried to sidetrack him by putting a less radical leader in his place. Rojas won a majority, however, among the peasants of the Cochabamba valley. Several leaders of the Ligas Camponeses had suffered attempts of assassination and some, such as Joao Pedro Teixeira of Sapé, fell in the struggle. Also in the Convención area, imprisonment, abusive treatment by the landlords and killings occurred. Many leaders of the Venezuelan FCV suffered considerable persecution or exile in the years between 1948-1958, which made some of them into martyrs. In all cases, the effort to create representative peasant organizations could only be undertaken by persons willing to risk their lives.

Awareness of Grievances and First Steps

After seeing some of the factors, common to the few important peasant movements in Latin America, as conditions favorable to their growth, some of the elements which played a role in the actual dynamics of this growth should be studied: 1) identification of an acutely felt need or grievance; 2) availability of leadership with some previous organizing experience able to rally the peasants around this need or grievance; 3) the creation and consolidation of a following as a cohesive group around this leader; and 4) the alliance with urban supporters who link the organization with forces at the regional or national level.

Most of the movements previously described started with action from below and were formed because of an acutely felt need or grievance existing among the peasants. In the case of the Zapata movement, the grievance resulted from the break up of a more or less tolerable status quo. There was a strongly felt need to recover the lands which had been usurped and the status of independent peasants which had been lost. In the cases of Galileia in northeast Brazil, La Convención in Peru, as well as the Ucureña syndicate, the most strongly felt need that stimulated the peasants to unite and struggle was the abolition of increasingly burdensome land tenure conditions. These were mainly the unpaid labor and services which had to be rendered to the landlord in exchange for a small plot of land, or an increasing rent which had to be paid.

The most acutely frustrating factor in these cases was that when the peasants, strongly influenced by modernizing factors, hoped to improve their situation, the landlords blocked this possibility and tried to maintain the old system with more rigidity than before.

After awareness of an acute problem existed, the first steps to come to a solution were undertaken jointly. In practically all cases studied, the initial activities of the peasant groups strictly followed the established and traditional legal channels to obtain the fulfillment of their needs. The village committee led by Emiliano Zapata, as well as the peasant syndicate of Ucureña, the peasant league of Galileia, and the unions of La Convención tried to defend their legitimate interests by appeals to the local courts or labor inspectors.

However, the local courts and rural labor authorities in many Latin American countries were, to a large extent, controlled or influenced by vested interests and only rarely decided in favor of the peasants. In the examples described above, the peasants soon learned that recourse to legal action gave no result and that power, primarily in the form of physical force—and not law—is decisive in cases of conflicting interest. One CIDA report called this the lawlessness which rules in most of rural Latin America.[4]

The high respect of the peasantry for law and order is indicated by the fact that in all cases peasants initiated their activities with some form of legal action. In view of the poor results of peasant efforts in this respect, one could even say that they have an exaggerated respect for the law and that they are overly legalistic. The need to overcome the generally prevailing lawlessness can be seen as one of the most strongly felt needs of the peasants and the fact that governments are not able or willing to enforce the existing legislation in cases where it protects the peasants rather than the landlords, is a strongly radicalizing stimulus in the rural areas. It is not surprising that among the demands expressed by peasants in the examples, in addition to the questions relating to a minimum of law and order and personal security (abolition of the most abusive and generally illegal practices of servitude), high importance was given to education. It is difficult to assess what the attractiveness of school education exactly means to the peasants, but it may well have important consequences for such elementary civil rights as the right to vote. In several Latin American countries, the peasants are denied these rights as long as they are illiterate. Another basic right, more directly related to the formation of peasant organizations, that of freedom of association is also denied to them in most countries.

In some countries, there seems to exist at the national level a willingness to apply legislation concerning freedom of association or labor protection, but an effective enforcement apparatus at the local level exists only precariously. In some cases, laws accepted at the national or federal level are not approved at the state level, or are applied at that level only after much delay and considerable weakening of the possible impact. There are many cases in the rural areas where the large landholders try—generally successfully—to impose their authority and power to circumvent national laws and international conventions, such as those of ILO regarding freedom of association. It is not only in very isolated areas that the wealthy landowners effectively control or have a strong influence over the local authorities in charge of justice and the execution of the law. Even in countries where peasant organizations and their leaders are legally protected, strategies to hamper such organizations can easily be applied. It seems that a strong agitating or politicizing factor is not only the unwillingness of the landlords to make concessions, but especially the opposition against peasant organization as such. In all cases described above, the intransigence of the rural power holders helped an initially moderate and timidly growing peasant organization to become conscious of the fact that there would be no solution of their problem or survival of their organization without a considerable change in the rural power structure.

The lack of basic civil rights and civil protection became immediately obvious after moderate efforts to achieve some improvements were initiated by the peasants. Opposition was of an intransigence and violence out of proportion to the moderation and legalistic approach of the peasants. It was as if the landed elite felt that the whole status quo and all their privileges were at stake once minor changes would be allowed. In several of the cases described above, the opposition of the landlords was directed not so much against the specific demands of the peasants, but against the fact that they made demands at all, or efforts to change their conditions. Even if one particular landowner was willing to give the peasants a change for improvement, his neighbors or relatives, out of some kind of class solidarity, became alarmed about this possibility of change in the status quo, and violently blocked its further progress, or reversed the trend. The cases of the Santa Clara estate in Ucureña and the *engenho* Galiliea in Pernambuco were obvious examples. It was this type of opposition then that made the peasants aware of the fact that they would not achieve any moderate improvements without changing the existing power structure as a whole.

The awareness among the peasants of a need for overall change is expressed in some cases spontaneously in their adherence to messianic or millenarian movements created by outsiders or by people from the peasantry. The difficulty is that, although peasants may see or feel the need for overall change, they do not clearly visualize ways and means through which this can be realized. It is at this crucial point that either peasants with urban experience, such as Zapata and José dos Prazeres, or urban leaders, such as Juan Guerra (the teacher in Ucureña) and Hugo Blanco, became important. They can channel the vague awareness of a need for change into a more concrete awareness of ways and means to change through organized effort.

It is obvious from the cases known that it is important to break through the isolation of the closed hacienda community in order that awareness of other possibilities can grow or be created among the peasantry. The growth of awareness of the need and possibilities for change that occurred in Ucureña, Anenecuilco (Zapata's village), and La Convención with great difficulties and after trial and error, can also be promoted through educational campaigns. Existing general grievances or needs of the peasants, without being particularly acute at a certain moment, can become so through abusive acts of the landlords and through teaching or explaining.

The growth or creation among the peasants of awareness of their basic needs and of the possibilities of demanding and struggling for the fulfillment of those needs has been called conscientization[a] in some countries, mobilization or agitation in others and also politicization.[5] One case was the Basic Education Movement sponsored by the Church in the northeast of Brazil. The letters to peasants published at times by Juliao or the orientation speeches given by Hugo Blanco and his elders in La Convención were other examples. The most important as-

[a]The Paolo Freire method of literacy teaching is called *Concientizaçao*.

pect of this process of creating awareness refers to the need to break through the impact of the traditional land tenure and power system, and the means through which this break may be accomplished.

One of the obstacles to the awareness of the need for radical change in cases where there are no blatant abuses is the fact that the traditional system has some more or less consciously applied defense mechanisms which prevent the peasants from seeing their situation clearly. Since the culture of repressions has prevailed for ages, certain elements have come up under this system which try to soften its impact. This is the role of patronage, dealt with in the first chapter. Landlords, as long as they are solidly in control, try to maintain the image of being good fathers and in some cases, they become godfathers to the children of their subjects, or at least some of them.

Such apparently benevolent patronage relations can be created easily since the hacienda system generally is the only frame of reference for the peasants who grew up in it. It should be stressed that those who belong to the traditional clientele of the *patron* of the estate where they were born have no alternative. Belonging to it was not a question of voluntary choice but simply one of ascription. One is born into it and one has practically no way of escaping from its impact.[b] One is completely dependent on the hacienda for survival and many coercive means exist to enforce this dependency. An additional difficulty is that the more able peasants often get special rewards, and are offered possibilities for individual improvement or special ties to the landlord, so that they refrain from stimulating group action. Such people become the foremen on the estates, rather than leaders of peasant interest groups.

It is clear that an important condition for the formation of a representative organization of peasants is to break through the closedness, dependence and cohesion of the traditional patronage system. This can generally only be done by the active stimulation of dissent and conflict and the creation of new loyalties outside and conflicting with the traditional ones.(This is even recognized in recent United Nations policy statement on community development.)[6]

The creation of dissent to overcome the traditional influence of the landlord implies the promotion of awareness of the peasants' rational interests as contrary to the traditional bonds existing in the hacienda system. The cases described above, particularly the syndicate of Ucureña and the unions of La Convención, show that the fear and intransigence of the landed elite were a help in this respect. In fact, the lawlessness and at times violent opposition from the landlords which the peasants encountered when they tried to form a representative organization within the traditional social climate, practically forced them to greater internal cohesiveness out of the need for self-defense or resistance.

In the sociology of conflict, it is a well-known fact that it is easier to form a

[b]In some countries this still goes so far that when a hacienda is sold, the people working on it are like the cattle and the stables, included in the sale. This happened, for example, with the Vicos hacienda when it was taken over by the Cornell University team.

group when there is an opposing force than to form a group when there is no opposition.[7] Thus, the fact that the formation of representative peasant organizations is strongly opposed and creates a conflict situation can be interpreted positively as a fact which may help to strengthen the cohesion of the new group.

As a result of the acute need for the defense of common interests, interpersonal conflicts which always exist in peasant communities tend to diminish. As indicated in Chapter 3, the strong orientation towards the family and inability to form peer groups have been noted by several observers as inherent characteristics of the peasantry. In reality, it seems that this inability often disappears in the face of a common enemy. However, some basic consensus within the peasant group before a conflict becomes open is an important condition for achieving cohesion in the face of an outside threat. If this basic consensus does not exist, an outside threat may cause general apathy rather than internal cohesion. Such consensus seems to be strong in several of the Andean countries where the comunidades have to face frequent conflicts with the landlords, although at times conflicts arise between the communities over boundaries. There is, generally, considerable cohesion within the traditional comunidades, which can be an asset for the formation of viable bargaining organizations.

This basic consensus existing among peasants in certain areas does not exist everywhere. In some of the cases described, there existed basic differences and even contrary interests among the peasants, such as between the *arrendires, allegados* and *agregados* in La Convención, and between the various types of peasants and peasant organizations in the northeast of Brazil in 1963-64. However, in a crucial struggle, it is not overly difficult to achieve common action. As we have seen, the examples of effective peasant organization described above show that the resistance to change of the peasantry can be overcome with relative ease, once they can participate in a movement which is clearly to their own and common interest. The resistance to change of the traditional elite can be taken as a point of departure in the strategy of formation of peasant organizations and as a negative reference group to stimulate cohesion among the peasants.

In some of the more isolated areas where the culture of repression of the hacienda system prevailed almost undisturbed by modernizing influences, it seems that guerrilla groups can have a function of creating awareness among the peasants of possibilities for change. This was at least the case with the group headed by Hector Bejar in some of the more isolated parts of the Ayacucho department of Peru in 1965. A small group of guerrilleros was able to win acceptance among the repressed peasants and became powerful and popular after an assault on the Chapi hacienda where the owner had been particularly abusive.[8] Several peasants joined the ranks of the small guerrilla group that created fear among the hacienda owners of the region, causing several of them to flee. Only considerable army and airforce intervention was sufficient to round up the group at the end of 1965.[9] The military-civic action program initiated in the region immediately after the defeat of the group brought the isolated communities and peasant groups under modernizing influences. Peasants seemed to be aware of the reasons that brought medical care and other modern facilities into their villages. They also realized that landlords were not as powerful as they had always appeared.

While in some respects peasant organizations in their formative stage can draw lessons from the syndical struggle of urban workers, it is important to note that there is considerable difference between a peasant movement and an urban labor organization involved in a conflict. While most industrial labor conflicts are solved in Latin America within the prevailing system, leaving the social structure of enterprises as such intact, solutions to the basic problems in rural areas can only come about through changes in the social structure. In labor conflicts, there is often a basic consensus between employers and workers, which can be maintained in spite of a conflict over details such as the size of wages. Between the majority of the landlords and the peasantry, however, such consensus generally exists only if maintained by coercion. This is a basic fact which must be taken into account.

In this respect also, the question of whether or not the struggle should be directed towards economic or political goals becomes important. The more or less successful peasant movements stress some kind of political struggle. Struggle for such concrete objectives as the return of usurped lands (the Zapata movement) or the possibility for small peasants to liberate themselves from servitude through the buying or renting of land (the movements in Ucureña and La Convención), encountered so much opposition from the local power elite that the struggle automatically became political. This appears to be the main characteristic of the agrarian struggle in Latin America to date and it would be illusory not to focus peasant organization activities accordingly.

An important aspect of the new groups, however, is that, if possible, they render certain services to the peasants. Some of the peasant leagues founded centers where medical assistance was given to members. The unions in La Convención did a great deal to foster education and agricultural extension, antidrinking habits and certain aspects of home economics such as the use of beds and shoes. It was thus noted that in Chaupimayo long after Hugo Blanco was jailed, peasants continued to wear beards (as their leader did) and shoes, in distinction from the areas farther away where the daily impact of the educational efforts had been less. Such services or activities are a means to guarantee loyalty of members in periods of calm in the struggle to solve more basic issues.

Among peasant and labor union leaders, it is an often discussed problem, how to gain enough concrete benefits to keep members interested and militant, but at the same time to keep the struggle for overall social change awake. Members sometimes tend to be content with minor adjustments and gains and forget about the basic social change needed to bring them a real and enduring improvement, such as redistribution of land. In La Convención as well as the northeast of Brazil, this problem came up. There were those who wanted to follow the more radical line (those who voted for Hugo Blanco to head the La Convención peasant federation), while the more moderate peasants preferred the older and less radical leaders. The Ligas Camponeses organized a good number of services for their members and gained direct benefits, but always emphasized the importance of the final purpose, agrarian reform rather than partial improvements. It seems that particularly where the basic needs of the peasants cannot be solved unless radical changes in the rural social structure are brought about, it is best to begin the struggle, and gain strength, through winning concrete minor changes: better tenancy rates, prevention of eviction, abolition of servitude conditions, etc. For the first time, gaining a case against a landlord is an encouraging experience and next steps will be easier to take. The opposition of the landlords to even minor changes which merely imply the execution of existing laws (regarding wages or tenancy) will enhance the will to struggle among the peasants once they see that this struggle is not completely hopeless. Small successes are essential for this process.

The Role of Leadership

A most important factor in the formative stages of a peasant organization is the quality of the leadership. As shown above, a primary objective in the formation of new organizations is to achieve independence from the traditional *patron*. This can take place when peasants become followers of a leader, with whom the relationship of dependency is less unilateral and monopolistic than with the hacienda patron. A peasant leader is as dependent on the support of the members as the members are dependent on his leadership. Such groups initially take the form of a following around an inspiring and strong personality, a local peasant. A feeling of togetherness grows at the same time as a feeling of supporting and following the respected and exemplary leader. The important point is that this following of peasant leaders has to grow in competition or even conflict with the already existing ties of the hacienda system.

This was to a large extent the case in the beginning of the peasant leagues in Brazil. The approach of José dos Prazeres, its initiator, as well as Francisco Julião, who later became the more or less charismatic leader of the leagues, was rather paternalistic. It should be noted, however, that this was the approach the peasants of the northeast best understood and which appealed to them. It was a form of protective and independence stimulating paternalism, which can be compared with the approach used by the team of the Cornell University in the ex-hacienda Vicos in Peru, described briefly in the first chapter. This type of paternalism and the patronage elements belonging to it are not aimed by maintaining themselves, but try to provoke increasing initiative and independency among the members of the group. The leaders of this new following purposely tried to create a social group climate with democratic or participatory tendencies, respecting the peasants and their opinions and defending their interests.

Francisco Julião, himself a son of a local landowner, used his and his brother's estates to hold the meetings of the leagues which were forbidden and persecuted on the surrounding estates and purposely stimulated the associational capacity of the peasants.

The innovating leader who is essential for political development and for stimulating the associational capacities of the people needs as a basic quality: ". . . the capacity for psychic mobility and the ability to mentally place oneself in other's roles."[10] This is particularly needed in situations where a justified distrust of all kinds of outside intervention prevails. To a large extent, Julião seems to have had this quality as one of his colleagues described him.

. . . Julião possessed certain personal qualities which day by day reconfirmed his position of leadership in the Peasant Leagues. He had the patience and humility to work well with the peasants, the energy to defend them without tiring, the openhandedness to distribute the favors and money that the peasants needed so badly, and a political style sufficiently paternalistic to permit him to relate successfully to peasants accustomed for generations to the paternalism of the great landowners.

His residence in the capital of Pernambuco, a *casa grande* (mansion) after the fashion of the sugar plantations, was large and comfortable, with extensive service areas and almost a hectare of land on which he cultivated mannioc, and raised pigs and poultry. Preserving the traditions of the feudal family from which he sprang, Julião retained numerous servants to cut wood for the kitchen, pump water, tend the pigs and poultry, carry messages, guard the house, guard his person (always under threat of death) and cook for the dozens of peasants who appeared each day at the house asking Julião's help in sorting out their legal problems.

The peasant arriving at Julião's home suffered no sense of dislocation from the familiar atmosphere of the *fazenda* (plantation). The physical surroundings were virtually the same, with one substantial difference: in Julião's home the peasant was a guest who sat about, ate and slept with absolutely no sense of discomfort, at times sojourning for several days, to work out a solution to his problems or to enjoy protection from the pursuit of the police or the landowner. In addition the peasant was able to converse for hours with the 'Boss' or 'chief' (Julião), who often attended his guests in pajamas, utterly free of any trace of stiff protocol. Although the peasant may not have resolved any of his problems, for all the long journey to the capital, he returned to his village satisfied, deeply pleased for having met this rich man, this 'Doctor' who treated him as an equal, with respect and great kindliness. For a whole generation of humble and downtrodden peasants this very natural posture of Francisco Julião was absolutely essential. Peasants went forth from his house spreading the word wherever they passed of the 'graciousness of Dr. Julião,' each day raising still higher the personal prestige of Julião among the dispossessed.[11]

Hugo Blanco went much farther in his identification with the peasants. He became a peasant himself and the farm where he lived became a training and radiation center for the whole Convención area. Generally, peasants seem to need a leader who through his personality gives them, as followers, a sense of strength and discipline and courage to overcome great odds.[c] The personal example set by such a leader has to represent these characteristics in an abundant way. This was apparently the case with Zapata, José Rojas, José dos Prazeres, Juliao, Hugo Blanco and others mentioned above.

These cases seem to confirm the view that peasants often (but not always) tend to see as an ideal political leader an imposing, masculine *(macho)* personality sufficiently strong to be able to overcome their fear of organizing and of getting involved in risky organizational efforts.[13] Practically all organizations and movements studied had in their initial stage such a leader with charismatic qualities who knew how to inspire people and bring them to united action. Sometimes, this implied the ability to be violent and aggressive so as to trigger off political action in spite of strong opposition.

It is characteristic of charismatic leaders that they themselves create or tolerate the creation of a myth around their personality.[14] They accept certain postures or terminology impressive to peasants. This becomes clear from Juliao's statements and letters to peasants, and from the fact that José Rojas refused to speak any language other than Quechua. Such messianistic elements may be helpful in the initial stage, but at a later stage, when the movement begins to develop and is gaining strength, these phenomena may become counterproductive.

A great deal depends on the qualities of the new leader as a patron of his group. He can become a dominating personality on whom the followers depend and the domination over his following can become almost as coercive as that of the traditional hacienda system. Particularly in the stage where the struggle of the organizations is difficult, and the leader depends on the willingness of his followers to participate actively and back him up, chances for such developments are relatively small. Then active support, sometimes the risking of lives, of the members is needed. Such a situation was recently observed for the position of the peasant leader in the los Cristales estate in Chile, which had been taken over by a peasant union.

Given the dominant position of the union president, the current administration of "Los Cristales" resembles the traditional system in which the owner completely dominates life on his fundo. But the resemblance is only superficial. Both the peasants and their president know that he—a man elected from their ranks—is ultimately subject to their veto. Furthermore, the peasants accept the system because it delivers results.[15]

---

c"In the potentially explosive political climate created by the preconditions and precipitants described above, social revolution breaks out only in the presence of revolutionary leadership."[12]

Because several successful peasant organizations have changed from a representative organization of struggle into a brokerage system by becoming part of a political clientele network, some observers tend to overemphasize the similarities between peasant organizations and the traditional hacienda patronage system. They suggest that leaders of peasant movements—be they peasants themselves or not—who have a personal following, such as José Rojas, Francisco Juliao and others use the peasants as tools for their personal purposes in ways which are not basically different from those employed under the hacienda system.[16] Such simplified and static interpretations of peasant organizations seem to overlook, however, the dynamics of peasant movements. Even those leaders of peasant organizations who have gained personal prestige, political influence and in some cases even personal wealth have challenged the monopoly of the traditional system and broken its rigidity. Patronage becomes a highly dynamic phenomenon, once the monopoly of the traditional hacienda patronage is broken. Under the traditional system, the peasants are so dependent that is almost impossible for them to develop an active horizontal solidarity based on common interests. This becomes feasible, however, as soon as a competing clientele is formed, based on the willingness of the peasants to stick together in support of a militant charismatic leader. Once the new group is strong enough to be a real challenge to the traditional system, efforts will be undertaken by the traditional forces to neutralize its impact. This is particularly the case where the new group tends to be directed not only towards some concrete benefits for its members, but towards a radical change in the rural social structure and the elimination of the landlords as a class.

As part of this effort, it seems quite logical that one of the first things peasant organizations, opposing the traditional hacienda system, try to organize for their members is the kind of services that landlords sometimes provide for their peasants to tie them to the hacienda and oblige them to conform to a basically disadvantageous and exploitative system. These are in some cases schools, elsewhere medical services (the peasant leagues in Brazil organized medical services for their members wherever they could). Once such services are taken care of through means outside the monopoly of the landlord, the true characteristics of the patron-worker relationship on the haciendas and the need and possibility to break with it becomes more obvious.

It is obvious that one possible disadvantage of this method is that a peasant organization that takes up such patronage functions, providing services to their members in exchange for support, may become dominated by those who control the resources. Rather than an organization of struggle to oppose the overall hacienda system, it may become a means to control the peasants to the benefit of a leader or a party. Particularly when looking at the influence of nonpeasants in the formation of peasant organizations, it is important to distinguish between those who identify with the peasants and their demands and those who try to exploit the peasants or use them for their own interests. It seems unjustified to suggest that all peasant leaders who are not peasants themselves intend to utilize the peasantry. Reality is less simple. There are many cases of outsiders who identified with the peasants and risked their lives for the peasant cause without a view of any significant benefit for themselves except the personal satisfaction of being a highly respected leader.[d]

It seems that the leaders who try to represent the peasants' interest rather than their own, tend to make their followings inclusive in such a way that peasants who do not directly belong to it as a member or client still find their interests defended. Such leaders are generally aware of representing the peasants as a class rather than as a particular personal following. Hugo Blanco in La Convención, Peru, Jacinto Lopez in the northwest of Mexico and to some extent Juliao were such leaders.

A clear distinction should be made between followings where the vertical forces, dependence of the clients on the patron, dominate and those where this is the case with horizontal forces, the solidarity between clients in order to make their patron; the leader of the organization, strong. While the first type of following is traditional, nonrational and authoritarian, the opposite type is rational, participatory and democratic. To facilitate the understanding of the dynamics of followings and their role in a beginning struggle to eliminate the hacienda system, one could imagine a continuum between the two ideal types (in the Weberian sense) of followings.

participatory	authoritarian
democratic	dependent
rational	traditional

Most organizations—and all peasant organizations as followings in some stage of their development—are somewhere between the two poles, and they move towards one or the other side.

The Mexican peasant organizations started on the left side and moved towards the extreme left before and during the Cardenas period, by becoming more and more participatory, rational and representative organizations. When they became part of the overall political system, dominated by the middle classes, they were drawn back towards the right side of the continuum.

From the above described examples, it can be seen that some peasant organizations remain close to the middle of this continuum. Horizontal solidarity is stimulated to some extent, but vertical ties to an overall political clientele system remain at least as important, if not predominant. The best example is the Federacion Campesina de Venezuela, appropriately characterized as a brokerage system.

[d]A striking example is Jacinto Lopez of the Union General de Obreros y Campesinos de Mexico (UGOCM) who once turned down a bribe of almost one million United States dollars and lives in modest conditions in spite of having become a national leader.

Political leaders and parties in Venezuela have been successful in building up a system of distribution of benefits, including at times land reform measures, to win the peasants' vote and support. At some stages, the benefits which the peasants received were so important and the confidence placed by the top in their active participation so significant that one could notice a change in the social climate among the peasantry from authoritarian to democratic. Later, these tendencies were reversed, as happened in Venezuela after 1961. Vertical elements gained importance, in a system in which peasant union leaders tried to obtain benefits for their followers (on whose support or votes they depended) through their relations with government agencies. Here, the leader or *patron* functioned clearly as a broker[17] and there remained a considerable degree of mutual dependency in the relationship between him and his followers. In order that a brokerage system may function to the satisfaction of the peasants as well as the brokers, abundant favors and services have to be available for distribution, which is the case in Venezuela.

In relation to the misunderstanding about the basic similarity of traditional followings and new, more participatory ones, the Ligas Camponeses of Northeast Brazil have been mentioned a few times.[18] Particularly in this case, however, there is a considerable difference in social climate in the following of a traditional *patron*, and in that of a new leader such as Juliao. These differences have to be taken into consideration since they are an important motivation of people to take the risk of joining a certain organization.

Initially, the joining of the new group gave no benefits and considerable risks and certainly no protection to the peasants who participated. Only after the Ligas had grown strong and militant and obtained benefits through organized action, did affiliation with this clientele became attractive to an increasing number of peasants. Then, the Ligas were able to support middle-class groups seeking to gain political control of the state of Pernambuco in exchange for more benefits, although the struggle against the traditional elite continued. Therefore, later new clienteles were sponsored by more conservative forces to compete with the Ligas. These were the rural unions created in some areas in the northeast by the Church.[e] Then, the syndicates sponsored by the federal government commission for the organization of the peasantry started under a new legislation to create its own clientele. During the period before April 1964 when these different clienteles were operating and competing for adherence among the peasantry, considerable benefits resulted. At one time, the groups united in radical action such as a mass strike in order to achieve an important wage increase. The more radical groups could set the tone in such a movement while the others had to participate, wholeheartedly or not, in order not to lose their following.

---

[e]It is interesting to note that Pearson qualifies the peasant groups organized by the priests as genuine peasant unions which protect the interest of their members against landowners, middlemen and government agencies, while he describes the Ligas Camponeses as tools of nonpeasants.

Although the government-sponsored structure of syndicates was gaining increasing control over the whole movement, there was considerable room for the articulation of various peasant interests within the system. The competitive aspects gave this system considerable dynamism, one group trying to outdo others in radically defending peasant demands. Probably, this was a reason that it was destroyed in April 1964 by the traditional forces. This proves the crucial distinction between the traditional clientele which monopolizes the adherence of the peasants through means which include coercion and the participatory clientele which competes with the traditional one, and tries to change the system of which the traditional clientele is a part.

While some of the new clienteles, such as the Peasant Leagues, gained adherence by striving for radical change of the whole system, others, such as the syndicates sponsored by priests, were more conformist towards the prevailing traditional system. Both groups, however, stimulated a participatory climate among the peasants, which as such was a first step to end the landlords' monopoly of power and decisionmaking. Once the moderate priests, generally also rather paternalistic (and thus quite fit to create a following among the peasantry) had formed unions and had given the peasants a frame of reference different from the traditional patron-dominated following, it seems to have been relatively easy for more radically oriented leaders to take over the control of the unions, unless the priests and their helpers became more radical themselves. The important step was to get the peasants out of the system in which there is only one patron who dominates their life completely. The second step is to stimulate the peasants towards increasing democratic participation in the new following. In this respect, it seems that the priests in the northeast have given an interesting contribution, in spite of their intentions.[f]

It seems that the people most suitable to lead their peers in the agrarian struggle are those persons with leadership qualities who have gone out of the village and returned with modern insights and new skills. An increasing number of actual and potential peasant leaders have had the chance to become acquainted with urban life. Many initiators and leaders of peasant organizations have had experience while doing compulsory military service, the most striking example being Emilio Zapata. Others have worked in the towns or in mines, or as migrant workers in highly developed areas. In Bolivia, Peru and Chile the influence of peasants who became miners and later went back to their villages has been important.[19] It should be noted that the difference between miners and peasants is vague in many instances, since many miners are recruited from peasant families and return to agriculture when silicosis or some other illness makes further work in the mines too dangerous for them.

In some more isolated communities a person who is literate and through that

---

[f]In this sense, the experience of the peasant unions led by the priests in the northeast of Brazil give an interesting clue that the Catholic Church can have considerable impact in favor of peasant organization.

capacity knows how to deal with the outside world, can become an outstanding leader, surpassing in importance the traditional leaders.[20]

An outstanding factor important in past and present cases of good leadership is the personal quality of the leader. Particularly, incorruptibility in the face of the manipulations of the opposing interests, is highly important. It seems that the personal qualities of leaders are often related to or influenced by their ideological orientation. Many of those who are outstanding because of their personal qualities adhere to religious or ideological groups that emphasize honesty, exemplary personal behavior, zeal and diligence, self-discipline, a great sense of justice and other characteristics crucial for good leadership. Thus, leaders are sometimes militant protestants, communists, or socialists or inspired by the social-christian tendencies renovating catholicism in some countries.

Among the outstanding leaders in the La Convención area of Peru were people who belonged to protestant sects, and as a result impressed their neighbors with exemplary behavior. In the Brazilian northeast, several outstanding leaders were members or exmembers of the Communist Party, while others were devout Catholics. Although belonging to a specific religion or ideology that requires a certain behavior and discipline from its adherents is not a prerequisite for being an exemplary leader, there is a frequent coincidence. A specially needed quality for leaders is the ability to resist cooptation by the overall political system, which in most countries is not favorable to effective peasant organization. Unfortunately, these personal qualities are difficult to rely upon and their development is hard to predict.

Naturally, personal characteristics can be an asset as well as a risk for successful peasant organization. A great deal depends on the social system in which the leaders are functioning. Generally, this overall system is not a guarantee that the best qualities of peasant leaders are stimulated, nor that the best natural leaders necessarily rise to the surface. On the contrary, one serious problem faced by peasant organizations is the tendency of leaders to utilize the organization to further their individual ambitions. Leaders do become coopted by the power elite of the country and in the process tend to cease defending the interests of the peasants. This could be called political corruption. Economic corruption is another temptation: the misuse of the resources of the organization or the acceptance of bribes. Another problem is that personal rivalry between leaders over power or economic gains may lead to internal struggles. Internal division may also arise from ideological rivalry. Such rivalries are often related to or stimulated by outside forces of some kind.[21]

Urban Support and Regional Organization

The leaders of the peasant organizations described all complemented the ability to rally people against an abusive landowner with the ability to build up and direct a broader organization. Several local peasant communities were brought together not only to face one specific landowner, but the hacienda-system as such, as it functioned in a whole area.

From the experience described above, it is clear that the formation of new groups at the community level, important as it may be, is not enough to break through the traditional system. The Vicos experiment in Peru indicated that one traditional hacienda can be transformed into a democratically led community without having much influence on the traditional system as a whole. Isolated pilot experience, where considerable improvements in the life of the peasants have been introduced or achieved, have existed in many countries, but their only effect lies in some degree of awakening the surrounding peasants to their potential—an increase in organizability as a result of frustration. As such, this does not lead to the effective formation of similar groups and the extension of the pilot experience to a large area.

It is at this critical stage that contact with urban sympathizers who are willing to be allies in the struggle against the traditional and vested rural interests becomes highly important. The linkage of local peasant organizations with a wider framework of mutual or outside support or a combination of both comes out in all examples as a crucial factor in the success of new groups.[g]

As indicated above, Zapata's movement began at the village level and initially integrated only a few communities. It gained momentum as participant in the overall revolutionary struggle and then found several sympathizers (such as the local school teacher and later the lawyer and politician, Díaz Soto y Gama) in the building up of an effective regional organization with some kind of legal basis (the *Plan de Ayala*). The syndicate of Ucureña was in its survival and spread through the area supported by school teachers and former miners. Later, the growing movement was related to political parties working at the national level such as the PIR and MNR. The peasant leagues in the Brazilian northeast were supported by lawyers and other professionals, who gave the organization a regionwide structure. The leagues were specially designed as a centralized body with nuclei in many places in order to increase their effectiveness. The unions of La Convención became influential after forming a federation when they were able to apply for help from urban lawyers and politicians, who helped to create a regional structure. The need for any local peasant organization to join with other similar groups and to form a federation of some kind is a *sine qua non* for gaining influence.

An important advantage of federation of local unions or other community or peasant organizations is that it is a definitive step in the break-up of the tradi-

---

[g]The distinction between allies and enemies of the peasants made by Landsberger is useful in this respect, although it should be emphasized that some enemies present themselves as allies of the peasants until they have a solid control over them. It is unfortunate that Landsberger has purposely given only little attention to the enemies in his framework for the study of peasant movements.[22]

tional social system dominated by the hacienda. The peasants become aware that in other communities in neighboring areas people have the same problems. This psychological factor may help to overcome an initial fear of resisting or breaking with the local system. The importance of forming federations of community organizations cannot be stressed enough.

An additional psychological effect of the broadening of peasant organization beyond the community level is the feeling of power which people get when belonging to a large-scale regional movement. It has been observed in many instances, e.g., at the First Congress of Peasants of Pernambuco, Brazil, and the Indian Congress in La Paz, Bolivia, in 1945, that peasants for the first time in their life get a feeling of power and importance when they have a regional meeting, and march by the hundreds through the streets of an important city to represent their interests and show themselves as a unified body. Mass meetings and parades of this type have an important function during the formation process of a peasant organization; to strengthen the self-esteem of the peasantry and to impress public opinion. Such occurrences helped the peasants overcome the effects of living for ages in the culture of repression.

In this respect, the importance could be observed of having a regional headquarters, which serves as an office and meeting place for the growing organization. Such physical amenities give the organization an identity. The name is written on a plate at the entrance, and any peasant, when coming to the main city of his region where the center is established, can always find peers and comrades from different places representing the same interests. For those who had been living in dependency of only one *patron*, and had the hacienda as their only point of reference, this is an important new experience of widening perspective.

Once a local group sees the need for joining a federation with other groups in similar conditions, the more or less charismatic peasant leader(s) who started the movement can be overshadowed by more sophisticated charismatic leaders or politicians. To some extent, this happened in Ucureña, Bolivia, when José Rojas took the leadership; it occurred very clearly in the peasant leagues of the Brazilian northeast where Juliao became increasingly important and in the peasant federation of La Convención where Hugo Blanco took over. In the movement directed by Zapata in Morelos, Mexico, the initial charismatic leader kept his position through the process of extension of the movement.

The federation can sometimes be seen as a system of different followings of several leaders who have joined together under one charismatic leader at the top. Initially, the presence of one strong personality to hold the movement together seems crucial. Such leadership may exist at the regional and the national level.

In order to prevent the total dependence of cohesion and strength of a large group on one strong leader, and to guarantee effective participation of the membership in the group, it is essential that charismatic leadership—the initially mobilizing factor in a movement—becomes institutionalized. This can occur when the inspiration a leader is able to give is transformed into what has been called party-charisma.[23] The membership starts to feel increasingly that it belongs to an organized and structured movement or a party with a more or less defined ideology, representing their needs. This process was initiated in the peasant leagues of Brazil, but was well on its way in the movement in La Convención, Peru. In Brazil, the leagues started a campaign to create a political organization of a leninist type within the local branches to give cohesion and a more defined structure to the whole movement, just before they were destroyed in April 1964.[24]

In Bolivia, the process of structuring the movement took place after the peasant federation in the area where it originated, Cochabamba, had shown its power. National political leaders, particularly Paz Estenssoro, used the Movimiento Nacional Revolucionario party and its activities to spread the peasant movement into the whole country and to institutionalize it into a national framework related to MNR interests.

The Venezuelan peasant federation was created and built up as a nationwide political structure from the outset, although officially the Federation was founded after local unions and state seccionales had been organized by activists of the Acción Democrática party.

While support from national political and ideological groups can be an asset and help to spread or strengthen a peasant organization, it can also be a source of weakness. Through the alliance with national movements over which they have no control, they can become involved in the political and sometimes ideological rivalries existing at that level. This was clear in the Venezuelan FCV, which purged the relatively radical original leadership in order to bring the federation policies in line with the overall national policies of the Acción Democrática party, increasingly identified with the middle class. The Mexican CNC in particular was transformed into a political clientele of the official middle-class dominated party to control the peasant vote rather than to defend peasant interests.

In the Peasant Leagues in the northeast of Brazil and in the Peasant Federation of La Convención, rivalries among the leaders produced divisions or confusion at the grass roots. Several pamphlets or periodicals published by exponents of the currents within and around the movements show these internal divisions. This was in part a result of ideological differences between leaders over strategy. In the Convención movement, one faction wanted to use a less radical approach than that advocated by Hugo Blanco. In the Ligas Camponeses, the division concerned the structure of the movement. For years, the Leagues expressed themselves mainly through agitation, while some groups internally advocated a tighter political organization, apparently against the wishes of Juliao. These divisions were not only along ideological lines but also a result of rivalry of personalities. Particularly in the case of the Leagues, when during certain stages political groups in power in Pernambuco or the country as a whole needed electoral support of the Leagues, political ambitions became a dividing issue between some of the top leaders.

It is natural that in Latin America the strong tradition of personalism or *caudillism* in politics should be reflected in the peasant organizations when they become a politically important force.

It is probably impossible to break away from the traditional coercive patronage system of the hacienda without passing through a stage where participatory organizations have to wage a difficult struggle not to become paternalistic. The degree of participation which is given to the base in the wider regional organization depends in part on the psychological liabilities of the top leaders. Morale can be strengthened considerably by occasional mass rallies and congresses, but even more by the frequency of local meetings, large enough to be impressive but small enough to give many peasant delegates a chance to participate actively in the deliberations. The more or less authoritarian or democratic social climate created in the organization will be a factor in the strength of participation. Organizations which start as small nuclei from below and spread out little by little with increasing force generally seem to enjoy a more democratic social atmosphere. The initial leaders have particularly strong roots among the base and interact almost constantly with them.

Particularly important in relation with this problem of competition or neutralization is the kind of demands brought forward by the organization and its leaders. While most movements described started by demanding moderate changes and improvements, the opposition of the landlords stimulated radicalization or escalation of the demands. No less than radical change in the overall power and land tenure structure became the main focus of struggle of the peasants in all cases described. In the escalation of the demands the urban supporters of the peasants have given considerable guidance. It seems that the movements derived part of their cohesion and strength from the overwhelming importance of the demand for land, rather than minor benefits. Peasant organizations which only focused on wage increases or similar adjustments in the status quo were easily liable to decay or were outstripped by more radical organizations. The first was the case in the vineyard workers movement led by Christian-Democratic politicians in La Molina, Chile, described by Landsberger[25] and the second possibility was visible in the church-sponsored unions in Pernambuco before 1964.

It seems that clear-cut, radical demands for land distribution or restitution, and leadership which in a rather uncompromising way leads the peasants in the struggle for these demands, ensures a strong cohesion in the organization and active participation of the peasants. The movements led by Zapata in Mexico, Hugo Blanco in La Convención, José Rojas in Ucureña, Jacinto López in the northwestern development area of Mexico and the 1958-1960 period of the FCV in Venezuela are cases in point. Simple slogans such as "Land and Freedom" ("Tierra y Libertad") or "Land or Death" ("Tierra o Muerte") rallied peasants into large-scale organized activities. This is no guarantee, however, that effective political peasant participation will continue after this main demand has been fulfilled, or is in the course of being fulfilled. This problem will be dealt with in the next section, which shows how peasant organizations developed strongly during the height of the struggle for land reform, but soon after success could be partly or wholly neutralized.

Once peasant movements become part of nationwide political institutions, the democratic and participatory atmosphere may continue at the local level (as in Bolivia) or suffer decline (as in Mexico), but is generally not extended to the national level.

The Demand for Land and Appropriate Means of Struggle

As is evident from almost examples and cases known in Latin America, the political role of peasant organizations in the struggle for land has generally not been very orderly, but often took a spontaneous and at times a violent form. Only after agrarian reform in some countries was well under way could peasant participation be channelled through newly created institutions, such as trade unions or political organizations. This is a direct result of the lawlessness and culture of repression prevailing in the rural areas and the severe obstacles created by the opposition of traditional vested interests to orderly and institutionalized, but dynamic reform of the land tenure structure.

It has been this resistance to change of the landed elite and its influence in the national governments which directly or indirectly provoked the drastic or even violent forms in which the peasantry acted often with guidance or leadership from urban groups. This is most obvious from the case of Mexico, where the first agrarian legislation (of 1915) was a result of a strong peasant reaction to evictions and abuses which was expressed in a violent revolutionary movement. Later, this legislation could only be applied because of the determined resistance of the peasantry in various regions of the country against the violent measures taken by landowners to block its application. Also, the Bolivian reform was inconceivable without the strongly organized pressure of the peasants in the Cochabamba area. In Venezuela, the pressure by the Federación Campesina de Venezuela, particularly the many peaceful land invasions after the fall of the Pérez Jiménez regime in 1958, were crucial to agrarian reform.

The examples of Mexico and Bolivia, countries which had a more or less sweeping land reform, indicate that such reforms come about only through a considerable transformation of society as a whole and particularly of the rural sector. In general terms, the position is stated below.

At this stage of events in Latin America, one seems faced with the dilemma that land reform, when seriously undertaken, is an explosive and unpredictable business, but may be much more explosive when left undone. It will be argued that rural tensions are likely to intensify as conditions of income and social justice continue to stagnate or to decline while the perception of the possibility of change increases. An attempt will be made to show that a certain amount of violence, unrest, and disorder is unavoidable and even necessary for successful reform measures, the initiation of which is likely to create further disturbing or unsettling elements.[26]

In those countries which have hesitantly initiated agrarian reform, the same explosive forces are at work which operated in the countries which have an effective program. It will be important to know what kind of disorder or unrest is unavoidable and how these different forces can be most effectively used. In this respect, it is particularly important to discuss the form of direct action by peasants through which agrarian reform legislation and its implementation has been achieved or accelerated. Forms of direct action and pressure were employed by peasant groups after they encountered insurmountable obstacles in presenting their demands through the normal legal channels. When dealing with the radical action methods used by peasants, it cannot be stressed enough that in all the examples studied these means were used only after the legal and institutionalized channels of problem solution had been consistently blocked because of intransigent landlord opposition.

Among the forms of direct pressure which the peasants exercised were sit-down strikes and occupations of unused land and those lands which the peasant petitioned for, or which were in dispute. These activities or even more drastic ones, such as armed revolt, were the only ways open to the peasants to pressure for reform. The cases described above give overwhelming evidence that practically all agrarian reform activity in Latin America, until today, is the direct or indirect result of such activities.

In some cases, such as Mexico in the Cárdenas period, Bolivia after 1952 and Venezuela after 1958, these organizational activities were supported, stimulated or tolerated by the government and/or the political party in power in spite of the fact that a certain amount of chaos sometimes resulted from this policy. This happened in Bolivia in 1952-1953, and was related to the fact that the reform efforts started there after six years of severe repression (1946-1952). A return to that situation was threatening as the landlords attempted to overthrow the reformist government. There was also organized direct action of peasants in Venezuela in 1958-1960 under somewhat similar conditions after ten years of repression (1948-1958). The land invasions were ostensibly disapproved but tacitly tolerated by the authorities; as the reform process got under way, they could be channelled and directed.

A careful study of the various forms of direct action taken by peasants to bring across their demands for agrarian reform measures points to some important factors. Most cases show a process of escalating demands. Land reform as such often became an issue after other, less drastic, demands had met with the intransigence of the landed elite. The escalation of the demands was generally accompanied by an escalation of the means used to pressure for those demands.

Initial demands often included abolition of practices which interfered with basic—and often constitutionally established—civil rights, such as personal freedom. Others concerned the recognition of traditional property rights, security of tenure or the compensation for improvements made if tenancy of a certain plot had to be given up. Most had a firm legal basis, but the law was, at the local and at times at the national level, either ignored or interpreted in favor of the landlords who had the power.

The peasants appear to be overly legalistic in their approach. As we saw, initially, the means used to present demands were always moderate: petitions, lawsuits, and complaints to the labor inspector. Since relief through these legally established channels was generally not obtained, wherever peasants had some organizing experience or could count on support from people with such experience, other means were tried, but only after the legal approach insistently proved fruitless. Examples are the years of legal struggle of the peasant communities headed by Zapata, before they joined the Revolution; the petitions for land and the legal struggle for the UGOCM in the Northwestern states of Mexico around 1957 concerning lands which were held by large owners in circumvention of the law; the legal arrangements achieved by the first peasant union in Ucureña in Bolivia in 1936, undone by the landlords in 1939; the year-long struggle in the court of Recife by the first Brazilian peasant league to avoid the illegal dislodgment of peasants from the plots that they had occupied for years. These are all cases in point that testify to the peasants' respect for legal and orderly means. To have existing laws respected, rather than overruled by the intransigent landlords, was often the basic issue around which peasants started to become active. Whether a growing peasant organization initiated its activities with a struggle for civil rights against illegal practices of the landlords, or for economic improvements, or for agrarian reform depended on the local situation. To start with issues which had the best chances of being successfully solved seemed sound strategy in the period when leaders and followers of an organization were gaining self-confidence.

The escalation of demands and of means used to pressure for them, appeared generally to have been a reaction to the uncompromising attitude of the landlords. If moderate demands and forms of pressure were completely ignored or even ridiculed by those in power, more radical forms were tried. More recently, having learned from past experiences, peasant organizations have begun to use the escalation of demands as a conscious strategy to achieve significant social reforms.

Agrarian reform has been among the main objectives of most peasant movements from their beginning. In some cases, this idea came up among the more alert peasant leaders—generally where peasants had been despoiled of their ancestral lands. In other cases, the idea of radical reforms was introduced by urban leaders and supporters of a peasant movement such as Hugo Blanco in Peru or Francisco Juliao in Brazil. Seeing that a radical agrarian reform was the only solution for the existing rural inequities, but that the majority of the peasants had not yet realized it, these leaders tried to create awareness of this need, this was done not only through *concientización*, teaching the explaining the social implications of rural underdevelopment, but also through the struggle itself. By showing time after time that the landlords would not grant moderate, legally guaranteed demands and civil rights, it was easily demonstrated to the peasants that only radical changes in the rural power structure could lead to fulfillment of their demands and redress of their grievances.

This escalation of awareness through struggle for civil rights and other basic needs has had in some cases considerable success. It had the additional advantage that the peasants learned gradually to overcome their traditional fear of opposing the rural elite; they started facing this opposition on issues where justice and common sense was so overwhelmingly on their side that they felt they could take the risk. These were also the issues where the attitude of the landlords was most flagrantly in conflict with law and order, and the landlords' refusal to give in to legitimate demands diminished their traditional prestige in the eyes of their workers and of public opinion.

In many areas, peasants had never contemplated the possibility of using means more radical than a petition or an appeal to justice. Radical means had not been tried consistently and their uselessness was almost accepted as a fact of life. Once it was demonstrated that following through on a case with dedicated legal help made the landlords uneasy and intransigent, the use of more radical means appeared to be feasible.

One of the means which in most countries fall well within the established legal framework is the strike. This usually consists of refusal to work at critical moments of the agricultural cycle after all demands had been bluntly refused.

The use of strikes is usually considered a more or less legitimate form of struggle. Where the peasants have become acquainted with the labor struggle, such as in areas of Peru and Bolivia where peasants work during certain periods of their life in the mines, the approach taken by labor organizations as a legitimate form of struggle had an impact on the organizations of the peasantry. It is generally recognized that in Latin America political bargaining rather than collective bargaining is the major instrument used by labor to achieve its economic and social demands. This tendency has been explained in the following terms. 1. The general economic weakness of the (labor) movement; and 2. the general weaknesses of the political and legal structure of Latin America. It was noted in this respect: "Legislative enactment has proved largely ineffective as a means of achieving trade union goals in Latin America, mainly because of inadequate administrative enforcement and/or insufficient financial resources."[27] For that reason, political action of some kind by the workers is needed to make collective bargaining and legal enactment meaningful. It was affirmed that under the political bargaining system, the success of labor is directly correlated with the amount of pressure which it can bring to bear at either the government or the party level.[28]

A study of the political bargaining process,[29] taking Peru as an example, in-dicated that this tactic works particularly well in a climate where the executive has an insecure position in the face of civilian opposition and violence.[h]

The basic dimensions of the system are unequivocally those of political bargain-ing. The workers employ tactics directed toward agitation and violence. The ex-ecutive is their target. And he responds in terms of this threat to his survival. In Peru, labor's primary weapon is neither votes nor economic pressure. It is is abil-ity to threaten an insecure executive with extinction.[31]

All kinds of manifestations, demonstrations, and even the use of noninstitu-tionalized violence are indicated as appropriate means to show political bargain-ing power.[i]

While the Latin American political process is becoming more complex, and such acts of civic disruption and violence are growing more serious and threatening in intent, in the classic pattern of Latin American political life, such techniques of demonstrating a power capability seem generally accepted as appropriate to the political system. Thus, when such techniques as manifestations, strike, and even violence are used symbolically, that is as the demonstration and not the use of a power capability, there would seem an a priori case that the appropriate re-sponse of government leaders should be conciliation and bargaining.[33]

Peasant strikes should also be seen in this light.

An important type of peasant strike is to refuse to provide free labor service to the landlord—obligations which are outlawed, but not eradicated in most countries. In Bolivia between 1939 and 1952, the peasants frequently went on sitdown strikes *(huelgas de brazos caídos)* against the landowners of varying lengths of time and sometimes for years. This nonviolent means of action con-trasted with the spontaneous and violent outbursts of protest that occurred fre-quently before in Bolivia.[j] A great number of complaints by the landowners in the press and to the authorities about these strikes indicated their effectiveness.

It seems that the violence potential of the peasants' direct action method is far less important than it is in the labor movement. In the peasants' *huelga de brazos caídos* (sitdown strike), the disadvantages are not on the side of the peas-

---

[h]Almond and Powell wrote of James Payne's book: "This work may be a landmark in the reassessment of the more ethnocentric views of possible roles of violence long held by West-ern political scientists."[30]

[i]Needler used the term "representational violence" to describe the role which can, and ap-parently has to be, played by the threat of violence expressed mainly in symbolic activities in order to articulate interests of groups who have no or little or no institutionalized repre-sentative way to do this.[32]

[j]"The actual demonstration of violence must occur from time to time in order to give credibility to its threatened outbreak, thereby gaining efficacy for the threat as an instru-ment of social and political change."[34]

ants but rather on the side of their opponents. The peasants have more time to work their subsistence plot. There is no danger for damage to anyone's goods or life involved, as there is in a street demonstration where shopkeepers or the city traffic can suffer damage whether intentionally or not.

A form of political bargaining used by the peasants more frequently than the sitdown strikes are the peaceful occupations or invasions of unused or underutilized lands belonging to large estates. Many of the agrarian reform efforts carried out in Latin America are direct or indirect result of this form of political bargaining. However, a great deal of misunderstanding exists about this approach.

Some observers believe that radical actions such as land seizures undermine the present system as part of an effort to destroy it.[35] It seems, that in most cases the present system is undermining itself, because of its lack of flexibility and refusal to consider legitimate peasant demands. The peasants in most countries seem to be relatively conservative in the sense that they do not easily embark upon new experiments which imply risks. However, they have to face such extreme conservatism and rigidity among the rural elite that they have no other alternative than to make their demands known through spectacular action.

Violence is one means by which the victims of a problem are able to bring that problem forcibly to the decisionmaker's attention. Thus, a peasant 'invasion' of unoccupied but privately owned lands may do much to stimulate consideration of the total problem of agrarian reform.[36]

... for a peasant movement, constantly seeking representational access to decisionmakers, and having exhausted procedural remedies, to occupy unused lands, held in private property only for purposes of speculation, may be a most suitable political tactic. This is particularly true where a strong legal presumption in favor of the 'social function' of property exists.[37]

The cases described above show that some form of actual or potential violence has in the past been the most important reason for governments to seriously consider and promulgate agrarian reform laws. It would be a mistake, however, to consider all peasant invasions as acts of violence. On the contrary, most acts of violence related to the agrarian reform issue have come from the landlords and violent action by the peasants has generally come as a reaction to the landlords' actions. The peasant guerrillas of Zapata, the rural defense units organized among the peasants by President Cárdenas in the late thirties in Mexico, the forceful take-over of estates, and the driving out of the most abusive landlords in the initial stage of agrarian revolution in Bolivia were reactions against landlord violence.

On the other hand, most occupations of unused lands have been of a nonviolent and at times explicitly peaceful nature. In cases where peasants occupied privately owned but unused land, the action could often be interpreted as a form of civil disobedience, an accepted form of nonviolent pressure.[k]

When governments are ill-informed of local conditions (or obdurate in the face of evidence) and legal channels are not equally open to all for redress of grievance, groups which see themselves as deprived may resort to civil disobedience thus making it impossible for their demands to be ignored. . . . Governments may respond by repression but if public opinion can be sufficiently mobilized for the cause of the disadvantaged, governments must—at the very least—attempt ameliorative projects.[38]

When considering the invasions as an appropriate means of struggle for the peasants, students must examine the problem of legitimacy of landed property. The CIDA study on Peru indicated that under invasions was understood the factual occupation of land in the hands of the haciendas by dispossessed peasants.[39] The CIDA report noted that the peasants did not see such invasions as illegitimate because they considered them as a recovery of lands which had been taken away from them illegally. Many of the lands occupied had been for years in litigation, but were factually occupied by the large landholders in the meantime, often under very extensive use, while peasants lived on surrounding, overcrowded mountain slopes. A definition of invasions given by a Colombian labor leader was: occupation of lands by more or less large groups of peasants who want to cultivate immediately the ground which they did not possess before.[40]

These two definitions indicate the implications of the invasions which vary from region to region. It seems that the invasions in many cases were an expression of the peasants' attachment to legality rather than an indication for subversion of the existing order. In many cases in Peru, peasants reasoned that the manner in which their traditional claims were honored benefited only the large landholder in forms which they considered illegitimate. In an attitude research among peasants in one area in Colombia, it emerged that the occupation of idle or underutilized land for agricultural exploitation was generally viewed not as an illegitimate act but as a possible activity for peasant unions.[41]

From the peasants' point of view, there appears to be a sound logic in the occupation and effective use of idle or underused lands. This is particularly so if they have been illegally despoiled as happened in many cases. It seems that in most cases where invasions have taken place, they were rather a constructive nonviolent reaction to violence, such as despoliation and efforts to assassinate

---

[k]The idea of civil disobedience was introduced by Henry David Thoreau in the middle of the last century in the United States in relation with the American war with Mexico and the abolition of slavery. Civil disobedience became a widely applied strategy for change in the struggle for independence from colonial rule, particularly in India, partly as a consequence of the teachings and activities of Gandhi.

leaders. Rather than taking vengeance on the landlord or destroy his goods, the peasants occupied unused or underused lands and brought them under cultivation.

Guatemala (1952-1954) seems to be the only country which in its reform program strongly emphasized the need to bring into use accessible but idle lands of private property. Expropriation by decree was generally followed rapidly by the occupation by peasants of the affected lands. Bolivia appears to be the only case where the government has encouraged the peasants to occupy lands of the privately owned estates which did not fulfill their social function (because they were exploited through servitude and similar unconstitutional systems).

In other countries, even if the lack of social function of private lands was recognized as a problem, occupation of such land by peasants was officially condemned. In Venezuela, the government officially took position against the invasions of estates which were not efficiently cultivated or which had been alienated from the peasants by illegal means, but the invasions were encouraged by the peasants' unions belonging to the government party. Most of the invaded estates in Venezuela were later purchased from the landlords and distributed among the peasants under the agrarian reform program. As was noted before, in Peru where return of formerly usurped land or distribution of estate land was promised to the peasants during election campaigns, a special clause was included in the 1964 agrarian reform law indicating that lands which had been invaded would not be considered for official land distribution. In fact, however, invasions were initially tolerated and several invaded estates were distributed among the peasants.

Hirschman called the land occupation approach a "direct problem-solving activity," and noted the following regarding Colombia.

For the past hundred years, peasants have occupied and are still occupying today lands that are not theirs. Sometimes they have used force and force has occasionally been used against them by those who claim ownership. But eventually, forcible appropriation of large areas has been sanctioned by the state through *ad hoc* intervention or general legislation. Thus, the willingness of the peasants to occupy uncultivated lands—a kind of entrepreneurial spirit—has powerfully contributed to reform legislation. Without the past experience of mass squatting and the threat of more to come, neither Law 200 of 1936 nor the land reform of 1961 would ever have been passed by the Congress.[42]

It should be noted that Hirschman does not make a clear distinction between peaceful occupation or bringing into cultivation of unused or underused lands, and acts of violence.

Thus the violence that is compatible with reform and frequently appears to be part and parcel of it is not the kind of decisive clash—force meets force in the principal square of the capital—which is usually associated with revolutionary violence. Rather it is a violence akin to guerrilla warfare, with the ability of the groups practicing it to now advance, now retreat, now lie low and now come forward with a new thrust.[43]

How seriously the legitimacy of private land property is taken by the peasant depends a great deal on how seriously it is taken by those who have the power to interpret and execute the laws. Coser noted

Whether feelings of hostility lead to conflict behavior depends in part on whether or not the unequal distribution of rights is considered legitimate. In the classical Indian caste system, intercaste conflict was rare because lower and higher castes alike accepted the caste distinctions. Legitimacy is a crucial intervening variable without which it is impossible to predict whether feelings of hostility arising out of an unequal distribution of privileges and rights will actually lead to conflict. Before a conflict between negatively and positively privileged groups can take place, before hostile attitudes are turned into social action, the negatively privileged group must first develop the awareness that it is, indeed, negatively privileged. It must come to believe that it is being denied rights to which it is entitled. It must reject any justification for the existing distribution of rights and privileges.[44]

Related to the problem of legitimacy is the question of payment. In Mexico, Bolivia, Cuba and Venezuela, the only countries with a more or less considerable agrarian reform at present, the peasants generally did not have to pay for the land they received. In Mexico and Bolivia, reimbursement to former owners was done by the government and was rather symbolic, although in some cases where it concerned a foreign estate, such as Cananea cattle estate in Mexico (in 1958), this could be a considerable amount.

It should be noted that it was a result of the nationwide organized peasant pressure during the crucial reform period in Mexico and Bolivia that the problem of payment for the expropriated lands was solved relatively easily. According to the law, agrarian debt bonds were issued. As value of the land was taken the amount that had been declared for tax purposes. The expropriated landlords were generally resigned to these measures once the law was enforced after their opposition had been broken. Until 1959 in Mexico, claims for only 220,000 hectares of expropriated land were made by former landowners.[45] Although the expropriation of foreign-owned estates was more complicated, even in those cases landlord pressure was limited. Between 1938 and 1955, 12.5 million dollars were paid as reimbursement for approximately 2 million hectares of foreign owned land.[46] In Bolivia, the Mexican example was followed and very little was paid to the former landowners. In Venezuela, the peasants did not have to pay but the landowners were rather lavishly reimbursed by the government.

Also in countries where land reform was carried out in specific areas or communities because only there had radical peasant actions such as land invasions occurred (while elsewhere in the country there had been no active peasant pressure), relatively high reimbursement was given to the landlords. This happened for example with the Algolan estate in Peru[47] after it had been occupied by the *comuneros* of the area. ("El negociado de Algolan," denounced this reimbursement as a national financial scandal.)[48] This could be done because the reform measures remained limited to relatively small areas. In most countries where peasant pressure has as yet not reached national proportions, reform laws include regulations for reimbursement that are so favorable to the landlord class that the law cannot be implemented on a large scale. In cases where the peasants were required to pay the reimbursement for the land in installments, new tensions arose.

It is clear that when militant peasant organizations have been temporarily contented by land distribution, the issue of payment for this land can be used to mobilize the peasants again. This happened in La Convención where peasants refused to pay for lands they claimed, occupied and believed to have paid for in many years of servitude. The problem of foreign ownership of land is important in this context. In some situations, such as Mexico under the Cárdenas regime, it seemed feasible and even advisable to expropriate foreign properties first, so as to neutralize local landlord opposition to some extent, while at the same time giving a nationalistic flavor to the whole reform program. Elsewhere, however, such as in Guatemala in 1952-1954, the expropriation of unused lands of the United Fruit Company and reimbursement over its delcared tax value provoked international intervention with the reform-oriented government. In Bolivia, few foreign landed properties existed and it seems that in most Latin American countries only some of the modernized plantations are foreign owned. With exception of Cuba and other Caribbean and Central American banana republics or sugar countries, the latifundia-minifundia problem is a national problem. This may change in some countries, such as Brazil where recently foreign interests have bought at a nominal price immense extensions of virgin land.

The problem of legitimacy of landed property should be seen in its historical context. Traditional titles continue to be respected by indigenous peasants in spite of their hopeless efforts to get them honored in the courts. Many *comunidades* in Latin America keep title documents that date from the colonial epoch. It was noted that in Guatemala in several municipalities with a predominant indigenous population, the Indians conserve with care and ceremony the municipal titles which they inherited from their forefathers. There is evidence that these officially invalid titles are more recognized than the titles of private property that have been issued some way or another since the end of the last century.[49]

Although most countries have adopted legislation, either as part of the agrarian reform law, or independently, regarding the traditional property rights of original *comunidades*, in practice not much has been done to return to those comunidades the status and dignity to which they feel they are entitled. The fact that existing laws in this respect are only slowly executed—if executed at all—has been identified as a main reason for the existence among *comuneros* of distrust in any government intervention or doubts regarding the legitimacy of the present rules of the game. Considerable feeling of injustice prevails in such areas.[50]

Anyway, in the cases of land invasions where property rights are in dispute or where the law or the constitution does not protect privately owned lands which do not fulfill their social function, occupations by peasants cannot be seen as acts of disobedience. In spite of this in many countries, the press, often related to or influenced by the landlords, denounces such activities as violence or violations of the law. On occasions where such acts take place, violence can sometimes occur because alarming publicity stimulates police or army intervention to be more drastic than necessary under the circumstances.

In order to analyze such cases, a clear concept of what is understood by the term violence is important. The social sciences have paid relatively little attention to this subject as yet. Gurr's recent working definition for civil violence reads

All collective, nongovernmental attacks on persons or property, resulting in intentional damage to them, that occur within the boundaries of an autonomous or colonial political unit.[51]

He also noted

Until recently, many political scientists tended to regard violent civil conflict as a disfigurement of the body politic, neither a significant nor a proper topic for their empirical inquiries. The attitude was in part our legacy from Thomas Hobbes' contention that violence is the negation of political order, a subject fit less for study than for admonition. Moreover, neither the legalistic nor the institutional approaches that dominated traditional political science could provide such insight into group action that was regarded by definition as illegal and the antithesis of institutionalized political life.[52]

Using this definition when idle lands are peacefully occupied by landless peasants and brought under cultivation, we may note that there is no question of intentional damage, and the term "violence" does not apply. On the other hand, the eviction of squatters from formerly unused lands which they have cleared and cultivated for years, often falls under the category of civil violence. One frequently used method of dislodging peasants is burning their houses. This is intentional damage, and thus falls under the definition of civil violence.

According to this definition of civil violence, it becomes obvious from almost all the cases of successful peasant movements, that violence, i.e., intentional destruction of life or property, has been used by only a few of them. Except for the Mexican Revolution (the Zapata movement and other peasant struggles related to that event) and the initial stages of the Bolivian agrarian revolution, most of the violence in the agrarian struggles came from the landlords. The proverbial attachment of the peasants to security, order and lawfulness explains that there were no more acts of vengeance and violence than sporadically occurred. This seems surprising in the light of the fact that the peasantry in many parts of Latin America lived permanently as victims of lawlessness, institutionalized violence and abusive behavior of the landlords.

There is considerable evidence from the known cases that where the peasants were given institutionalized opportunities to bring about a radical change in the rural power structure, they used these opportunities with moderation and with respect for those who were to lose their privileged position rather than with vengeance. The best example is the Bolivian agrarian reform, which was the most drastic. Although for many years in the preliminary struggle, numbers of peasant leaders had been assassinated, once the power relationships had changed, the lives, and, in most instances, the personal property of the landlords were respected. Only where the landlords themselves engaged in violent opposition were their lives endangered. No cases are known (but some cases probably did occur) where landlords were persecuted for their former abuses or crimes after the power relationships had changed. Generally, the peasants felt that having been given land was enough. In the most radicalized areas, they merely refused to let the abusive landlords return to their former estates. In some of these cases, peasant leaders visited the former landlords in their town houses in order to make deals or arrangements related to the transfer of land. Some landlords even received payments or contributions from their former subjects without this being necessary according to the law. There was no call for popular justice or anything similar, although landlords in some areas feared this.[1] This fear, however, was probably more a result of the landlords' bad conscience than of their understanding of the peasants' attitudes.

There is some evidence that the violent resistance of the landlords to moderate peasant demands is related to their irrational fear of the peasants' vengeance once they would be free of their bondages. The saying of not giving a finger, because then they take the whole hand, is a conscious and openly expressed element in the approach of the rural elite in many cases.

When comparing the various movements in which strikes or land occupations of some kind had an important role, it is apparent that most of them were limited to specific geographic regions. The most successful movements did not take place spontaneously in one community, but rather were carried out in a coordinated way in a whole region, such as the upper Cochambamba valley in Bolivia, the Convención valley in Peru, the state of Morelos and the northwestern development area in Mexico, and some of the densely populated states

---

[1]Only in the earliest period of the Mexican agrarian revolution in the beginning of the century did cases of vengeance on the landlords by the peasants occur, as was noted by MacLean y Estenos:
"The destruction, the pillage, the burning and devastation of the large farms, was a punishment which spontaneous and untenable popular justice imposed upon the abuses and crimes of the large landowners. A horrible warning which should be benefited from by those who still maintain an agrarian system of latifundios, similar to the conditions in Mexico before 1910."[53]

of Venezuela. In some of those regions, the movements were more intense, and more successful than in others, but generally, they had a sufficient geographic concentration to give the peasants the feeling that their region was on the move, and that their efforts were not just scattered and uncoordinated protest actions. This explains the relative success in most of these regions of such efforts as were made to mobilize the peasants for development after land reform had been carried out. Specifically, in some areas of Mexico in the Cárdenas period and in the Convención valley, this was the case. But as a rule, peasant mobilization was not utilized to bring about a really sustained regional development.

On the whole, it seems that the means used by the peasants were generally such that, with a minimum of extralegality, a maximum of concrete benefits or security could be achieved, mainly the possession of the land which they tilled. As soon as the peasants' demands were satisfied, and the land they worked was in their possession, in most cases, they lost interest in the political movement as a whole. Hugo Blanco declared on various occasions after his movement had been calmed through military action and land distribution, that he was disappointed in the revolutionary spirit of the peasants.[54] The peasants of the Galileia estate in Pernambuco, Brazil, are another case in point. It seems, however, that the landlords have so much fear for change that they take a stand which provokes the peasantry to use increasingly radical means. Thus, the peasant movement became in some cases a revolutionary factor in the society as a whole, in spite of the originally limited demands and the moderate attitude of the peasants. In those areas, where the peasants took to radical forms of action, their civil violence occurred generally as a direct response to landlord intransigence and violence, and because no other ways were open to them.

Only where full citizen rights have been conquered by all significant strata of the population, that is, only where there exist open channels of political communication through which all groups can articulate their demands, are the chances high that political exercise of violence can be successfully minimized. Where this is not the case the political use of violence is a recurring potentiality. Where political structures are incapable of accommodating all political demands there is an ever-present chance that violence will be resorted to by those who feel that they cannot get their voice heard, as well as by those who have vested interests in suppressing this voice.[55]

7

Summing Up of Political Implications: An Increasing Revolutionary Potential?

The whole issue of escalation of peasant demands as a reaction to landlord intransigence clearly demonstrates that peasants are not revolutionaries by birth, but neither are they the passive victims of traditional or modern forms of patronage. They let themselves be repressed, exploited and utilized, but the frustration which results brings an increasing awareness that other ways are open to them. In the present chapter, an effort will be made to show that the culture of repression in Latin America seems to become increasingly felt by the peasants as illegitimate and out of harmony with other possibilities that modernizing societies seem to offer. Peasants have had a variety of experiences which have promoted their awareness of possibilities for change. In some cases, peasant groups that have tried to overcome the effects of acute frustrations were halted in their spread or repressed (in the Convención valley in Peru and the Northeast of Brazil). It seems that in such cases, conditions for more radical movements are being created. Elsewhere, movements growing from below gained sufficient "power capability" to achieve important benefits and an institutionalized role on the national political scene. This happened in Mexico and Bolivia (after 1952), but particularly in Mexico, the influence of the organized peasantry was later neutralized by cooptation and integration in a dependent political patronage system. Only in Cuba, it seems that the peasantry has achieved or been given an active share in the national development effort and its benefits. In some countries, more or less populist or reform-oriented governments have at times made their appearance and have contributed to an awakening of the peasants. The latter were allowed or even stimulated to organize from above, as happened in Venezuela, Guatemala (before 1954) and Brazil (1963-1964), but as soon as the possibility for effective change grew, these populist governments were overthrown by conservative forces. This was possible because there was no strongly organized peasantry to defend the government, as happened at times in Mexico, Bolivia and Cuba. The period of repression that followed in these cases seems, however, to be a main condition for a radicalization of the peasants who will probably come into action at a later stage more strongly than ever (as occurred in Venezuela in 1958 after the repressive military government was overthrown). The various ways in which the peasantry of Latin America experiences frustration may well make them increasingly willing to participate in radical or revolutionary movements as happened in some past cases. Whether this revolutionary potential will be utilized depends on the extent to which urban allies will be prepared to support and guide such movements effectively.

179

The Culture of Repression and
Illegitimacy

At present, even the peasants in remote areas get an idea of political forces at the national level through the modern means of mass communication. This factor counted little in the past, when only such events as the Chaco War (Bolivia, 1933-1936), or la Violencia (Colombia, 1948-1958) shook up the peasant society sufficiently to create awareness regarding national political forces and conflicts. In areas where repression has been severe and where not only the local government and police, but also the national government through the army has taken a position against the peasants, awareness sometimes takes the form of resentment, if not hatred. Precisely in countries such as El Salvador, where repression has been extremely severe (the genocide of between 20,000 and 30,000 people in the early thirties) a constant semimilitary control over the rural areas has to be maintained in order to prevent the hatred from becoming overt aggression.

Also in areas where repression is less acute and obvious, the more subtle forms of the culture of repression are increasingly felt as such. Peasants learn about elections and popular participation, but serious doubts and distrust remain. In this respect, it seems important to take into account an observation by Charles Anderson.

A frequent point of departure for analysis of Latin American politics is to note that in this region there is imperfect consensus on the nature of the political regime, that the legitimacy of the formal political order is weak.[1]

Most regimes seem to be distrusted because they are repressive. Horowitz defined:

... legitimacy is the perception of the State as a service agency rather than an oppressive mechanism, and ... this perception is cemented by a common adhesion to either legality or mass mobilization. The norm of illegitimacy, on the contrary, is the perception of the State as primarily a power agency, which is cemented by a common reliance on illegal means to rotate either the holders of power or the rules under which power is exercised.[2]

Particularly when a regime, felt as repressive and thus illegitimate, breaks down, the peasants easily seem to take the law into their own hands and give up their on the whole, overly legalistic attitude. Once the lid is off, the peasants defend their interests by means uncontrollable even by their own organization leaders.

This happened to a large extent in Bolivia after the years of repression during 1946-52 and in Venezuela to some extent after 1958, when the repression climate suddenly disappeared for reasons which were not directly influenced by the peasants. In such cases, among the peasants who felt repression most acutely, those who had in earlier periods enjoyed some improvement or had justified expectations were the first to take action (not those who had always been repressed in a more or less constant way under the traditional system). The relatively more prosperous and developing areas of Cochabamba in Bolivia and the states of Aragua and Carabobo in Venezuela became the scenes of spontaneous radical peasant action.[a]

From the several cases studied, one could indicate three forms of frustration or repression which have led to radical peasant movements.

1. One is the intervention of the landlords which provokes the acute deterioration of a traditionally existing situation. The violent extension of sugar plantations at the cost of the traditional indigenous *comunidades* in the state of Morelos in Mexico in the later part of the last century is one example.
2. The second is the introduction of possibilities for considerable improvement, while for the majority of the peasants, the situation remains the same, worsens or improves very little. This was the case with the introduction of huge irrigation schemes in the northwestern development area of Mexico that benefited only the agricultural entrepreneurs and not the landless peasants who had legal claims to irrigated lands.
3. The third possibility is the achievement of improvements by the peasants in their economic or social conditions which suddenly become abruptly blocked and reversed. This was the case in the Convención valley in Peru, in the Galileia estate in the Northeast of Brazil, in some coffee-growing areas of Colombia such as Viotá, in Ucureña where the first Bolivian peasant syndicate was founded, and the densely populated areas of Venezuela before and during the Pérez Jimenez regime.

These three possibilities are shown graphically in Figure 7-1:

The success, or failure, of such radical movements at the national political level depends on several factors that will be dealt with briefly. Some of these movements were so limited in their impact that they could be considered as unsuccessful as a national political force. They grew as a protest against frustration but did not have enough impact to provoke changes in the overall political system because of repression or other limiting factors.

The peasant federation in the Convencion valley in Peru was neutralized partly by ceding to its demands and partly by severe measures of repression. The purpose of the movement, to bring about radical change at the national level, was not achieved. This may be because the most spectacular show of power

---

[a]This seems to be in conformity with the observations of de Tocqueville regarding the French revolution; he indicated that peasant movements were strongest in the areas that had undergone improvements but where discontent was strong as a result of frustrated expectations and relative deprivation.[3]

Figure 7-1
Ways in Which Peasant Frustration Occurs

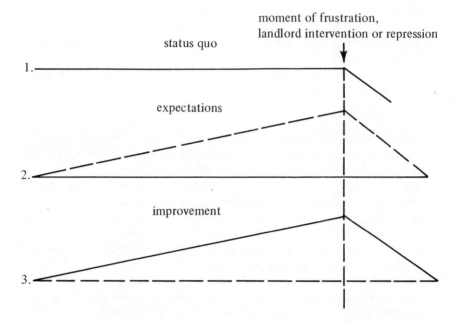

capability, the climax of a systematic campaign to escalate peasant action, came at a moment when the peasantry in other areas of the country was not yet prepared to take over and spread the movement. The action in the Convención area was premature and could be limited by government action (a localized land reform and military intervention).[4] The land reform agency, Oficina Nacional de Reforma Agraria (ONRA) immediately tried to transform the highly participatory following of Blanco into a clientele dependent on the flow of government benefits. Coffee growers cooperatives were organized and an effort was made to stimulate cooperative leadership which was not identical with the leadership of the militant unions, a large part of which was imprisoned. This government effort was only moderately successful. Later, when new problems and grievances arose, for example, the drop in coffee prices which meant losses to the peasant cooperatives, the old militant leaders were able to reestablish considerable influence. Protest demonstrations and mass meetings were organized about this issue in the capital of the valley, Quillabamba. One of the demands was to free Hugo Blanco from jail.[5]

The growing bargaining power of the Ligas Camponeses in the northeast of Brazil provoked the neutralizing efforts by more establishment oriented unions created by the Church and later by the populist government. When these unions, partly under influence of the activities of leaders or former leaders of the Ligas, became more and more radical, the whole system of new organizations was destroyed after a *coup d'état* in 1964. Only a skeleton of the former unions and federations was left, which did not even serve as a dependent patronage system to the peasants.[b]

Neutralization or Mobilization:
Mexico, Bolivia and Cuba

The effects of the more successful radical peasant movements were generally limited, in the end, after a new, middle-sector elite had established itself in power with peasant support. Anderson noted the following about this subject.

New contenders are admitted to the political system when they fulfill two conditions in the eyes of existing power contenders. First, they must demonstrate possession of a power capability sufficient to pose a threat to existing contenders. Second, they must be perceived by other contenders as willing to abide by the rules of the game, to permit existing contenders to continue to exist and operate in the political system.[7]

Some peasant movements had sufficient power capability to be able to gain considerable influence at the national level. Some peasant organizations were enabled by reformist governments to demonstrate their power capability in an institutionalized way either because peasant support was needed by such a government to remain in power, or because the peasants had already, through their "political bargaining" methods, shown to have so much "power capability" that they could threaten the whole system, if they would not be satisfied. Mexico, particularly in the Cárdenas period (1934-1940), and Bolivia around 1953 were cases where peasants were allowed to organize and were provided with the means of power to protect themselves against the violence of the landowners.

In Mexico, where the *de facto* reform in most cases came years after the legal arrangements were worked out for the transfer of property, the landlords had every chance to boycott the legal procedure and at the same time use a great variety of violent means to halt the reform process. One effect of this was the death of many peasant leaders, among them outstanding regional leaders such as Primo Tapia. More recently, around 1958, only the formal threat by peasant organizations to take revenge prevented continued assassinations in the north-

---

[b]Peasants who participated in the cooperative training programs sponsored by the unions under guidance of the American Institute for Free Labor Development explained that they were well aware that this kind of activity was not what they needed, but they utilized the facilities as part of a preparation for "better days," when radical action would be possible again.[6]

western development area while the peasants were strongly campaigning for reform laws. During the Cárdenas regime, the situation was so hazardous that the government felt obliged to distribute 60,000 weapons among the organized peasants for their self-protection and as a guarantee that the legal procedures would be respected by the landowners. Legal provisions for the distribution of arms to the peasants had existed since 1926 when the white guards of the landlords were particularly active in frightening the peasants not to petition for land as the law stipulated. The armed peasants constituted according to the regulations a reserve army to guarantee internal order in the rural areas.

Provisions for the armed self-defense of peasants in countries where radical agrarian reforms encountered intransigent opposition from the traditional landowners not only turned out to be important for the implementation of the reform legislation as such. It was also a sign of the almost absolute confidence of the government in the peasants' loyalty. This gave the peasants considerable self-confidence and a chance to prove their loyalty by supporting the reformist government at a time when conservative forces tried to overthrow it. In Mexico, the peasantry came to the rescue of the reform-oriented government in 1923, 1929, 1935 and almost in 1940.

Now a crucial point is whether the peasant organizations with their armed force or with the freedom to show other forms of power capability are effectively mobilized and given ample participation (contributing as well as benefiting) in an overall development effort? Or are these peasant organizations neutralized and subjected to the support of middle-class interests, receiving only minor benefits and favors. It seems that in most cases where at some stage the peasantry has played an important role, their force was later neutralized more or less successfully through making the peasant organizations dependent on the distribution of benefits through a political patronage system that had been created essentially to serve classes other than the peasantry.

How new groups based on class solidarity can be neutralized and controlled by the overall system, strongly influenced by the traditional forces is also demonstrated by the Mexican case after 1940. During the Cardenas regime of the late thirties, a monolithic peasant organization was created out of several regionally organized groups to form part of the overall political structure. Several militant and strong groups were brought together in one organization, the Confederación Nacional Campesina, and thereby linked with the political system as a whole. After 1940, this structure was increasingly controlled by the middle sector, not identified with the peasants, but rather opposed to them. The bargaining power of the peasantry disappeared or was left unused. The main function of the official peasant organization, the CNC, was then to keep the peasants within the fold of the official party and mobilize support for the government at elections.

The relatively small middle sector, although larger than the traditional ruling class, reaps the benefits from modernization in Mexico, while the majority of the population and particularly the peasants, fell back into conditions not too different from those before the Revolution. New forms of internal colonialism appeared. It should be noted that the reversal of the radical reformist policies after 1940 is partly (but only partly) a result of outside pressures, particularly from the USA which was interested in a politically stable Mexico in a period when fascist forces were becoming dangerously strong in their opposition to the radical experiments carried out during the Cárdenas regime.

In the overall post-1940 context, the CNC has lost its function as a promotor of a dynamic agrarian policy. Many of the CNC's regional or state leaders are politicians, often not of peasant origin, who function as brokers, or intermediaries between the government and the peasants and through whom individual peasants or groups can obtain favors or facilities in exchange for political support. Roads, schools, water supply or loans are used by officials to gain a political clientele at the local level. For many local leaders who know to adapt well to this system, it is advantageous to their personal social mobility. Since they conform, in order to be successful, to the standards set by the top leaders who identify with the middle-sector interests, these local leaders generally have little or no effectiveness in the long run as defenders of peasant interests. The overall system became so overpowering that the peasants were left in a state of dependency again. In many areas, the new political system of which the peasant organization was a part became so monopolistic and coercive that for the majority of the peasants the new situation became in some respects similar to the traditional hacienda system.

This is the main reason why considerable violence continues to prevail in the rural areas in Mexico and why at times radical movements occur which are repressed by army intervention. The assassination of the peasant leader Rubén Jaramillo in 1962, the massacre of peasants in Acapulco in 1967, the guerilla forces in the highlands of Chihuahua in Madera[8] and Guerrero (led by Genaro Vazquez), both still in operation, are symptoms of a potential for considerable unrest.

In Bolivia, some of the same forces were at work as in Mexico, but had less impact because of the shorter postrevolutionary period, and because the revolutionary change in the rural areas was considerably more profound and immediate than in most of Mexico.

During the carrying out in Bolivia of the peasant organization drive and the land distribution according to the law, there were few victims and violence was largely avoided. As we have seen, this was partly due to the fact that the peasants were effectively armed, so that they could defend themselves and those government functionaries who came to execute the laws in the few cases where landlords might have offered violent opposition. Special legislation was issued to regulate the rural security service in the hands of the peasants to guarantee a proper execution of the reform procedures. At present, the peasants in Bolivia still have a large part of their armed defense structure and have maintained the possibility of using political bargaining power to a much larger extent than in Mexico.

In Bolivia, there is also a great deal more competition among the leadership, and the organization as a whole appears less monolithic than that of the Mexican CNC. The Bolivian Confederación Nacional de Trabajadores Campesinos de Bolivia (CNTCB) is also less solidly controlled by a firmly established political party, dominated by middle-sector interests. It must be kept in mind that there has not yet been an opportunity in Bolivia for a new type of commercial farmers' class to arise whose interests conflict with the peasants' as in Mexico. This is largely because commercial-scale farming is virtually limited to the tropical lowlands where agrarian reform has been marginal to date. Particularly at the local level, peasant unions play a more important role in Bolivia than in Mexico, and there is probably more active participation of the rank and file in the management of local and regional affairs, although in this area, the degree of peasant participation still leaves much to be desired. While the peasant organizations increasingly assume the characteristics of a brokerage system, the flow of benefits is small, as are the available resources. They seem more and more to serve the purpose of merely maintaining clienteles of local or national leaders.

It should be noted that the peasant organization structure in Bolivia could possibly have been used to mobilize the peasantry behind a national development effort. Particularly after the radical land distribution, there was great enthusiasm among the peasants for new undertakings at all levels. It seems, however, that efforts were undertaken to calm and control this fervor rather than to channel it in effective ways. Many of the forces which try to prevent dynamic participation of the peasantry in the national economy could recover or remain in control.

This is particularly the case in the marketing system which remained in the hands of the townsmen who do not operate to the benefit of the peasants or of national development. International observers noted that the climate for effective community and regional development in Bolivia was exceptionally good compared with that of most other Andean countries because the institutional and psychological obstacles against full popular participation had disappeared.[9] But the new structure of peasant organizations was not sufficiently utilized. Instead, new and competitive organizations were created in which the townsmen had considerable influence.

The fact that the rank and file are often able to make their demands known through the use of political bargaining power is an indication that it would not be difficult to build on to the syndical structure. It seems that the Bolivian unions could still be used as a means of effective peasant mobilization for development and change rather than merely as a means of political manipulation of the peasantry.

Only one country, Cuba, as yet very little studied, has apparently been successful in giving the peasants a place in a new system which came about as a result of revolutionary change. It also has mobilized the peasantry effectively in a new development venture. New institutions have been fashioned in such a way that they keep a spirit of movement for change and development alive among broad masses of the people.[10]

Before 1959, Cuba was already a country in which about 60 per cent of the population lived in urban areas and where bargaining organizations of workers had gained considerable strength. This was also the case among the sugarmill workers, but an estimated 500,000 farm laborers, including seasonal sugar cane workers, were practically unorganized and lived under minimal conditions. Also the sharecroppers, squatters and the 65,000 tenants who grew sugar cane had hardly any organization and lived at the margin of society as a whole.[11]

Active participation in the forces which brought a new regime to power in 1959 came from the poor peasants in the mountain region of the Sierra Maestra. Many of these people were squatters who were continuously threatened by the large landowners and frequently evicted from the plots they tilled. It was in this area that already in 1958 a land reform program was carried out, giving secure title to the squatters. After the Revolution was victorious, a sense of participation in a new national venture was created among the whole peasantry. Through the agrarian reform law of May 1959, more than 100,000 tenants, sharecroppers and squatters became owners of their plot, without any obligation to pay for the land.[12] In addition to this land distribution, the agrarian reform program transformed the large-scale enterprises (many of which were owned by foreign companies) into collective or state farms.

After the reform, about one-third of those working in agriculture were small cultivators, working altogether 42 per cent of all farm land. In this important sector, new institutions were also created. More than 150,000 small farmers were organized into local associations and cooperatives, which in 1961 were brought together into the National Association of Small Cultivators (ANAP). This association acts as an intermediary in the supply of credit in the sale of products at fair prices. ANAP has been particularly effective in channelling cheap credits (with 4 per cent interest) to the small farmers in a system which gives over the supervisory task mainly to the local organization. Requests for credit are made to the bank through a local cooperative organization which guides, approves and supervises the cultivation plan of each member.[13] The available data do not indicate to which extent the planning of the local organizations is integrated into the national plan.

In addition to organizing the peasants' participation in credit and other agricultural promotion efforts, ANAP forms part of a wider system of popular mobilization through the so-called mass organizations. These are associations for farmers, workers, women, students and other categories covering the whole country with an estimated direct participation of one out of every two adult Cubans. (Before the Revolution of 1959, there was in Cuba, a high degree of solidarity among several categories of workers.)[14] A special place is taken among the organizations by the Committees for the Defense of the Revolution (Comites de Defensa de la Revolución) which date from the period when the regime was threatened from various sides. They became multipurpose citizens' groups used by the national leadership for recruiting support as well as for promoting sanitation drives and other civic campaigns. Official reports claim that these committees have a membership of 1,500,000 persons, one out of every five Cubans, organized in a network of over 100,000 committees all over the country.[15] From the presently available information, it is difficult to assess whether the flow of influence from the people to the top in this system is as effective as the influence from the top downward.

In addition to the new institutions, the mass media are amply used to keep a spirit of participation in a national struggle alive among broad layers of the population. The mass media, since long extensively spread in Cuba, keep the people continuously informed about national problems and make an almost direct influence by the charismatic national leadership possible. Apparently, another important factor is the two-way flow between city and countryside, since as many urban people go to work temporarily in the rural areas as *vice versa*.[16] That the sweeping nature of the land reform in 1959 had a nation-moving impact which reached well into the urban areas can be concluded from a public opinion poll carried out within a year of the reform by a team of the Princeton University. Of a countrywide sample of urban Cubans, 86 per cent indicated at that time that they supported the new government, and agrarian reform was mentioned most often as the "best aspects of life in Cuba today," with honest government as a second item.[17]

It would be highly useful if up-to-date studies could be made of the mobilization of the peasantry and their participation in the national development effort in Cuba. It seems clear that the main impulse for mobilization came from above, after the revolutionary government had come to power. Unlike Mexico and Bolivia, the peasant protest movement from below, although crucial in the initial stages of the guerrilla struggle in the Sierra Maestra, was not of such large proportions as to force the government to take the peasants into account once a new regime was established. However, the new government felt itself ideologically committed to a radical reform program and mobilized the peasants rather than neutralizing them as in Mexico and Bolivia. It possibly also felt the need for mass peasant support. It should be noted that the peasantry in Cuba was only one-third of the population as a whole and not the overwhelming majority it was in the days of revolution and turmoil in Mexico and Bolivia.

The Creation of Organizations from Above: Populism and Patronage

In the light of the later developments of peasant organizations in Mexico and/or Bolivia, it can be understood that other governments and parties have tried or are trying to create peasant organizations which have considerable vertical ties to the overall political system from the outset. This means that the peasants can be rallied in ways which give them some political bargaining power in a controlled way, opposing or neutralizing the traditional landholding interests.

Such vertically stimulated peasant organizations received benefits for their members before they had sufficient bargaining power to get such benefits on their own account. Such organizations are as clienteles dependent on those who manipulate the benefits, while the followings growing from below gained benefits in an independent way. It has been noted that in the Latin American labor movement, the dependent organizations which are stimulated from above, are quite common.[18] The government often creates such organizations as a clientele that depends on a flow of benefits, in order to prevent the rise of independent organizations that may try to gain influence through the use of their own political bargaining power.

Several Latin American governments have at some stage tried to mobilize the peasantry in a controlled way. These are Venezuela, Brazil (before 1964) and Guatemala (before 1954). However, this mobilization was carried out less wholeheartedly than in Mexico, Bolivia or Cuba where peasants received arms to defend their interests and the regime that benefited them.[c] The governments of Venezuela, Brazil and Guatemala that promoted peasant mobilization could be considered populist. Such regimes maintain that there is unity among the people, rather than a division (and struggle) along class lines.[19] They try to content all classes and power contenders (in the terms of Anderson). Mexico and Bolivia can also be considered populist in this sense, particularly after a new equilibrium between different classes had been established.

Venezuela is apparently a case in point. The Federación Campesina de Venezuela, (FCV) was, from its foundation, dependent on the flow of certain benefits from the government to the peasants. Once a strong organization existed, and particularly after this organization had suffered several years of frustration under a repressive regime, the FCV reacted in a way not unlike the first peasant movements in Mexico and Bolivia. It displayed considerable political bargaining power through effective land invasions. But once the most militant groups were contented through land distribution, the Federación Campesina de Venezuela became a brokerage system through which benefits flow to the peasant groups in exchange for their electoral support.

Only at one point did this system come close to running out of hand (during the invasions of 1958-1960) and this was as a reaction to the fact that the military dictatorship in power for ten years had come to repress even this well-controlled political patronage system. It is clear that one of the most important factors that keeps this system functioning in Venezuela with some degree of effec-

---

[c]One can only speculate what would have happened to reform-oriented governments in Venezuela (1948), Guatemala (1954) and Brazil (1964), and the agrarian reform program they were executing or initiating had there been a loyal and powerfully organized peasantry to support them against *coups* staged by the military forces.

tiveness is the availability of the considerable financial resources coming from oil revenues. Through these resources, the opposition of the landlords could be overcome in the first place and then the peasantry could be kept in expectation of benefits by a careful and strategic distribution of benefits in those areas where dissidence might develop. It should also be noted that Venezuela is different from most other Latin American countries in that its rural population represents only about one-third of the total.

In Brazil, a similar approach was tried in 1963-1964 when the government created a national system of peasant organizations in order to guarantee electoral support and to overshadow the peasant leagues and other militant peasant organizations that existed in some regions. However, through elections within the unions, the new structure came under control of their most radical elements, which was probably one of the reasons why the traditional elites and the army eliminated the whole political system in 1964.

A similar thing had happened ten years before in Guatemala in the counter-reform of 1954. However, the process of repression after a more or less controlled peasant mobilization had taken place led to an awakening of the peasants to their interests as a class similar to what happened as a result of the *violencia* in Colombia (and what could possibly happen in Brazil).

It is clear from the Guatemalan case, but particularly from the Venezuelan (1948-1958) and Bolivian (1946-1952) cases, that severe repression after a period of populist regime (which gave certain benefits and hopes to the peasantry) creates a climate favorable for radical peasant movements. Such movements then can only be contained by considerable concessions, if not overall reform or revolution favorable to the peasants. The conservative reaction of the traditional elites to the moderate reforms of the more or less populist regimes of Villaroel in Bolivia (1943-1946) and of Betancourt in Venezuela (1945-1948) created the conditions for the rise of radical peasant movements that came close to being revolutionary in 1952 and 1958, respectively.

In Guatemala, a similar development can at present be halted only by a considerable show of force and repression. As noted in Chapter 5, a great number of peasants and peasant leaders have been assassinated between 1962 and today and yet the unrest in the rural areas prevails. One could say that the intransigent reaction of the landed elite, repressing the peasant organizations or followings, even though these were stimulated from above by a reformist government brought a higher degree of class consciousness to the peasants. This consciousness could not have been brought about by the vertically created peasant organizations as such, dependent as they were on official patronage. For an organization living on a flow of benefits from government sources, it is difficult to maintain militancy as a class organization. As can be seen in Venezuela after 1960 and Mexico after 1940, such a dependent peasant organization can be manipulated so as not to harm middle-sector interests, even when these interests are not identical or even contrary to those of the peasants.

Some scholars have maintained the view that the force of vertical patronage ties is a reason why there is a lack of solidarity among peasants and little class-consciousness. Without going into a discussion of concepts introduced by Marx such as class-for-itself, class struggle, which may not apply in the same manner to the Latin American reality as they did to the European one during the first part of the last century, some correction should be given to this overly pessimistic view on the possibilities for the peasant struggle.[20]

If a proper distinction is made between various types of patronage, it can be seen that some forms have an important function in the creation of solidarity among peasants. Peasant solidarity is as little an inherent peasant characteristic as is resistance to change or distrust or the encogido syndrome. As was shown in earlier chapters, some counterpoint elements exist in the overall culture of repression, characteristic for the hacienda system in Latin America. These counterpoints reveal themselves in distrust and resistance, but they can be utilized and rallied for effective struggle. Solidarity and class-consciousness can emerge during the struggle and as an integral part of it. Efforts to prevent solidarity from growing, such as the use of vertical patronage influences, are factors in the struggle.

As we have seen, populist governments such as existed in Brazil before 1964 and Guatemala before 1954 may create vertically controlled peasant organizations, but the struggle in which these organizations unavoidably get involved once they defend peasant interests, brings to increasingly large sections of the peasantry a greater solidarity and class-consciousness. This is not a natural growth phenomenon, but a result of the intransigent reaction of those whose interests are opposed to the peasants. Except for countries where huge resources exist to maintain a brokerage system that is reasonably beneficial to the peasants while, at the same time, sufficient to content the landlords (as happened in Venezuela), the growth of peasant clienteles independent from the traditional hacienda clientele seems an important step in the creation of a class-conscious or even revolutionary peasantry. How the populist system will develop depends mainly, as it seems, on the willingness of the traditional elite to give in to legitimate demands and to conform to the need for radical change. If they resist the pressures from the peasants, as they mostly do, the peasants will radicalize and escalate their demands and tactics of struggle. The peaceful coexistence of various vertical clienteles within the populist system will then collapse. Repression of the peasants follows, but this makes clear to them where their basic interests lie, and chances that they will be controlled again by a vertical clientele system and without repression, appear small. Guatemala, where the peasantry was highly traditional and isolated, is a case in point. There are many indications that conditions for a mobilization of the indigenous peasants for a radical reformist or revolutionary action are better than ever. This is quite understandable after the developments described above. Particularly important is the fact that populist governments stimulate a high-level expectation, but are unable to realize the promises because of the unwillingness and resistance of the traditional elite to adapt to new situations. Frustration, radicalization and repression leading to greater radicalization seem to be a recurrent theme in present Latin American peasant politics.

Other Factors Promoting the Revolutionary Potential

For those who see in revolutionary changes of the Latin American societies the only way to dynamic development, the present tendencies in the rural areas seem to offer good chances in the long run. As was noted

There exists an ideologically unfocused quasiinsurgency of peasant uprisings as one aspect of the violence that is an endemic feature of political life in many Latin American countries. Usually these have sought a remedy for a specific grievance or have been the attempt of land squatters to protect their claims against the government forces. This shades into rural banditry. Peasant-connected incidents of this type are not insurgency but can develop into it. Legitimate guerillas often utilize peasant unrest or incorporate rural bandits into their ranks.[21]

Ironically enough, this observation was made in the context of a top-level debate on foreign policy of the United States. It is well-known, and at times recognized, that this policy has tried to make impossible consistent populist reforms in several Latin American countries where United States interests were at stake. The counterreform in Guatemala in 1954 is the most renowned case. In several countries, such as Mexico (where during 1934-1940 many United States estates were expropriated) or Bolivia (where few United States landed interests existed), populist governments were left alone to carry out land reforms. Although the subject has hardly been studied systematically, there is some evidence that the United States favored the neutralization of the peasantry and the deemphasis on land reform during the post-1940 governments in Mexico, particularly during the term of president Miguel Aleman (1946-1952).[22] In Bolivia, USAID community development advisors were influential in neutralizing to some extent the peasant syndicate structure by creating parallel community councils for the promotion of community projects, rather than relying for this on the existing peasant unions. Only in Cuba, where United States influence, after it had tried to subvert or overthrow the revolutionary government, was completely cut off, could a consistent mobilization of the peasantry and their participation in a national development effort be achieved. United States policies have not always been consistent. While in the early sixties, the Declaration of Punta del Este emphasized the need for agrarian reform as a precondition for overall development in Latin America and for receiving United States aid, several governments which allowed forces to develop that might be helpful in the promulgation or carrying out of effective land reform, such as the Goulart regime in Brazil in 1964, were overthrown with the tacit or active support of the United States.

United States aid to peasant organizations is generally channelled only to those movements that do not strongly emphasize the need for radical land reform. In some cases, however, such as Venezuela in the early sixties, land reform and peasant organization is strongly supported, because this helped to prevent "Castro's attempts at insurgency."[23]

The extent to which populist governments are liable to foreign pressures depends on the type of foreign interests involved, which varies from country to country. At the United States policy level, one increasingly hears voices that denounce the rigidly antireformist United States pressures of the last few years, particularly the various forms of military aid given to Latin American governments. However, the tendencies to defend stability at all costs rather than to allow significant reforms to occur, seem to continue. In the long run, this policy, emphasizing economic development without social reform, may enhance the revolutionary potential of the peasantry even more than the populist reform policies.[24]

It is not only the populist regimes that create instability and frustration among the peasantry. Almost any development policy has this effect since it upsets the status quo and often creates relative deprivation rather than improvement. A recent study on the chances for civil violence gave the following hypothesis.

The occurrence of civil violence presupposes the likelihood of relative deprivation among substantial numbers of individuals in a society; concomitantly, the more severe is relative deprivation, the greater are the likelihood and intensity of civil violence.[25]

Additional factors not directly related to the rural situation are summarized by Kling.

Legal and formal concomitants of violence. Not surprisingly, there are legal and formal corollaries of the patterns of violence in Latin America:

1. frequent replacement and revision of written constitutional documents;
2. conspicuous departures from prescribed constitutional norms in political behavior;
3. recurrent suspensions of constitutional guarantees, declarations of states of siege, and the conduct of government by decree; and
4. the institutionalization of procedures for exile, including the right of asylum.[26]

The Colombian land reform program, emphasizing technical improvements and infrastructure building, can be considered typical for the half-hearted development efforts that create frustration among the peasants. This program was often propagandized as the example of the new Alliance for Progress reform strategy. The failure of this program to bring about any significant social reform has been recognized.[27] As a result continuous peasant unrest is a characteristic of Colombian rural life.[28]

As was noted in a recent evaluation of the Colombian Agrarian Reform Institute (INCORA), it ". . . had achieved a degree of success in its various activities (in agricultural improvement, irrigation facilities and infrastructure building among others) but has not, in the aggregate, achieved any appreciable success in effectively transforming the maldistribution of land in Colombia."[29] The fact that this approach in Colombia enhances the organizability of the peasants was recently noted in a technical study on the potential for insurgency in Latin American countries.[30]

Wherever new and modernizing influences enter into the rural areas, relative deprivation makes its appearance. This is often an unplanned result of a variety of development projects and programs, including irrigation schemes, settlement projects, and community development efforts. The traditional status quo is changed in such cases mostly in ways which give little participation to the peasantry. Frequently, the established elite or a privileged minority gets such a large share of the benefits that a development program loses its appeal and effect for the peasants. In addition, there are often the directly opposing traditional interests which detain any program that tends to lead to effective social change at the local level.

In the first chapters of this study, it was demonstrated that the commonly shown distrust of peasants regarding local development projects is not an irrational aspect of traditional peasant behavior, but rather the result of an awareness of the severe limitations of such projects which basically cover up unbearable conditions rather than bring improvement. Through effective involvement in three such projects, in rural areas in Central America, Sicily (where the situation has many similarities with Latin America) and Chile, I was able to learn gradually that this peasant distrust is quite rational and justified and that if properly utilized, it can be a condition for effective and militant peasant organization. Distrust is a logical reaction of the peasant to the resistance to change of the landed elite.

Ironically, it appears that it is precisely the landlord opposition and the resulting frustration among the peasants that is one of the main factors leading to the emergence of radical movements which cannot be contented unless really significant reforms have been brought about.

While the short-term effect of many community projects, such as the one in which I participated in El Salvador, seems to be increasing frustration, in the long run, such effort may have the positive effect of enhancing the organizability of the peasants. The more radical leaders of newly created organizations that appeal to the most basic and strongly felt needs of the peasantry, including the desire for basic structural reforms, will increasingly find response as was the case in the Punitaqui project in Chile that I assisted.

In the rural areas where some form of half-hearted change or development takes place, frustration and relative deprivation will grow and so will the chances for protest, civil disobedience, or even civil violence. This fact, occurring with increasing frequency in Latin American countries, conforms to a general trend: the more expectations are aroused and, relatively, frustrated, the more the apathy and tradition-bound conformity which dominated the rural areas for ages will make place for an aggressive attitude.

For this reason, the approach of those traditional groups that try to avoid any change at all in order to maintain their privileged position is understandable, but preventing change from taking place becomes more and more impossible in the Latin American countries these days. Even in isolated regions, there are modernizing influences. Roads, school teachers, a transistor radio, villagers who have worked in urban areas or mines and return to their birthplace are all factors which are the beginning of the erosion of the status quo. The state of violence is inherent in a society with a rigid social structure that divides the population into a few holders of power and a majority which has little or no share in economic benefits and political power. The situation of the peasant becomes increasingly unbearable after modernizing changes occur. And, as was noted above, turning the clock back after certain changes favorable to the peasants have been made can be achieved by increasing repression, but seems to have a radicalizing effect in the long run.[31]

Whether the increasingly favorable climate for militant peasant movements will be utilized depends to a large extent on the willingness of urban allies to support and guide the peasant organizations. Since the forces that oppose representative peasant organizations, the traditional landed elite, are highly sophisticated and do not hesitate to use any possible means to block peasant pressures to emerge, it is logical that the peasants need allies of equal sophistication to help defend their legitimate interests. Practically all cases of known strong peasant movements have had such allies.

In this respect, it is important to note that an erosion of the status quo is also taking place within the traditional elite itself. There seems to be an increasing number of sons of the wealthier classes, including the landed elite, who rather than inheriting status and wealth from their forefathers want to build a career and serve their country in ways which refute their background. Some of them become advisors to popular pressure groups, others take even more risky and spectacular approaches and join movements of armed resistance against the established order. According to Vega, a good number of participants in guerrilla movements come from the circles of the traditional elite.[32] As a result of the latter, some of the most backward areas of Peru and Guatemala have been or are being opened up through military-civic action programs which entered those regions in order to eliminate foci of guerrillas which had chosen those areas for their operation. These forces of modernization appear to bring about the erosion of the status quo in areas where the impact of population increase, urban contacts, and natural erosion are not yet strongly felt. For revolutionary movements of the past, similar phenomena have been noted. The loss of self-esteem among the ruling class as well as the transfer of allegiance of the intellectuals were important factors.[33] These forces are presently working with increasing strength in Latin America. Fidel Castro, Francisco Juliao, and Hugo Blanco are examples of popular leaders who were, by birth, members of elite classes. Part of the strategy for promoting peasant organization might be directed towards increasing the number of dissidents among the traditional elites. As we have seen, some of the younger members of the traditional elites seem to be willing and eager to accept new constructive roles in which they can find self-esteem and status and which are more in step with dynamic development needs of their countries than the traditional roles of their fathers. One could imagine that many young members of the traditional elite potentially feel that self-esteem derived from personal effort and capacity in the fulfillment of such new roles is more satisfactory than status derived from inheritance and the copying of outdated patterns of seignorial life. As yet, few systematic efforts have been made to tap the potentialities of disconformity and adventure of those youths.

It seems that the restlessness of youth and student groups in many countries is not unrelated to an attitude of protest against the traditional value system which upholds the overall status quo, most sharply visible in the rural areas.[34] A factor of great importance in this respect is that it becomes increasingly clear that the most conservative and repressive governments in Latin America are supported in the name of stability by foreign influences, particularly the United States. Especially in those countries where agrarian reform and peasant organization efforts or plans were frustrated, e.g., Guatemala in 1954 and Brazil in 1964, such outside interventions were more or less obvious, but they are increasingly recognized in most countries. In academic circles in Latin America,[35] criticism of United States intervention and economic domination has become a rallying point for protest action, but as yet, few links have been made between these intellectual protests and the actual or potential peasant resistance. The few guerrilla groups which have operated in some Latin American countries seem on the whole to have failed to make proper contact with the peasantry and convince them that their causes coincided. There is a considerable gap between the urban intellectuals, defected young members of the upper classes, and students on the one hand—and the distrustful peasantry on the other. One proof of this gap seems to be the expectation that once a group starts to organize a focus of revolutionary resistance to the overall system in some region, the peasantry will follow the call for revolt without much preparation and without going through several stages of conscientization and organization. The feasibility of collaboration between those urban political forces engaged in radical change and the peasantry and its leaders is demonstrated by the examples of this study.

Up to the present, few programs exist where university students were stimulated on a large scale to participate actively in rural organization efforts. However, where this has been done, some groups of young people of the educated classes have responded enthusiastically and shown ability to establish relationships with the peasantry which differ from the traditional pattern. The *Promoción Popular Universitaria* in Peru and some university-sponsored rural promotion programs in Chile were interesting examples. The first was practically discontinued because of its renovating or even radicalizing impact, particularly among the students.

Another group that has drawn attention as a powerful potential ally of the peasants are the local priests who have been influenced by new social teachings currently becoming important. Several groups of priests, interested and actively engaged in work in this field, have been formed in Colombia and Peru. The fact that students as well as priests belong to a kind of patronage system (university and church, respectively) that can be made independent from the overall traditionally controlled patronage system could be an advantage. Altogether, it seems that a broad field for experimentation in peasant organization lies open.

How "revolutionary" future peasant movements will be seems to depend largely on the measure of intransigence of the traditional "elites" and the national and international forces that support them. Past experience suggests that the more resistant to change the Latin American "elites" will be, the more radical the demands and the means of struggle of the peasantry will become.

Notes

Notes

Notes to Introduction

1. See particularly Raul Prebisch, *Towards a Dynamic Development Policy for Latin America*, United Nations, ECLA, 1963.
2. United Nations, "1967 Report on the World Social Situation" (E/CN.5/417/Add. 2, Dec. 1967).
3. For a broader discussion of this problem, see Gerrit Huizer, "Het woord Moet Actie Worden," *Sociologische Gids*, Vol. VIII, No. 3 (Mei/Juni 1961).
4. Howard S. Becker, "Problems of Inference and Proof in Participant Observation," *American Sociological Review*, Vol. XXIII, No. 5 (October 1958), pp. 659-660.
5. Some theoretical implications of the study of peasant mentality and behavior through these methods are analyzed in Gerrit Huizer, "Evaluating Community Development at the Grassroots," *América Indígena*, Vol. XXV, No. 3 (1965), pp. 279-301.
6. Gerrit Huizer, "Some Notes on Community Development and Rural Social Research," *América Latina*, Vol. VIII, No. 3 (1965), pp. 128-144.

Notes to Chapter 1

1. One such massacre, which took place in 1768 in the state of Veracruz in Mexico is described in Gonzalo Aguirre Beltran, *El Séñorio de Cuauhtochco, Luchas Agrarias en Mexico durante el Virreinato* (Mexico: Edic. Frente Cultural, 1940).
2. I.L.O., *Indigenous Peoples*, Studies and Reports, New Series No. 35, Geneva, 1953, p. 295.
3. Jean Piel c.s., "Les mouvements paysans au Perou de la Fin du 18e siècle à nos jours," (Enquête sur "Mouvements Paysans et Problèmes Agraires de la Fin du 18e Siècle à nos Jours," Commission Internationale d'Histoire des Mouvements Sociaux et des Structures Sociales, 1969), p. 11.
4. See Lucio Mendieta y Nuñez, *El Problema Agrario de México (Mexico: Séptima Edición, Editorial Porrua, 1959)*, pp. 53-54.
5. Roberto Mac-lean y Estenos, "La Revolución de 1910 y el Problema Agrario de Mexico," *Estudios Sociologicos*, Tomo II (IX Congreso Nacional de Sociología, México, 1958), pp. 31-33.
6. For a list of most of the uprisings after 1820, see Jean Meyer, "Mexique. Mouvements Paysans et Probèmes Agraires de 1810 à la Révolution" (Enquête sur "Mouvements Paysans et Problèmes Agraires de la Fin de 18e Siècle à nos Jours,") pp. 3-7, from which the following data in Mexico are mainly derived.

7. Jean Meyer, "El Ocaso de Manuel Lozada," *Historia Mexicana*, Vol. XVIII, No. 4 (abril-junio 1969) gives a detailed account of the campaign of this peasant leader, covering several states of Mexico.

8. I.L.O., *Indigenous*, pp. 298-299.

9. Jean Meyer, "Lozada," p. 9.

10. Ramiro Condarco Morales, *Zárate, El "Temible" Willka*, Historia de la Rebelión Indígena de 1899 (La Paz, 1966), pp. 41-44, 48.

11. See Richard Wilbur Patch, "Social Implications of the Bolivian Agrarian Reform" (Thesis, Microfilm, 1956), p. 126.

12. Luis Antezana E., *El Movimiento Obrero Boliviano (1935-1943)* (Bolivia: 1966), p. 16.

13. Maria Isaura Pereira de Queiroz, "O Sitiante Brasileiro e as Transformacões de sua Situacão Socio-Economica" (Colloques Internationaux sur les Problèmes Agraires des Amériques Latines, Paris, 11-16 Octobre 1965), Editions C.N.R.S., 1967, pp. 287-298.

14. Rui Facó, *Cangaceiros e Fanaticos, Genese e Lutas*, (Rio de Janeiro: Editora Civilizacao Brasileira, 1965).

15. Ibid., p. 49, 132.

16. Maria Isaura Pereira de Queiroz, *Movimientos Mesianicos Brasileños: Instrumentos u Obstaculos a la "Participacion"* (Simposio sobre la Participacion Social en America Latina, Mexico, 14-16 de Octubre de 1969), International Institute for Labor Studies.

17. Rui Facó, *Cangaceiros*, pp. 200-219.

18. See Anibal Quijano O., "Contemporary Peasant Movements," *Elites in Latin America*, ed. Seymour Martin Lipset and Aldo Solari, (New York: Oxford University Press, 1967), p. 301 for an interesting typology of peasant movements; Eric J. Hobsbawm, *Primitive Rebels: Studies in Archaic Forms of Social Movements*, (Manchester: 1959).

19. Albert O. Hirschman, *Journeys towards Progress*, (New York: Twentieth Century Fund, 1963), p. 102.

20. Special Operations Research Office, *U.S. Army Area Handbook for Venezuela* (Washington D.C.: American University, 1964), p. 100.

21. Anton Blok, "Mafia and Peasant Rebellion as Contrasting Factors in Sicilian Latifundism," *European Journal of Sociology*, Vol. X (1969), pp. 95-116; see also Eric J. Hobsbawm, *Rebels.*

22. Solon Barraclough and Arthur Domike, "Agrarian Structure in Seven Latin American Countries," *Land Economics*, Vol. XLII, No. 4 (Nov. 1966), LTC Reprint No. 25, (Land Tenure Center, University of Wisconsin), p. 392.

23. Ibid., p. 398.

24. Tenth FAO Regional Conference for Latin America, *"Main Conclusions and Policy Implications of the IWP Regional Study for South America"* (Kingston, Jamaica, 2-14 December 1968), LARC/68/4, pp. 4-5.

25. Thomas F. Carroll, "The Land Reform Issue in Latin America," *Latin*

American Issues, Essays and Comments, ed. Albert O. Hirschman, (New York: Twentieth Century Fund, 1961), p. 169.

26. Ernest Feder, *"Societal Opposition to Peasant Movements and its Effect on Farm People in Latin America,"* *Latin American Peasant Movements*, ed. Henry A. Landsberger; (Ithaca: Cornell University Press, 1970).

27. CIDA, *Ecuador, Tenencia de la Tierra y Desarrollo Socio-Económico del Sector Agricola* (Washington D.C., 1965), p. 87.

28. Ernest Feder, "Opposition."

29. Allan R. Holmberg, "Some Relationship between Psychobiological Deprivation and Culture Change in the Andes" (Cornell Latin American Year Conference, March 21-25, 1966); see also Paul L. Doughty, "The Interrelationship of Power, Respect, Affection and Rectitude in Vicos," "The Vicos Case: Peasant Society in Transition," *American Behavioral Scientist*, ed. Allan R. Holmberg et al., Vol. VIII, No. 7 (March 1965).

30. Ibid.

31. About the role of counterpoints in prevailing value systems, see W.F. Wertheim, *East-West Parellels*, (The Hague: W. van Hoeve, 1964), Chapter 2.

32. For some such legends among peasants in Peru, see Aníbal Quijano "El Movimiento Campesino del Peru y sus Lideres," *América Latina*, Vol. VIII, No. 4 (1965), pp. 43-66.

33. Paul L. Doughty, "The Interrelationship of Power, Respect, Affection and Rectitude in Vicos," p. 14.

34. Edward M. Dew, "Politics in the Altiplano: A Study of Provincial Political Change in Peru" (Dissertation, University of California, 1966, University Microfilms), p. 108.

35. About the safety-valve institutions in conflict, see Lewis Coster, *The Functions of Social Conflict*, (Glencoe: Free Press, 1964), p. 41.

36. Gonzalo Aguirre Beltrán, *Regiones de Refugio, El Desarrollo de la Comunidad y el Proceso Dominical en Mestizo America*, (Mexico: Instituto Indigenista Interamericano, 1967), pp. 11-17.

37. United Nations, "1967 Report on the World Social Situation" (E/CN.5/ 417/Add. 2, December 1967), pp. 51, 65.

38. Rodolfo Stavenhagen, "Clases, Colonialismo y Aculturación," *America Latina*, Vol. VI, No. 4 (1963), p. 93; for a discussion of the term internal colonialism which is increasingly used by scholars (such as René Dumont, C. Wright Mills), see Pablo Gonzalez Casanova, "Sociedad Plural, Colonialismo Interno y Desarrollo," *America Latina*, Vol. VI, No. 3 (1963), pp. 15-32.

39. David Chaplin, "Peru's Postponed Revolution," *World Politics*, Vol. XX, No.3 (April 1968), p. 400.

40. CIDA, *Brazil. Land Tenure Conditions and Socio-Economic Development of the Agricultural Sector* (Washington D.C., 1966), p. 15.

41. Ibid., pp. 15-19.

42. Dwight B. Heath, "The Changing Social Structure of Inter-Ethnic Drink-

ing in Two Bolivian Communities" (Paper prepared for Symposium on Drinking Patterns in Latin America, 132nd Annual Meeting of the American Association for the Advancement of Science, 29-30 December, 1965, Berkeley, California), p. 7.

43. Charles P. Loomis, *Turrialba. Social Systems and the Introduction of Change*, (Glencoe: Free Press, 1953), p. 281.

44. Ibid., p. 48.

45. Ibid., p. 46.

46. Ibid., p. 206.

47. Ibid., p. 57.

48. Ibid., p. 58.

49. Olen E. Leonard and Roy A. Clifford, *La Sociologia Rural para los Programas de Acción* (Instituto Interamericano de Ciencias Agricolas, 1960), p. 44.

50. Charles P. Loomis, *Turrialba*, p. 90.

51. Benno Galjart, "Old Patrons and New," Some Notes on the Consequences of Patronage for Local Development Projects, *Sociologia Ruralis*, Vol. VII, No. 4 (1967), p. 335.

52. Ibid., "Itaguaí. Old Habits and New Practices in a Brazilian Land Settlement" (Dissertation, Wageningen, 1968), p. 88.

53. Charles Wagley, *The Brazilian Revolution: Social Changes since 1930, Social Change in Latin America Today*, ed. Richard Adams, et al., (New York: Vintage, 1960), p. 183.

54. Benno Galjart, "Class and 'Following' in Rural Brazil," *America Latina*, Vol. VII, no. 3 (1964), p. 3. Charles Wagley, "Luso-Brazilian Kinship Patterns: The Persistence of a Cultural Tradition," in *Politics of Change in Latin America*, ed. Joseph Maier and Richard W. Weatherhead, (New York: Frederick A. Praeger, 1964), pp. 174-189.

55. Ibid., p. 6.

56. Ibid., p. 6.

57. Benno Galjart, "El Sociologo ante la Reforma Agraria," *America Latina*, Vol. VI, No. 3, 1963, p. 77.

58. B.F. Galjart, *Itaguaí*, pp. 89-92.

59. Francisco Juliao, *Cambao, La Face Cachée du Bresil*, Cahiers Libres 129, (Paris: François Maspero, 1968), pp. 68-71.

60. Benno Galjart, "A Further Note on 'Followings': Reply to Huizer," *America Latina*, Vol. VIII, No. 3 (Julho-Setembro 1965), pp. 146-147.

61. For a discussion of some of these factors, see CIDA, *Brazil*, p. 144.

62. Ibid., pp. 228-261.

63. Ibid., pp. 142-144, 148-149. See also Manoel Correia de Andrade, *A Terra e o Homen no Nordeste*, (São Paulo: Editora Brasiliense, 1963), p. 246.

64. Information supplied by Father Paolo Crespo, syndical leader in Pernambuco.

65. Belden H. Paulson, "Difficulties and Prospects for Community Develop-

ment in Northeast Brazil," *Inter-American Economic Affairs*, vol. XVII, no. 4 (Spring 1964), p. 26.

66. Belden H. Paulson, "Local Political Patterns in Northeast Brazil: A Community Case Study" (Land Tenure Center, University of Wisconsin, August 1964), p. 53. One recent case-study where this problem is discussed is Jean Casimir, "Juazeiro e Petrolina. Um Polo de Crescimento" (SUDENE-Centro Latinoamericano de Pesquisas em Ciencias Sociais, Rio de Janeiro, 1967), pp. 64-74, 128-135.

67. Beldon H. Paulson, "Difficulties," p. 49.

68. See Everett M. Rogers, "Motivations, Values and Attitudes of Subsistence Farmers: Toward a Subculture of Peasantry" (Paper delivered at A/D/C Seminar on Subsistence and Peasant Economics, Honolulu, March 1, 1965).

Notes to Chapter 2

1. For an earlier description of this experience, see also Gerrit Huizer, "A Community Development Experience in a Central American Village, *International Review of Community Development*, No. 12 (1963), pp. 161-186.

2. See "Selected Findings and Queries. American Friends Service Committee," in *Community Development Review*, ICA, No. 4 (March 1957), about the advantages of the independent position of volunteers in a similar project in India.

3. See Carlos Campos Jimenez, *Una Experiencia de Organización de la Comunidad en el Valle de la Esperanza*, Serie sobre Organización de la Comunidad, No. 6 (Diciembre 1953), Union Panamericana, Washington, D.C., included as No. 20 in the *Coleccion de Estudios*, published by United Nations, UNESCO and OAS, 1954.

4. Ibid.

5. Ibid., pp. 6, 7.

6. Ibid., p. 8.

7. Ibid., p. 3.

8. Huizer, "Central American Village," pp. 172-174. For a comparison of the effects of undernourishment in Jamaica and the Netherlands during World War II, see G.J. Kruijer, "The Impact of Poverty and Undernourishment on Man and Society in Rural Jamaica," *Mens en Maatschappij*, Vol. XXXII, No. 5 (May 1957), p. 284.

9. Rafael Humberto Hasbun Hasbun, "La Cuestion Agraria en El Salvador," (Tesis, Universidad Nacional Autónoma de México, Escuela Nacional de Ciencias Políticas y Sociales, 1963), pp. 65-67.

10. OIT, *Los Problemas del Trabajo en El Salvador*, por Marguerite Thibert, (Ginebra, 1952); OIT, *Informe al Gobierno de El Salvador sobre los Asalariados Agrícolas*, por Jean Ambrosini (Ginebra, 1954).

11. Daniel Goldrich, "Toward the Comparative Politicization in Latin America," *Contemporary Cultures, and Societies of Latin America*, ed. Dwight B. Heath and Richard N. Adams (New York: Random House, 1965), p. 363.

12. Galjart, "Old Patrons and New," p. 337.

13. Ibid., p. 338.

14. Coser, *Social Conflict*, pp. 92, 95.

15. Galjart, *Itaguai*, p. 93.

16. Edward C. Banfield, *The Moral Basis of Backward Society* (Glencoe: Free Press, 1958), p. 85.

17. Ibid., pp. 31, 175.

18. Ibid., p. 85.

19. Ibid., pp. 172, 175.

20. See Anton Blok, "South Italian Agro-towns," *Comparative Studies in Society and History*, Vol. XI, No. 2 (April 1969), pp. 121-135.

21. The importance of *mafia* as a force of social and political control supporting the traditional elite in Sicily has been noted by Anton Blok, "Mafia and Peasant Rebellion as contrasting Factors in Sicilian Latifundism," *European Journal of Sociology*, Vol. X, No. 1, 1969, pp. 95-116; see also Jeremy Boissevain, *Poverty and Politics in a Sicilian Agro-town* (Preliminary report, Université de Montreal, 1964), pp. 45-50.

22. For a brief description of my community development activities in Partinico, see Gerrit Huizer, "Some Community Development Problems in Partinico, Western Sicily," *International Review of Community Development*, No. 10 (1962), pp. 47-56; about the initial stage of the work, Gerrit Huizer, "An Approach to Community Development in Partinico," *Mens en Maatschappij*, Vol. XXXVI, No. 1 (Jan./Feb., 1961), pp. 22-27.

23. Charles P. Loomis, *Turrialba. Social Systems and the Introduction of Change* (Glencoe: Free Press, 1953), ch. III and IV. The importance of this kind of informal groups, also called cliques, for communication of ideas and community development has been stressed also by Marian Rogers, "Autonomous Groups and Cultural Milieux," *International Review of Community Development*, No. 6 (1960), p. 146.

24. The importance of this project is demonstrated in several studies contained in Danilo Dolci, *Waste* (London: MacGibbon & Kee, 1963).

25. Regarding the developments of the Dolci Centro over the years, see James McNeish, *Fire under the Ashes, The Life of Danilo Dolci* (London: Hodder and Stoughton, 1965).

26. See Danilo Dolci, *Difficulties in the Development and Stimulation of New Initiatives in Western Sicily* (Text of a conference held at Yale University, 9 March 1961), published in Italian as: "Difficoltá di sviluppo e nuove iniziative nella Sicilia occidentale," in *La Cultura Populare* (Milano, April 1961). Peasant leader Turiddu Carnevale was described by Carlo Levi, *Words Are Stones* (New York, 1958), and union leader Accursio Miraglia by Dolci, *Waste*, chap. III.

27. Joseph E. Shatil, "Report on a Visit to Western Sicily," *International Review of Community Development*, No. 12 (1963), pp. 122-123.

28. Gavin Maxwell, *The Ten Pains of Death*, New York, 1960, p. 115.

29. See also a confirmation of this in Shatil, *Sicily*, p. 128.

30. The importance of competition in the process of building a clientele in Sicily was noted by Jeremy Boissevain, "Patronage in Sicily," *Man*, Vol. I, No. 1 (March 1966), p. 24.

31. Banfield, *Backward Society*, pp. 34, 38.

32. Ibid., p. 34.

33. Coser, *Social Conflict*, p. 95.

34. Banfield, *Backward Society*, p. 37.

35. F.G. Friedmann, "The World of 'La Miseria'," *Community Development Review*, I.C.A., Washington, D.C., No. 10, September 1958, p. 26.

36. Sybel F. Silberman, "Agricultural Organization, Social Structure and Values on Italy: Amoral Familism Reconsidered," *American Anthropologist*, Vol. LXX, No. 1 (February 1968), pp. 1-20.

37. Sidney G. Tarrow, *Peasant Communism in Southern Italy* (New Haven: Yale University Press, 1967), p. 58.

38. J.M.G. Thurlings, "The Dynamic Function of Conflict," *Sociologia Neerlandica*, Vol. II, No. II (Summer 1965), p. 144.

39. W.F. Wertheim, "Sociology between Yesterday and Tomorrow," *Comparative Studies in Society and History*, Vol. IX, No. 2 (January 1967), p. 184.

40. United Nations, Technical Assistance Recruitment Service, Request from the Government of Chile, Job-description, CHI-64-D, 23 December 1964.

41. For a more detailed description of the origin and present situation of the *comunidades* in Chile, see Gerrit Huizer, "*Comunidades agricolas*, Internal Colonialism and Agrarian Reform in Chile," *America Latina*, Vol. XI, No. 4 (Outubro-dezembro 1968), pp. 110-128.

42. Eric J. Hobsbawm, "Peasants and Rural Migrants in Politics," *The Politics of Conformity in Latin America*, ed. Claudio Veliz (New York: Oxford University Press, 1967), p. 55.

43. Several conversations with José Campusano, president of the FCI, who was himself born in one of the *comunidades* of Coquimbo.

44. "Levantamiento Campesino," *La Provincia*, Ovalle, 13 de Febrero 1969; "Triunfaron los Campesinos," Ibid., 14 de Febrero 1969.

Notes to Chapter 3

1. For many peasant uprisings in Russia before the 1917 Revolution, see David Mitrany, *Marx against the Peasant* (Chapel Hill: University of North Carolina Press, 1951) and Launcelot A. Owen, *The Russian Peasant Movement 1906-1917*, (London: King, 1937).

2. Lewis Coser, *The Functions of Social Conflict* (Glencoe: The Free Press, 1956), pp. 15-31.

3. W.F. Wertheim, "Sociological Aspects of Corruption in Southeast Asia," *Sociologia Neerlandica*, Vol. I, No. 2 (1963), p. 129.

4. See Anton Blok, "Enige Problemen bij het Onderzoek naar de Siciliaanse Mafia," *Sociologische Gids*, Vol. XIV, No. 6 (Nov./Dec. 1967), pp. 378-387.

5. For a brief comparative description of some similar experiments on a small or large scale, see Gerrit Huizer, "Community Development, Land Reform and Political Participation," *American Journal of Economics and Sociology*, Vol. XXVIII, No. 2 (April 1969), pp. 159-178.

6. George M. Foster, *Empire's Children. The People of Tzintzuntzan*, Smithsonian Institution, Institute of Social Anthropology, Publ. No. 6, 1948.

7. George M. Foster, "Peasant Society and the Image of Limited Good," *American Anthropologist*, Vol. LXVII, No. 2 (April 1965), pp. 296, 303.

8. Pascual Calderón Caballero, *Semblanza de un Pueblo de Michoacán: Cucuchucho* (CREFAL, Pátzcuaro, Mexico, Thesis, 1958), pp. 14-18.

9. For an extensive description of the fascist-inspired *sinarquista* movement which started in rural Mexico in the late thirties, see Nathan Whetten, *Rural México* (Chicago: University of Chicago Press, 1948), Chapter XX; about sinarquism in Tzintzuntzan: Foster, *Empire's Children*, pp. 181-185.

10. Rudolf A.M. van Zantwijk, *Lastdragers en Hoofden. De Sociale en Culturele eigenheid van een Taraskische Gemeenschap* (Dissertatie, Amsterdam, 1965), pp. 47, 74 and 167. This dissertation appeared in English as, *Servants of the Saints: The Social and Cultural Identity of a Tarascan Community in Mexico* (Assen, Netherlands, van Gorcum, 1967).

11. Ibid., p. 47.

12. Apolinar Martinez Mugica, *Primo Tapia, Semblanza de un Revolucionario Michoacano* (Mexico: Segunda Edición, 1946).

13. Paul Friedrich, "A Mexican Cacicazgo," *Ethnology*, Vol. IV, No. 2 (1965), p. 205.

14. Anibal Buitron, "Community Development in Theory and in Practice," *Community Development Review*, Vol. VI, No. 3 (September 1961), pp. 14-21.

15. For an interesting evaluation of community development programs in South East Asia partly based on United Nations documentation and on scholarly studies, see W.F. Wertheim, *East-West Parallels* (The Hague: Van Hoeve, 1964), Chapter 12.

16. Lewis A. Coser, *Continuities in the Study of Social Conflict* (New York: Free Press, 1967), p. 59.

17. Charles J. Erasmus, *Man Takes Control: Cultural Development and American Aid* (Minneapolis: University of Minnesota Press, 1961).

18. Charles J. Erasmus, "Community Development and the Encogido Syndrome," *Human Organization*, Vol. XXVII, No. 1 (1968), p. 70.

19. Erasmus, *Control*, p. 319.

20. Ibid., p. 316.

21. For more details about the reasons for the creation of this organization, see Gerrit Huizer, *Peasant Organization in the Process of Agrarian Reform in Mexico*, Studies in Comparative International Development, Monographic Series, Vol. IV, No. 6 (1968-1969), pp. 138-140.

22. Erasmus, *Control*, p. 238.

23. Various conversations with Jacinto Lopez; see also Karl M. Schmitt, *Communism in Mexico* (Austin: University of Texas Press, 1966), p. 14; Howard F. Cline, *Mexico: Revolution to Evolution: 1940-1960* (New York: Oxford University Press, 1962), p. 211; Martin C. Needler, *Mexico: Revolution as a Way of Life, Political Systems of Latin America*, ed. Martin C. Needler (Princeton, N.J.: Van Nostrand Political Science Series, 1964), pp. 23-24.

24. Erasmus, "Encogido Syndrome," p. 70.

25. Jorge L. Tamayo, *El Problema Fundamental de la Agricultura Mexicana* (Instituto Mexicano de Investigaciones Ecónomicas, 1964), p. 118.

26. Interviews with peasants in the area.

27. Data from local newspapers, such as *El Sol de Sinaloa*, Culiacán, from interviews and from the archives of UGOCM.

28. Erasmus, *Control*, pp. 220, 263. In another context, in Dwight W. Heath, Charles J. Erasmus and Hans C. Buechler, "Land Reform and Social Revolution in Bolivia" (University of Wisconsin: Land Tenure Center, 1965), p. 584.

29. Ibid., p. 631.

30. Heath, Erasmus, and Buechler, Reform, p. 665.

31. The ethnocentrism of Erasmus was also noted by Rudolf van Zantwijk, "Tarascan," p. 171.

32. Field visit to this ejido, Quechehueca in the Yaqui valley, and conversations with the leader, Bernabé Arana; Salomon Eckstein, *El Ejido Colectivo en Mexico* (Mexico: Fondo de Cultura Economica, 1966), p. 154.

33. George M. Foster, *Traditional Cultures: and the Impact of Technological Change* (New York: Harper & Brothers, 1962), p. 57, partly quoting from Charlotte Viall Wiser and William H. Wiser, *Behind Mud Walls* (New York: Agricultural Missions Inc., Yang Hsin-Pao, 1951), p. 160.

34. Foster, "Limited Good," p. 110.

35. Charles J. Erasmus, *Culture Change in Northwest Mexico*, ed., Julian Steward, *Contemporary Change in Traditional Societies*, Vol. III (Urbana: University of Illinois Press, 1967), p. 17.

36. Ibid., p. 113.

37. Ibid., p. 111.

38. Edward Banfield, *The Moral Basis of Backward Society* (Glencoe: The Free Press, 1958), p. 85.

39. Ibid., p. 10.

40. Ibid., p. 147.

41. Ibid., p. 153.

42. Foster, "Limited Good," p. 297.

43. Benno Galjart, *Itaguaí, Old Habits and New Practices in a Brazilian Land Settlement* (Wageningen, Netherlands, 1968), p. 85.

44. Charles J. Erasmus, "Upper Limits of Peasantry and Agrarian Reform: Bolivia, Venezuela and Mexico Compared," *Ethnology*, Vol. VI (1967), p. 378.

45. Benno Galjart, "Old Patrons and New," *Sociologia Ruralis*, Vol. VII, No. 4 (1967), p. 336.

46. George M. Foster, "Interpersonal Relations in Peasant Society," *Human Organization*, Vol. XIX, No. 4 (Winter 1960-61), p. 178.

47. Erasmus, "Encogido Syndrome."

48. Ibid., p. 70.

49. Ibid., p. 72.

50. Banfield, "Backward Society," p. 67.

51. Ibid., p. 174.

52. Allan R. Holmberg, "Changing Community Attitudes and Values in Peru: A Case Study in Guided Change," *Social Change in Latin America Today*, Richards Adams et al. (New York: Vintage 1961), pp. 80-81; Allan R. Holmberg et al., "The Vicos Case: Peasant Society in Transition," *The American Behavioral Scientist*, Vol. VIII, No. 7 (March 1965).

53. Ibid., p. 83.

54. Allan Holmberg, "Land Tenure and Planned Social Change: A Case from Vicos, Perú," *Human Organization*, Vol. XVIII, No. 1 (1959), p. 9.

55. Harold D. Lasswell, "Integrating Communities in More Inclusive Systems," *Human Organization*, Vol. XXI, No. 2 (Summer 1962), p. 117.

56. Henry B. Dobyns, Carlos Monge M., and Mario C. Vásquez, "Summary of Technical Organizational Progress and Reaction to It," Ibid., pp. 109-115.

57. Mehmet Beqiraj, *Peasantry in Revolution* (Cornell University: Center for International Studies, 1966), pp. 92-93.

58. This statement followed the generally accepted United Nations definition of community development in *Community Development and Related Services*, E/2931 Annex III, United Nations, 1960, par. 3.

59. United Nations, *The Future Evolution of Community Development*, draft 1967, par. 5, p. 4.

60. Ibid., par. 15.

61. Foster, *Limited Good,* pp. 301-302.

62. W.F. Wertheim, "Sociology between today and tomorrow," *Comparative Studies in Society and History*, Vol. IX, No. 2, Jan. 1967., p. 185.

Notes to Chapter 4

1. Henry A. Landsberger, "The Role of Peasant Movements and Revolts in Development: An Analytical Framework," *Bulletin*, International Institute for Labor Studies, No. 4 (February 1968), p. 20.

2. Many data used in this section are taken from Gerrit Huizer, "Los Movimientos Campesinos en Mexico" (Centro de Investigaciones Agrarias, Mexico, 1968); see also Gerrit Huizer, "Peasant Organization in the Process of Agrarian Reform in Mexico," *Studies of Comparative International Development*, Monographic Series, Vol. IV, No. 6 (1968-1969), pp. 115-145.

3. Ernest Gruening, *Mexico and its Heritage* (New York: The Century Company, 1928), p. 142.

4. Frank Tannenbaum, *The Mexican Agrarian Revolution* (New York: Macmillan, 1929), p. 158.

5. Pastor Rouaix, *Génesis de los Articulos 27 y 123 de la Constitución Políticade 1917* Instituto Nacional de Estudios Historicos de la Revolución Mexicana, Mexico, 1959).

6. Tannenbaum, *Agrarian Revolution*, p. 322.

7. Frank Tannenbaum, *Peace by Revolution: Mexico after 1910* (New York: Columbia University Press, 1933, 1966), p. 178.

8. See p. 52 ff above.

9. Paul Nathan, "México en la Epoca de Cárdenas," *Problemas Agrícolas e Industriales de México*, Vol. VII, No. 3 (Mexico, 1955), p. 99.

10. Ibid.; see also Moisés T. de la Pená, *El Pueblo y su Tierra. Mito y Realidad de la Reforma Agraria en Mexico* (Cuadernos Americanos, Mexico, 1964), pp. 320-323.

11. Frank Ralph Brandenburg, "Mexico: An Experiment in One-Party Democracy" (Dissertation, University of Pennsylvania, 1956, University Microfilms), p. 174.

12. About the political function of the CNC, see Confederación Nacional Campesina, *Declaración de Principios, Plan de Acción y Estatutos* (Publicaciones de la CNC, No. 1, Mexico, 1965), p. 138, Capitulo XXII, *de la Militancia Política*.

13. *Seis Anós de Gobierne al Servicio de México*, 1934-1940 (El Secretario de Governacion, 30 Noviembre 1940, La Nacional Impresora), pp. 95-96.

14. Artemio Arrelano Cruz, "Las Defensas Rurales Como Fuerza Militar de Protección de los Derechos Agrarios" (Tesis, Universidad Nacional Autónoma de Mexico, 1950), pp. 55, 96, 94, referring to the Primer Reglamento de Organización y Funcionamiento de las Defensas Rurales, 1 de enero de 1926.

15. For a comparison of the Cardenas presidential period with the fervor of the French Revolution, see James W. Willkie, *The Mexican Revolution: Federal Expenditure and Social Change since 1910* (Berkeley: University of California Press, 1967), p. 74.

16. William P. Tucker, *The Mexican Government Today* (Minneapolis: University of Minnesota Press, 1957), pp. 44, 56-58.

17. L. Vincent Padgett, *The Mexican Political System* (Boston: Houghton Mifflin, 1966), p. 127.

18. Leon Vincent Padgett, "Popular Participation in the Mexican 'One-Party' System" (Diss., Northwestern University, 1955, University Microfilms), p. 196.

19. Ronald Waterbury, "Politicization and Factionalism in a Zapotec Community in the Valley of Oaxaca" (Paper presented at the 66th Annual Meeting of the American Anthropological Association in Washington, D.C., November 30–December 3, 1967).

20. Oscar Lewis, *Life in a Mexican Village: Tepoztlan Restudied* (Urbana: University of Illinois Press, 1963), pp. 221-252.

21. Paul Friedrich, "A Mexican Cacicazgo," *Ethnology*, Vol. IV, No. 2 (April 1965), pp. 204-205; see also p. 52 above.

22. Steven Albert Reinheimer, "A Socio-Economic Study of Two Ejdos in Hidalgo State, Mexico" (Thesis, University of Wisconsin, 1967), pp. 23-27, 62-63.

23. See about the role of cooptation in Mexico: Bo Anderson and James D. Cockroft, "Control and Co-optation in Mexican Politics," *International Journal of Comparative Sociology*, VII, No. 1-2, March 1966, Leiden, Netherlands, pp. 11-28.

24. Padgett, *Political System*, p. 83.

25. Pablo González Casanova, *La Democracia en Mexico* (Mexico: Ediciones ERA, 1967), p. 35.

26. Ibid., pp. 193-194.

27. Padgett, *Political System*, p. 120.

28. See for example, Victor Manzanilla Schaffer, *Reforma Agraria Mexicana* (Universidad de Colima, 1966), p. 184.

29. Eric R. Wolf, "Aspects of Group Relations in a complex Society: Mexico," *American Anthropologist*, Vol. LVIII, No. 6 (1956), p. 1071.

30. Ibid., p. 1072.

31. González Casonova, *La Democracia*, p. 120.

32. Ibid., pp. 39-42.

33. Linda S. Mirin and Arthur L. Stinchcombe, "The Political Mobilization of Mexican Peasants" (Paper presented to the annual meeting of the American Sociological Association in Montreal, September 1964), pp. 20-21; Peter P. Lord, "The Peasantry as an Emerging Political Factor in Mexico, Bolivia and Venezuela," L.T.C. No. 35 (Land Tenure Center, University of Wisconsin, May 1965), p. 30.

34. Lola Romanucci Schwartz, "Morality, Conflict and Violence in a Mexican Mestizo Village" (Diss., Indiana University, 1962, University Microfilm), p. 177.

35. Ibid., p. 181; an interesting description of how ejido leaders can convince the people and their competitors of the need for a certain advantage such as electrification or a health center, and the ways such benefits can be obtained, is given in Pedro Félix Hernández, "An Analysis of Social Power in Five Mexican Ejidos" (Diss., Iowa State University of Science and Technology, 1965, University Microfilms), pp. 217-225.

36. François Chevalier, "Ejido y Estabilidad en México," *American Indigena*,

Vol. XXVII, No. 2 (Abril 1967), pp. 186-188; see also René Dumont, *Terres Vivantes* (Paris: Plon, 1961), pp. 93-97; a description of the conflicts between the peasants and this sugarmill run by the Banco Nacional de Crédito Ejidal (BNCE) can be found in Ruben M. Jaramillo y Froylan C. Manjarrez, *Autobiografía y Asesinato* (Editorial Nuestro Tiempo, Mexico D.F., 1967).

37. Michael Maccoby, "Love and Authority," *Man Against Poverty: World War III*, ed. Arthur I. Blaustein and Roger R. Wook (New York: Vintage, 1968), p. 348; about the alcoholism problem, see: M. Maccoby, "El Alcoholismo en una Comunidad Campesina," *Revista de Psicoanálisis, Psiquiatría y Psicología*, Vol. L, No. 1 (1965).

38. Judith Adler, "The Politics of Land Reform in Mexico with Special Reference to La Comarca Lagunera" (Thesis, London School of Economics, 1970), Chapter II. See also p. 55 ff above.

39. Gerrit Huizer, *Los Movimientos Campesinos en México*, Centro de Investigaciones Agrarias, Mexico D.F., 1968, pp. 93-95; also Henry A. Landsberger and Cynthia N. Hewitt, "Preliminary Report on a Case Study of Mexican Organizations" (Cornell University), p. 29.

40. Victor Manzanilla Schaffer, *La Reforma Agraria*, in *México: Cincuenta Años de Revolución*, III, La Política, XL, Appendix, Mexico: Fondo de Cultura Economica, 1965, pp. 43-44.

41. Carlos Manuel Castillo, "La Economía Agrícola en la Región del Bajío," *Problemas Agricolase Industriales de Mexico*, Vol. VIII, No. 3-4, p. 159.

42. For a collection of articles of various newspapers, see Manjarrez, *Asesinato*, pp. 123-167.

43. Periodicals of the epoch, around 20 August 1967.

44. *New York Times*, 29 December 1967.

45. Partido Revolucionario Institucional, IV *Asamblea Nacional Ordinaria*, Documentos No. 1, Mexico, 1965; *Ultimas Noticias*, (7 February 1968).

46. Adolfo López Mateos, *Documentos*, Vol. II, No. 8 (Julio-Sept. 1960), p. 226.

47. Rodolfo Stavenhagen, "Los Jornaleros Agrícolas," *Revista del Mexico Agrario*, Confederacion Nacional Campesina, No. 1 (Noviembre-Diciembra 1967), pp. 163-166.

48. COTPAL (Comite Tecnico Permanente de Asuntos Laborales), "Income Distribution in Mexico" (Panamerican Union, without date).

49. González Casanova, *La Democracia*, p. 130.

50. Ibid.

51. See Fernando Carmona y Alonso Aguilar, *Mexico: Riqueza y Miseria* (Mexico, 1968), Editorial Nuestro Tiempo.

52. Richard W. Patch, "Bolivia: U.S. Assistance in a Revolutionary Setting," *Social Change in Latin America Today*, Council of Foreign Relations (New York: Vintage, 1960), pp. 115-116.

53. CIDA, Draft Report on Bolivia, p. 10.

54. Jorge Dandler Hanhart, "Local Group, Community, and Nation: A Study of Changing Structure in Ucureña, Bolivia (1935-1952)" (Thesis, University of Wisconsin, 1967), p. 52.

55. Jorge Dandler Hanhart, p. 71.

56. Patch, *Bolivia*, pp. 120-121.

57. Ibid.

58. The data regarding 1943-1952 are taken mainly from a CIDA study of the history of peasant organization in Bolivia by Luis Antezana, "Bosquejo Histórico del Movimiento Sindical Campesino en Bolivia" (La Paz, Agosto 1968).

59. Ñuflo Chavez Ortiz, "Monografía sobre el Movimiento Sindical Campesino" (Ponencia III Congreso Indigenista Interamericano, La Paz, Agosto 1954), p. 5.

60. Carter Goodrich, *Revolution and Economic Development, Economic Development, Evolution or Revolution?* ed. Laura Randall (Boston: Heath, 1964), p. 17.

61. Patch, *Bolivia*, p. 118.

62. Ñuflo Chavez Ortiz, p. 6.

63. Patch, *Bolivia*, pp. 121-122.

64. Report of Ministerio de Asuntos Campesinos, 3 July 1953, Luis Antezana, "La Revolución Agraria del Año 1953" (CIDA-LTC Manuscript), pp. 37-42.

65. Patch, *Bolivia*, p. 123.

66. El Diario 3-VIII-53, p. 5, Luis Antezana, La Revolución, p. 60.

67. Robert J. Alexander, *The Bolivian National Revolution* (New Brunswick, N.J.: Rutgers University Press, 1958), p. 64.

68. El Diario 2 and 8-IV-53, Luis Antezana, La Revolución, p. 75.

69. Ibid., p. 66.

70. Ibid., p. 73.

71. Alexander, *Revolution*, p. 274.

72. Legislative Decree No. 03464, 1953 (FAO translation); italics added.

73. Edmundo Flores, "La Reforma Agraria en Bolivia" (Informe presentado a la Junta de Asistencia Tecnica de las Naciones Unidas y al Gobierno de Bolivia, March 1955).

74. Hernan Siles Suazo, *Boletín Indigenista,* Vol. XIV, No. 3 (Mexico D.F., Sept. 1954), p. 211.

75. Ernesto Ayala Mercado, *Gaceta Campesina*, Año 4, No. 5, p. 112.

76. *El Libro Blanco de la Reforma Agraria* (La Paz, 1953), p. 167; Luis de la Puente Uceda, *La Reforma del Agro Peruano* (Lima: Ediciones Ensayos Sociales, 1966), p. 102.

77. *La Nación*, 26 de julio 1953; Amado Canales, *Mito y Realidad de la Reforma Agraria* (La Paz-Cochabamba: Ed. Los Amigos del Libro, 1960), p. 162.

78. Richard W. Patch, "Freedom and Development, Rural Decision-Making and Agricultural Development," LTC No. 22 (Land Tenure Center, University of Wisconsin, July 1966), p. 12.

79. Luis Antezana y Hugo Romero, "Origen, Desarrollo y Situacion Actual del Sindicalismo Campesino en Bolivia" (CIDA-LTC, La Paz, 1968, Parte I), p. 97.

80. Oscar Delgado, "Reforma Agraria y Desarrollo Rural en un Area del Altiplano Norte de Bolivia" (Estudio de Caso, CIDA-LTC, La Paz, 1967), p. 415.

81. Luis Antezana y Hugo Romero, Campesino, Parte II, p. 147.

82. Ibid., Parte I, pp. 145-157.

83. Special Operations Research Office, *U.S. Army Area Handbook for Bolivia* (Washington, D.C.: American University, 1963), p. 340.

84. Dwight B. Heath, Charles J. Erasmus and Hans C. Buechler, "Land Reform and Social Revolution in Bolivia" (Land Tenure Center, University of Wisconsin, 1965), p. 637.

85. Dwight B. Heath, "The Aymara Indians and Bolivia's Revolution," *Inter-American Economic Affair*, Vol. XIX, No. 4 (Spring 1966), p. 37.

86. Field visit and talks with leaders in Quillacollo, dept. of Cochabamba, September 1967.

87. This came out in a debate that I attended in the Bolivian Chamber of Deputees where the subject of maintaining the peasants armed was discussed and defended by the government and the peasant delegates; see also *Presencia*, 2 de octubre 1968.

88. Several interviews in 1966 and 1967.

89. For indications of economic improvement for the peasants in a sample of 51 former estates, see Ronald J. Clark, "Land Reform and Peasant Market Participation on the North Highlands of Bolivia," *Land Economics*, Vol. XLIV (May 1968), pp. 168-172.

90. See Laurence Whitehead, *The United States and Bolivia. A Case of Neo-Colonialism* (London: Haslemere Group Publication, 1969).

Notes to Chapter 5

1. John D. Powell, "Peasant Society and Clientelist Politics" (Research paper, Center for International Affairs, 1968), p. 19.

2. John Duncan Powell, "The Politics of Agrarian Reform in Venezuela: History, System and Process" (Thesis, University of Wisconsin, 1966), p. 37; John D. Powell, "Preliminary Report on the Federación Campesina de Venezuela: Origins, Organizations, Leadership and Role in the Agrarian Reform Program" (Research paper, Land Tenure Center, Wisconsin University No. 9, Sept. 1964).

3. Powell, "The Politics," p. 95.

4. See John D. Powell, "The Role of the Federación Campesina de Venezuela and Related Political Aspects," (Manuscript prepared for CIDA study).

5. International Labour Office, *Freedom of Association and Conditions of Work in Venezuela*, Studies and Reports, New Series No. 21, Geneva, 1950, p. 40.

6. Ibid., p. 41.

7. Powell, "The Politics," p. 14.

8. I.L.O., *Freedom*, p. 85.

9. Ibid., p. 104.

10. Powell, "The Politics," etc., op. cit., p. 150.

11. Ibid., p. 151.

12. Ibid., pp. 154-155.

13. Romulo Betancourt, *Frente a Problemas del Campo Venezolano*, Secretariá General de la Presidencia de la República (Caracas: Imprenta Nacional, 1959), pp. 29-31; for evidence that the president of the FCV declared himself at that time to be against the use of land invasions, see Ramón Quijada, *Reforma Agraria en Venezuela* (Caracas: Editorial Arte), pp. 163-164.

14. Interviews with leaders in *asentamientos* La Julia-Jobo Dulce and in Burro Negro, both at some period the scene of a land invasion, presently pilot projects of CORDIPLAN's national community development program in coordination with agrarian reform.

15. CIDA-CENDES, *Reforma Agraria Venezuela*, Vol. I, *El Proceso de Adquisicion de Adquisición de Tierras*, Documento de Trabajo, por Luis Ratinoff, p. 83.

16. For speeches, press interviews and other statements, see Quijada, *Reforma*.

17. Special Operations Research Office, *Area Handbook for Venezuela* (Washington, D.C.: American University, 1964), quoted in Peter P. Lord, *The Peasantry as an Emerging Political Factor in Mexico, Bolivia and Venezuela*, LTC Paper No. 35 (Madison: Land Tenure Center, University of Wisconsin, 1965), p. 77.

18. About the purge, see John Duncan Powell, "The Peasant Movement in Venezuela" (Paper prepared for Seminar of Latin American Peasant Movements, Cornell University, 8-10 Dec. 1966), p. 25.

19. John R. Mathiason, "Political Organization and Attitudes among Venezuelan Peasants" (Diss., M.I.T., Cambridge, Mass., 1967, draft).

20. I.L.O. *The Landless Farmer in Latin America* (Studies and Reports, New Series, No. 47, Geneva, 1957), pp. 51-52.

21. For general information see Eric J.E. Hobsbawm, "Problèmes Agraires à La Convencion (Pérou)" (Communication présentée au Colloque International C.N.R.S. sur les Problèmes Agraires en Amérique Latine, Paris 11-16 Oct. 1965); CIDA, *Peru. Tenecia de la Tierra y Desarrollo Socio-Económico del Sector Agricola* (Washington, D.C., 1966), p. 215; Eric J.E. Hobsbawm, "A Case of Neo-Feudalism: La Convencion," *Journal of Latin American Studies*, Vol. I, No. 1 (1969), pp. 31-50.

22. Wesley W. Craig, "The Peasant Movement of La Convencion, Peru; Dynamics of Rural Labor Organization" (Paper presented to Seminar on Peasant Movements in Latin America, Cornell University, 8-10 Dec., 1966), p. 16.

23. Ibid., pp. 17-18.

24. A list of the cruelties and abuses committed by this specific landlord and his relatives came out in a document issued later by the peasant union and published in part in Mario A. Malpica, *Biografía de la Revolución* (Lima: Ediciones Ensayos Sociales, 1967), pp. 445-447. A good number of these facts were later revealed during the prosecution of the main peasant leader of La Convencion, Hugo Blanco in 1966-67, and were partly reported in Victor Villanueva, *Hugo Blanco y la Rebelion Campesina* (Lima: Editorial Juna Mejía Baca, 1967); see also the analysis by Roberto Mac-Lean y Estenas, *La Reforma Agraria en el Perú* (Cuadernos de Sociología, Instituto de Investigaciones Sociales, U.N.A.M., 1965), pp. 29-40, with data based mainly on reports of the Ministry of Labor and Indigenous Affairs.

25. Gonzalo Añi Castillo, *Historia Secreta de las Guerrillas* (Lima: Ediciones "Mas Allá," 1967), p. 54.

26. Eric J.E. Hobsbawm, "Problèmes Agraires."

27. Mac-Lean y Estenos, *La Reforma*, pp. 110-111.

28. Hugo Blanco, *El Camino Nuestra Revolución* (Lima: Ediciones Revolución Peruana, 1964), pp. 37-40.

29. Eric J.E. Hobsbawm, "Problèmes Agraires," p. 13.

30. Interview with Hugo Blanco, Oct. 1967.

31. Hugo Neira, *Cuzco: Tierra y Muerte*, Reportaje al Sur, (Lima: Editorial Problemas de Hoy, 1964), pp. 82-113.

32. CIDA, *Peru*, p. 397.

33. The data about the movements in Cerro de Pasco are partly derived from Mac-Lean y Estenos, *La Reforma*, pp. 109-139, and partly from interviews with leaders and peasants involved.

34. Carlos Malpica, "Antecedentes Económico-Sociales de las Guerrillas," Mario A. Malpica, *Biografía de la Revolución*, p. 438.

35. *La Prensa*, 1-7 August 1963, and personal interviews.

36. Mac-Lean y Estenos, *La Reforma*, p. 126.

37. Ministerio de Guerra, *Las Guerrillas en el Perú y su Represión* (Lima: Departamento de Relaciones Publicas del Ejercito, 1966), pp. 16-17.

38. Hugo Neira, *Cuzco*.

39. Ibid., p. 55.

40. Ibid.

41. For a highly interesting account covering the guerrilla movements, see Americo Pumaruna, "Peru: revolución: insurrección: guerrillas" *Cuadernos de Ruedo Iberico*, No. 6 (Abril-Mayo 1966), pp. 62-86.

42. Data from several conversations with Dario Cabrera, Secretary-general of the Satipo peasant federation, after his release from jail in 1967.

43. Luis de la Puente Uceda, "The Peruvian Revolution: Concepts and Perspectives," *Monthly Review*, Vol. XVII, No. 6 (Nov. 1965), pp. 23-24; Luis F. de la Puente Uceda, *La Reforma del Agro Peruano* (Lima: Ediciones Ensayos Sociales, 1966).

44. Manoel Correia de Andrade, *A Terra e o Homem no Nordeste* (Saõ Paolo: Editora Brasiliense, 1963), pp. 241-255.

45. Conversations with José dos Prazeres and Clodomir Santos de Morais (former lawyer of the leagues who participated in their formation).

46. Anthony Leeds, "Brazil and the Myth of Francisco Julião," *Politics of Change in Latin America*, ed. Joseph Maier and Richard Weatherhead (New York: Praeger, 1964), p. 195.

47. Clodomir Morais, *Queda de uma Oligarquia* (Recife: Edicoes Gersa, No. 2, 1959), p. 115.

48. These and some of the following observations are taken from a study by Clodomir Santos de Morais, "Las Ligas Campesinas" (Santiago de Chile: 1965), which appeared in English in Rodolto Stavenhagen, editor, *Agrarian Problems and Peasant Movements in Latin America* (New York: Doubleday, Anchor Books, 1970), pp. 453-501; see also Clodomir Santos de Morais, "Comportamiento Ideologico de las Clases del Campo en el Proceso de Organización" (Santiago de Chile: ICIRA, 1966).

49. Francisco Juliao and Clodomir Santos de Morais, *Que son las Ligas Campesinas* (Montevideo: Ediciones ARCA, 1963), especially Chapters 2, 3 and 5. Francisco Juliao, *Escucha Campesino*, with a foreword by Edgardo Carvalho (Uruguay: Ediciones Presente, 1962); about the communication techniques used by the Ligas, see Clodomir Santos de Morais, "Comportamiento."

50. A detailed account of this assassination and many other examples of the difficult and dangerous struggle of the growing leagues are given by CIDA, *Brazil, Land Tenure Conditions and Socio-Economic Development of the Agricultural Sector* (Washington, D.C.: Panamerican Union, 1966), pp. 309-329.

51. CIDA, *Brazil*, pp. 313-315.

52. Julião, *Campesinas*, pp. 89-97; T. Lynn Smith, editor, *Agrarian Reform in Latin America* (New York: Borzoi, 1965), pp. 119-121; Francisco Julião, *Brazil. Antes y Después* (México: Editorial Nuestro Tiempo, 1968), pp. 55-56.

53. Maria Julieta Calazans, "Realidade e Tendencias do Sindicalismo Brasileiro no Campo" (Seminario de Estudios Realidade Sindical Brasileira, Rio de Janeiro, 5-8 de marco de 1964), Folheto No. 2, Centro de Educaçao e Cultura Operária (CECO), p. 18.

54. Procopio Camargo, *O Movimiento de Natal* (Bruxelles: Centre de Documentation sur l'Action des Eglises dans la Monde, 1968), pp. 101-104.

55. Ibid., pp. 148-149.

56. Ibid.; Laura de Oliveira Lima, *El Methodo Freire: Proceso Acelerado de Alfabetización de Adultos*, Documento No. 64 (Santiago: Instituto de Capacitación e Investigación en Reform Agraria).

57. Ibid., pp. 176-177.

58. Interviews with Fathers Crespo and Melo in 1967 and 1966, respectively; Mary E. Wilkie, "A Report on Rural Syndicates in Pernambuco, Brazil" (Thesis, University of Wisconsin, 1967), p. 42.

59. Padre Paulo Crespo, "Pequeno Resumo do Movimiento Sindical Rural em Pernambuco" (Servico de Orientaçao Rural de Pernambuco–SORPE, Recife, Maio 1966); for an interesting account of the struggle between the different kinds of organizations, see Cynthia N. Hewitt, "An Analysis of the Peasant Movement of Pernambuco, Brazil: 1961-1964" (Paper presented at Seminar on Latin American Peasant Movements, 8-10 Dec. 1966, Cornell University).

60. Emanuel de Kadt, "Religion, the Church and Social Change in Brazil," *The Politics of Conformity in Latin America*, ed. Claudia Veliz (New York: Oxford University Press, 1967), p. 214.

61. Wilkie, "Rural Syndicates," pp. 47-49.

62. Father Francisco Lage, in several conversations; "Los Sindicatos Campesinos del Brasil," entrevista al Padre Francisco Lage Pessoa por Padre Alfonso Gortaire Iturrialde, *Comunidad*, Vol. 1, No. 1 (Cuadernos de Difusión Cultural, Universidad Ibero-Americana, Marzo, 1966), pp. 69-76.

63. Wilkie, "Rural Syndicates."

64. Camargo, *Movimiento*, pp. 104, 205; Sergio Maturana, "An Attempt to give a Sociological Interpretation to the Brazilian Coup d'Etat of April 1, 1964" (University of Wisconsin, The Land Tenure Center, 1966); Juliao, *Brasil:*, p. 83; Antonio Callado, "Les Ligues Paysannes du Nord-Est Brésilien," *Les Temps Modernes*, 23e année, No. 257 (Octubre 1967), pp. 751-760.

65. Albert O. Hirschman, *Journeys Towards Progress* (New York: Twentieth Century Fund, 1963), p. 102; Otto Morales Benítez (former Minister of Agriculture and Minister of Labor) gave an interesting and revealing collection of statements about this in his *Reforma Agraria Colombia Campesina* (Bogotá: Imprenta Nacional, 1962), pp. IX and LXXXIII, particularly.

66. German Guzman Campos, *La Violencia en Colombia*, (Cali: Ediciones Progreso, 1968) Parte Descriptiva.

67. See Eric Hobsbawm, "Peasant Movements in Colombia" (Enquête sur "Mouvements Paysans et Problèmes Agraire de la Fin du 18e Siecle à nos Jours," Commission Internationale d'Histoire des Mouvements Sociaux et des Structures Sociales).

68. CIDA, *Colombia Tenencia de la Tierra y Desarrollo Socio-Económico del Sector Agricola* (Washington, D.C.: Panamerican Union, 1966), pp. 257-260.

69. See Pierre Gilhodes, *Agrarian Struggles in Colombia, Agrarian Problems and Peasant Movements in Latin America*, ed. Rodolfo Stavenhagen, (New York: Anchor, 1970).

70. Guzmán, *La Violencia*, pp. 341-350; a summary of material, made available by Guzman about this period can be found in CIDA, *Colombia*, Appendix C., pp. 337-340.

71. Camilo Torres Restrepo, *La Violencia y los Cambio Socio-culturales en las Areas Colombianas* (Bogota: Memoria del Primer Congreso Nacional de Sociologia, 1963), p. 143.

72. Ibid., pp. 112, 137.

73. Ibid., p. 149.

74. Pierre Gilhodes, *Struggles*.

75. Ibid.; Guzman, *La Violencia*, p. 159.

76. Eric J. Hobsbawm, "The Anatomy of Violence," *New Society*, No. 28 (11 April 1963), p. 17.

77. For one interesting case study, see the publication of INCORA: Victor Daniel Bonilla, "De la Lucha por la Tierra al Atlántico 3," *Tierra, Revista de Economía Agraria*, No. 4 (abril-junio 1967); Vicente Andrade Valderrama, S.J., *Juicio Moral sobre la Invasión de Tierras*, Publicaciones FANAL No. 3, 1963.

78. Leo A. Suslow, *Aspects of Social Reforms in Guatemala, 1944-1949* (Hamilton: Colgate University Area Studies, Latin American Seminar Reports, No. 1, 1949), p. 93.

79. Neale J. Pearson, "The Peasant Movement in Guatemala, 1944-1954" (Paper prepared for Seminar on Peasant Movements in Latin America, Cornell University, December 8-10, 1966), pp. 3, 32.

80. Ibid., p. 33.

81. Ibid., p. 36.

82. Ibid., p. 57.

83. Ibid., p. 24.

84. Nathan L. Whetten, *Guatemala. The Land and the People* (New Haven: Yale University Press, 1961), p. 154; José Luis Paredes Moreira, *Reforma Agraria. Una Experiencia en Guatemala*, Universidad de San Carlos de Guatemala, Facultad de Ciencias Economicas, 1963, pp. 153, 48.

85. Whetten, *Guatemala*, p. 157.

86. CIDA, *Guatemala, Tenencia de la Tierra y Desarrollo Socio-Económico del Sector Agrícola* (Washington, D.C., 1965), pp. 41-42.

87. Moreira, *Reforma*, pp. 61-62, 121.

88. Richard Adams, "Social Change in Guatemala and US Policy," *Social Change in Latin America Today*, Richard Adams et al. (New York: Random House, Vintage Books, 1960), p. 270; Alain Dessaint, "Effects of the Hacienda and Plantation Systems on Guatemala's Indians," *America Indigena*, Vol. XXII, No. 4 (October 1962), p. 335; Alain Dessaint, "Papel que juegan la hacienda y la plantación en el cambio socio-cultural: Guatemala y Brasil," *Guatemala Indigena* Vol. II, No. 2 (1963), p. 33.

89. Richard Adams, *Introducción a la Antropología Aplicada* (Guatemala: Seminario de Integración Social Guatemalteca, publicación No. 13, 1964), p. 377.

90. CIDA, *Guatemala*, p. 53.

91. Ibid., p. 45.

92. Thomas and Margie Melville, "Guatemala: The Doing and Undoing of Land Reform" (Paper presented to Seminar on Latin America, American University, Washington, D.C., 1969), p. 100.

93. For an account of several hundreds of persons, mainly peasants, killed

between July 1966 and July 1967, see *La Violencia en Guatemala*, (México: Ediciones Hora Cero, Cuaderno No. 1, 1967), pp. 38-76.

94. Stokes Newbold, "Receptivity of Communist Fomented Agitation in Rural Guatemala," *Economic Development and Cultural Change*, Vol. 5, No. 4 (1957), pp. 338-361.

95. Ibid., p. 354.

96. Ibid., pp. 360-361.

97. CIDA, *Guatemala*, pp. 90, 117.

98. Adolfo Gilly, "The Guerrilla Movement in Guatemala," *Monthly Review*, Vol. XVII, No. 1, 2 (May, June 1965); Eduardo Galeano, *Guatemala. País Ocupado* (Mexico: Editorial Nuestro Tiempo, 1967).

Notes to Chapter 6

1. For case studies confirming this observation, see Orlando Fals Borda, *Campesinos de Los Andes: Estudio Sociológico de Saucio* (Bogota: Universidad Nacional, 1961), pp. 285-304 and Gerrit Huizer, "A Community Development Experience in a Central American Village." *American Indigena*, Vol. XXIV, No. 3, July 1964.

2. Pierre Gilhodes, "Luchas por la Tierra en Colombia" (Unpublished paper, 1968), p. 34.

3. Emilio Maspero, "Latin America's Labor Movement of Christian Democratic Orientation as an Instrument of Social Change," *Religion, Revolution, and Reform*, ed. William V. D'Antonio and Frederick B. Pike (New York: Praeger, 1964), p. 166.

4. CIDA, *Brazil. Land Tenure Conditions and Socio-Economic Development of the Agricultural Sector* (Washington, D.C.: Panamerican Union, 1966), p. 574.

5. See Daniel Goldrich, "Toward the Comparative Politicization in Latin America," *Contemporary Cultures and Societies of Latin America*, ed. Dwight B. Heath and Richard N. Adams (New York: Random House, 1965), pp. 361-378.

6. See United Nations, *The Future Evolution of Community Development*, draft, 1967, par. 17: "... until that happens conflict and dissensus, rather than cohesiveness, may be a true and more realistic measure of the development of communities and similarly of the success of community development activities."

7. Lewis A. Coser, *The Functions of Social Conflict* (Glencoe: Free Press, 1956).

8. Hector Bejar, *Informe 65* (Mimeo. Lima, 1966).

9. Ministerio de Guerra, *Las Guerrillas en el Perú su Represión* (Lima: Departamento de Relaciones Publicas del Ejercito, 1966), pp. 68-69.

10. Lucian W. Pye, *Aspects of Political Development* (Boston: Little, Brown and Company, 1966), pp. 99-100.

222

11. Clodomir Moraes, "Peasant Leagues in Brasil," in *Agrarian Problems and Peasant Movements in Latin America*, ed. Rodolfo Stavenhagen (New York: Doubleday, Anchor Books, 1970), pp. 470-471.

12. Cole Blaisier, "Studies of Social Revolution: Origins in Mexico, Bolivia and Cuba," *Latin American Research Review*, Vol. II, No. 3 (Summer 1967), p. 39.

13. Eric R. Wolf, *Patrones Politicos entre Campesinos Latino-Americanos* (Colloque International sur les Problèmes Agraires des Ameriques Latines, Paris 11-16, Oct. 1965), Editions du CNRS (Paris, 1967), p. 190.

14. For an interesting study of charismatic leadership in the formation of new nations, see Ann Ruth Willner and Dorothy Willner, "The Rise and Role of Charismatic Leaders," *Annals of the American Academy of Political and Social Sciences*, Vol. CCCLVIII (March 1965), pp. 77-88.

15. Terry McCoy, "The Seizure of 'Los Cristales,' " *Inter-American Economic Affairs*, Vol. XXI, No. I (1967), p. 87.

16. Neale J. Pearson, "Latin American Peasant Pressure Groups and the Modernization Process," *Journal of International Affairs*, Vol. XX, No. 2 (1966), pp. 309-317.

17. See Jeremy Boissevain, *Patrons as Brokers* (Paper, Spring Conference on the Patronage, Section for Nonwestern Sociology, Dutch Sociological Association, Amersfoort, 6-7 Juni 1969), published in *Sociologische Gids*, Vol. XVI, No. 6 (Nov./Dec. 1969).

18. Pearson, "Pressure Groups"; Anthony Leeds, "Brazil and the Myth of Francisco Juliao," in Joseph Maier and Richard W. Weatherhead, editors, *Politics of Change in Latin America* (New York: Praeger, 1964), p. 190-204; Benno Galjart, "Class and 'Following' in Rural Brazil," *America Latina*, Vol. VII, No. 3 (1964), pp. 1-22; Gerrit Huizer, "Some Notes on Community Development and Rural Social Research," *America Latina*, Vol. VIII, No. 3 (1965), pp. 128-144; Benno Galjart, "A Further Note on 'Followings': Reply to Huizer," Ibid., pp. 145-152.

19. See James Petras and Maurice Zeitlin, "Miners and Agrarian Radicalism," *Latin America: Reform of Revolution?* , ed. James Petras and Maurice Zeitlin (New York: Fawcett, 1968), pp. 235-248.

20. See Matthew Edel, "El Ejido en Zinacantan," *Los Zinacantecos*, ed. Evon Z. Vogt (Instituto Nacional Indigenista, Mexico, 1966), pp. 175-176.

21. Henry A. Landsberger and Cynthia N. Hewitt, "Ten Sources of Weakness and Cleavage in Latin American Peasant Movements" (Paper read at the Second International Congress of Rural Sociology, Enschede, Netherlands, August 5-10, 1968) gives little attention to outside forces.

22. Henry A. Landsberger, "The Role of Peasant Movements and Revolts in Development: An Analytical Framework," pp. 64-71.

23. See the interesting discussion of this concept by Irving Louis Horowitz, "Party Charisma," *Studies in Comparative International Development*, Vol. I, Monograph No. 7 (1965).

24. LIGA, 22 March 1964.

25. Henry A. Landsberger, "A Vineyard Workers' Strike: A Case Study of the Relationship between the Church, Intellectuals and Peasants in Chile," in *Latin American Peasant Movements*, ed. Henry A. Landsberger (Ithaca: Cornell University Press, 1970), pp. 210-273.

26. Thomas F. Carroll, "Land Reform as an Explosive Force in Latin America," *Explosive Forces in Latin America*, ed. J.J. Te Paske and S.N. Fisher (Ohio State University Press, 1964), p. 84.

27. U.S. Congress, Senate, Committee on Foreign Relations, Survey of the Alliance for Progress, *Labor Policies and Programs*, 1968, Doc. 87-782, pp. 2-3.

28. Ibid.

29. Quoted in Ibid.: James L. Payne, *Labor and Politics in Peru: The System of Political Bargaining* (New Haven: Yale University Press, 1965).

30. Gabriel A. Almond and G. Bingham Powell, "Comparative Politics: A Developmental Approach" (Boston: Little, Brown and Company, 1966), p. 82.

31. James L. Payne, *Labor and Politics*, p. 57, pp. 12-14.

32. Martin C. Needler, *Political Development in Latin America: Instability, Violence and Evolutionary Change* (New York: Random House, 1968), pp. 47-49.

33. Charles W. Anderson, *Toward a Theory of Latin American Politics*, LTC Reprint No. 10, Land Tenure Center, University of Wisconsin, 1964, p. 5.

34. H.L. Neiburg, "Uses of Violence," *Journal of Conflict Resolution*, Vol. VII, No. 1 (March 1963), p. 20, quoted in Coser, *Continuities*, p. 107.

35. McCoy, "Los Cristales," p. 76.

36. Charles W. Anderson, " 'Reformmongering' and the Uses of Political Power," *Inter-American Economic Affairs*, Vol. XIX, No. 2 (Autumn 1965), p. 27.

37. Ibid., p. 38.

38. William C. Thiesenhusen, "Grassroots Economic Pressures in Chile: An Enigma for Development Planners," *Economic Development and Cultural Change*, Vol. XVI, No. 3 (April 1968), pp. 412-429.

39. CIDA, *Peru*, p. 395.

40. Jaime Santander, "Las Invasiones Agrarias," *Avanzada Obrera* (Organo official de UTRAL (Colombia), 20 de julio de 1964), quoted in Miguel A. Hernandez, "Invasión Campesina: Implicaciones Legales," *Jornadas Venesolanas de Derecho Agrario* (Septiembre 1968).

41. John D. Powell, "Organizing Colombian Peasants" (Research report, Center for Rural Development, Cambridge, Mass., 1968), pp. 35-47.

42. Albert O. Hirschman, *Journeys towards Progress*, Studies of Economic Policy-Making in Latin America (New York: Twentieth Century Fund, 1963), p. 259.

43. Ibid., p. 258.

44. Coser, *Social Conflict*, p. 37.

45. Edmundo Flores, *Tratado de Economía Agrícola*, Fondo de Cultura Económica Mexico (1961), Chapter 16.

46. Ibid., Chapter 17.

47. Gamaliel Carrasco, *Algolan. Análisis Económico y Financiero de un Proyecto de Reforma Agraria en el Peru* (Washington, D.C.: CIDA, Trabajos de Investigacion sobre Tenencia de la Tierra y Reforma Agraria, 1968), p. 15.

48. Roberto MacLean y Estenos, *La Reforma Agraria en el Peru* (Mexico: Instituto de Investigaciones Sociales, U.N.A.M., 1965), pp. 158-166.

49. Margie Melville, "Alteration of Land Tenure as a Factor for Change in Maya Indians of Guatemala" (Unpublished paper, Washington, D.C.: American University, 1969).

50. For a case study of some *comunidades* in the province of Coquimbo, Chile, see Gerrit Huizer, *"Comunidades agrícolas*, Internal Colonialism and Agrarian Reform in Chile," Vol. XI, No. 4 (1968), pp. 110-127.

51. Ted Gurr, "Psychological Factors in Civil Violence," *World Politics, A Quarterly Journal of International Relations*, Vol. XX, No. 2 (January 1968), p. 247.

52. Ibid., p. 245.

53. Roberto MacLean y Estenos, "La Revolución de 1910 y el Problema Agrario de Mexico," *Estudios Sociologicos* Tomo II (Mexico: IX Congreso Nacional de Sociologia, 1958), p. 51.

54. For a brief discussion of this problem, see David Chaplin, "Peru's Postponed Revolution," *World Politics*, Vol. XX, No. 3 (April 1968), p. 414.

55. Lewis A. Coser, *Continuities in the Study of Social Conflict* (New York: Free Press, 1968), pp. 106-107.

Notes to Chapter 7

1. Charles W. Anderson, "Toward a Theory of Latin American Politics," LTC Reprint, No. 10 (Madison: Land Tenure Center, University of Wisconsin, 1964), p. 2.

2. Irving Luis Horowitz, "The Norm of Illegitimacy: Toward a General Theory of Latin American Political Development" (Paper prepared for 62nd Annual Meeting of the American Sociological Association, San Francisco, Calif., August 1967).

3. See James C. Davies, "Toward a Theory of Revolution," *American Sociological Review*, Vol. XXVII, No. 1 (Feb. 1962), pp. 5-19.

4. Interview with Hugo Blanco, Nov. 1968.

5. Interviews with peasants in the area, Oct. 1968.

6. Interviews at Carpina, Pernambuco, Summer 1967.

7. Anderson, "Politics," p. 8.

8. About this movement, see José Santos Valdes, *Madera* (Mexico) 1967.

9. Caroline F. Ware, "Desarrollo de la Comunidad en Bolivia" (CEPAL, Seminario Regional Latinoamericano sobre el papel del Desarrollo de la Comunidad en el Desarrollo Económico y Social, 1964), p. 1.

10. Richard Fagan, "Mass Mobilization in Cuba: The symbolism of Struggle," *Journal of International Affairs*, Vol. XX, No. 2 (1966), p. 257.

11. Boris Goldenberg, *The Cuban Revolution and Latin America* (New York: Praeger, 1965), pp. 123-125.

12. Antonio Nuñez Jimenez, "La Reforma Agraria de Cuba" (Academia de Ciencias de Cuba, 1966), p. 19.

13. Ibid., p. 55; Cuba, "Report on Land Reform" WLR/C/66/19 (National paper World Land Reform Conference, Rome, 1966).

14. Fagan, "Mobilization," p. 261; Maurice Zeitlin, "Political Generations in Cuban Working Class," *Latin America. Reform or Revolution?* , ed. James Patras and Maurice Zeitlin (New York: Fawcett, 1968), pp. 264-288.

15. Ibid., pp. 260-261.

16. United Nations, *1967 Report on the World Social Situation*, p. 54.

17. Lloyd A. Free, *Attitudes of the Cuban People towards the Castro Regime* (Princeton: Institute for International Social Research, 1960), pp. 5, 10.

18. For some examples, see Henry A. Landsberger, "The Labor Elite: Is It Revolutionary? ," *Elites in Latin America*, ed. Seymour M. Lipset and Aldo Solari (New York: Oxford University Press, 1967), p. 260.

19. See Peter Worsley, *The Third World* (London, 1964); W.F. Wertheim, "Patronage, Vertical Organization and Populism" (Paper presented at 8th Internat. Congress of Anthropology and Ethnology, Tokyo, 1968).

20. See particularly Benno Galjart, "Class and 'Following' in *Rural Brazil*," *America Latina*, Vol. III, No. 3 (1964), pp. 1-22. For discussion on the use or misue of Marxist terminology (in answer to this article by Galjart), see Gerrit Huizer, "Some Notes on Community Development and Rural Social Research," *America Latina*, Vol. VIII, No. 3 (1965), pp. 128-144.

21. U.S., Congress, Senate, Committee on Foreign Relations, *Insurgency in Latin America*, Doc. 86-406, 1968, p. 8.

22. Frank R. Brandenburg, *The Making of Modern Mexico* (Englewood Cliffs: Prentice-Hall, 1966).

23. U.S., Congress, Senate, Committee on Foreign Relations, *Military Policies and Programs in Latin America*, Doc. 31-629, 1969, p. 18.

24. Ibid., particularly interventions of Ralph Dungan, former Ambassador to Chile, and George C. Lodge.

25. Ted Gurr, "Psychological Factors in Civil Violence," *World Politics*, Vol. XX, No. 2, 1968, p. 254.

26. Merle Kling, "Violence and Politics in Latin America," *Latin American Radicalism*, ed. Irving Louis Horowitz, Josué de Castro and John Gerassi (New York: Vintage, 1969), p. 200.

27. E. Feder, "When is Land Reform a Land Reform? The Colombian

Case," *The American Journal of Economics and Sociology*, Vol. XXIV, No. 2 (April 1965), pp. 113-134.

28. See Roger E. Soles, "Rural Land Invasions in Colombia" (Research proposal, Land Tenure Center, University of Wisconsin, 1968).

29. U.S. Congress, Senate, Committee on Foreign Relations, *Colombia – A Case History of US AID*, Doc. 21-145, 1969, p. 121.

30. Ibid., *Insurgency in Latin America*, Doc. 86-406, 1968, p. 4.

31. Arpad von Lazar and Luis Quiros Varela, "Chilean Christian Democracy: Lessons in the Politics of Reform Management," *Inter-American Economic Affairs*, Vol. XXI, No. 4 (Spring 1968), pp. 66-67, give an interesting example how this happened recently in Chile with another popular participation program.

32. See Luis Mercier Vega, "The Myth of the Guerrilla," *Dissent*, Vol. XV, No. 3 (May-June 1968), pp. 210-215.

33. Crane Brinton, *The Anatomy of Revolution* (New York: Vintage, 1965), pp. 39-66.

34. About this subject, see United Nations, Commission for Social Development, *Preliminary Report on Long-term Policies and Programmes for Youth in National Development*, E/CN. 5/434 (New York, 1969), par. 67-76.

35. Also in the United States itself, as can be seen from Committee on Foreign Relations, *Military Policies*.

Bibliography

Bibliography

Some of the experiences described or material used in this study have been the subject of articles or papers that have been published by the author. The more important ones are listed below.

"Some Community Development Problems in Partinico, Western Sicily." *International Review of Community Development* No. 10 (1962).

"Some Observations on a Central American Village." *América Indígena* Vol. XXIII, No. 3 (July 1963).

"A Community Development Experience in a Central American Village." *América Indígena* Vol. XXIV, No. 3 (July 1964).

"Some Notes on Community Development and Rural Social Research," *América Latina* Vol. VIII, No. 3 (July-Sept. 1965).

"Evaluating Community Development at the Grassroots: Observations on Methodology." *América Indígena* Vol. XXV, No. 3 (1965).

"Community Development and Land Reform, Preliminary Observations on Some Cases in Latin America." *International Review of Community Development* Nos. 15, 16 (1966).

"The Role of Community Development and Peasant Organization in Social Structural Change." *International Review of Community Development* Nos. 17, 18 (1967).

"On Peasant Unrest in Latin America." Mimeographed. CIDA, Panamerican Union, Washington, D.C., UP-G5/071, 1967.

"Community Development and Conflicting Rural Interests. Some Observations on the Programme of the National Indian Institute in Mexico." *América Indígena* XXVIII, No. 3 (July 1968).

"Peasant Organizations and Agrarian Reform in Latin America." Paper presented to Second World Congress of Rural Sociology. Enschede, Netherlands, August 1968.

"Comunidades Agricolas Internal Colonialism and Agrarian Reform in Chile." *América Latina* Vol. II, No. 4 (1968).

"Los Movimientos Campesinos en México." Mimeographed. Centro de Investigaciones Agrarias, Mexico, 1968.

"Peasant Organization in the Process of Agrarian Reform in Mexico." *Studies in Comparative International Development*, Monograph Series, Vol. IV, No. 6, St. Louis, Missouri: Washington University, 1968-1969.

"Community Development, Land Reform and Political Participation." *The American Journal of Economics and Sociology*, Vol. XXVIII, No. 2 (April 1969).

For an extensive general bibliography on peasant movements and organizations in Latin America, see Gerrit Huizer and Cynthia N. Hewitt, "Bibliography on Peasant Movements." In *Latin American Peasant Movements*, edited by Henry A. Landsberger. Ithaca, New York: Cornell University Press, forthcoming. A bibliography of the most important literature used in this study follows.

Adams, Richard N. "Rural Labor." In *Continuity and Change in Latin America*, edited by John J. Johnson. Stanford University Press, 1964, pp. 49-78.

Adams, Richard. "Social Change in Guatemala and US Policy." In *Social Change in Latin America Today*, by Richard Adams, et al. New York: Council of Foreign Relations, 1961.

Adler, Judith. "The Politics of Land Reform in Mexico: The Case of La Comarca Lagunera." Master's thesis, London School of Economics, 1970.

Aguirre Beltrán Gonzalo. *Regiones de Refugio, El Desarrollo de la Comunidad y el Proceso Dominical en Mestizo America*. Mexico: Instituto Indigenista Inter-americano, 1967.

Alexander, Robert J. *The Bolivian National Revolution*. Rutgers University Press, 1958.

Alexander, Robert J. *Organized Labor in Latin America*. New York: Free Press, 1965.

Anderson, Charles W. "Reformmongering and the Uses of Political Power." *Inter-American Economic Affairs* Vol. XIX, No. 2 (Autumn 1965).

Anderson, Charles W. "Toward A Theory of Latin American Politics." Reprint No. 10. University of Wisconsin: Land Tenure Center (1964).

Antezana, Luis. "Bosquejo Histórico del Movimiento Sindical Campesino en Bolivia." Mimeographed. La Paz, Agosto 1968.

Antezana, E. Luis. *El Movimiento Obrero Boliviano (1935-1943)*. Bolivia, 1966.

Antezana, Luis, y Romero Hugo. "Origen, Desarrollo y Situación Actual del Sindicalismo Campesino en Bolivia." Mimeographed. CIDA-LTC, La Paz, 1968.

Banfield, Edward C. *The Moral Basis of Backward Society*. Glencoe: Free Press, 1958.

Barraclough, Solon and Domike, Arthur. "Agrarian Structure in Seven Latin American Countries." *Land Economics* Vol. XLII, No. 4 Nov. 1966 (LTC Reprint No. 25. University of Wisconsin: Land Tenure Center).

Blanco, Hugo. *El Camino de Nuestra Revolución*. Lima: Ediciones Revolución Peruana, 1964.

Blok, Anton. "Mafia and Peasant Rebellion as Contrasting Factors in Sicilian Latifundism." *European Journal of Sociology* Vol. X (1969).

Boissevain, Jeremy. "Patronage in Sicily." *Man* Vol. I, No. 1 (March 1966).

Bourricaud, François. *Cambios en Puno*. Mexico: Instituto Indigenista Inter-americano. Ediciones Especiales 48, 1967.

Brandenburg, Frank. *The Making of Modern Mexico*. Englewood Cliffs, N.J.: Prentice-Hall, 1964.

Camargo, Procopio. *O Movimiento do Natal*. Bruxelles: Centre de Documentation sur l'Action des Eglises dans le Monde, 1968.

Carroll, Thomas F. "Land Reform as an Explosive Force in Latin America." In *Explosive Forces in Latin America*, edited by J.J. TePaske and S.N. Fisher. Ohio University Press, 1964.

Carroll, Thomas F. "The Land Reform Issue in Latin America." In *Latin American Issues, Essays and Comments*, edited by Albert O. Hirschman. New York: The Twentieth Century Fund, 1961.

Castillo, Carlos Manuel. "La Económía Agrícola en la Región del Bajío." Problemas Agrícolas e Industriales de Mexico, Vols. VIII, Nos. 3, 4.

CIDA. *Brazil. Land Tenure Conditions and Socio-Economic Development of the Agricultural Sector*. Washington, D.C.: Pan American Union, 1966.

CIDA. *Colombia, Tenencia de la Tierra y Desarrollo Socio-Económico del Sector Agrícola*. Washington, D.C.: Union Panamericana, 1966.

CIDA. *Guatemala, Tenencia de la Tierra y Desarrollo Socio-Económico del Sector Agrícola*. Washington, D.C.: Union Panamericana, 1965.

CIDA. *Peru, Tenencia de la Tierra y Desarrollo Socio-Económico del Sector Agrícola*. Washington, D.C.: Union Panamericana, 1966.

Chaplin, David. "Peru's Postponed Revolution." *World Politics* Vol. XX, No. 3 (April 1968).

Chevalier, François. "Ejido y Estabilidad en México." *América Indígena* Vol. XXVII, No. 2 (abril 1967).

Chevalier, François. "Un Factor Decisivo de la Revolución Agraria de México: El Levantamionto de Zapata (1911-1919)." *Cuadernos Americanos* Vol. XIX, No. 6 (November-December 1960).

Condarco, Morales Ramiro. *Zárate, El "Temible" Willka*. Historia de la Rebelión Indígena de 1899, La Paz, 1966.

Correia de Andrade, Manoel. *A Terra e Homen no Nordeste*. Sao Paolo: Editora Brasiliense, 1963.

Coser, Lewis A. *Continuities in the Study of Social Conflict*. New York: Free Press, 1968.

Coser, Lewis A. *The Functions of Social Conflict*. Glencoe: Free Press, 1956.

Craig, Wesley W. "The Peasant Movement of La Convención, Peru: Dynamics of Rural Labor Organization." In *Latin American Peasant Movements*, edited by Henry A. Landsberger. Cornell University Press, forthcoming.

Dandler Hanhart, Jorge. "Local Group, Community, and Nation: A Study of Changing Structure in Ucureña, Bolivia (1935-1952)." Master's thesis, University of Wisconsin, 1967.

Delgado, Oscar. "Reforma Agraria y Desarrollo Rural en una Area del Altiplano Norte de Bolivia." Mimeographed. CIDA-LTC, Estudio de Caso, 1968.

Delgado, Oscar, ed. *Reformas agrarias en América Latina Procesos y perspectivas*. Mexico: Fondo de Cultura Económica, 1965.

Dew, Edward. *Politics in the Altiplano: The Dynamics of Change in Rural Peru*. Austin: University of Texas Press, 1969.

232

Dolci, Danilo. *Waste*. London: Macgibbon and Kee, 1963.

Duran, Marco Antonio. *El Agrarismo Mexicano*. Siglo Veintiuno Editores, 1967.

Eckstein, Salomón. *El Ejido Colectivo en México*. Mexico: Fondo de Cultura Económica, 1966.

Erasmus, Charles J. "Community Development and the Encogido Syndrom." *Human Organization* Vol. XXVII, No. 1 (Spring 1968).

Erasmus, Charles J. *Man Takes Control, Cultural Development and American Aid*. Minneapolis: University of Minnesota Press, 1961.

Erasmus, Charles J. "Upper Limits of Peasantry and Agrarian Reform: Bolivia, Venezuela and Mexico Compared." *Ethnology* Vol. VI (Jan. 1967).

Facó, Rui. *Cangaceiros e Fanaticos*. Rio de Janeiro: Editora Civilizacão Brasileira, 1965.

Fals Borda, Orlando. *Campesinos de los Andes: Estudio Sociológico de Saucio*. Bogotá: Universidad Nacional, 1961.

Feder, Ernest. *Societal Opposition to Peasant Movements and its Effect on Farm People in Latin America*. In *Latin American Peasant Movements*, edited by Henry A. Landsberger. Ithaca: Cornell University Press, 1970.

Flores, Edmundo. "Land Reform in Bolivia." *Land Economics* Vol. XXX, No. 2 (May 1954).

Flores, Edmundo. *Tratado de Economía Agrícola*. Mexico: Fondo de Cultura Económica, 1961.

Foster, George M. *Empire's Children. The People of Tzintzuntzan*. Publ. No. 6. Washington, D.C.: Smithsonian Institution, Institute of Social Anthropology, 1948.

Foster, George M. "Peasant Society and the Image of Limited Good." *American Anthropologist* Vol. LXVII, No. 2 (April 1965).

Friedrich, Paul. "A Mexican Cacicazgo." *Ethnology* Vol. IV, No. 2 (April 1965).

Galjart, Benno. "Class and 'Following' in Rural Brazil." *America Latina* Vol. VII, No. 3 (1964).

Galjart, Benno. *Itaguaí, Old habits and new practices in a Brazilian land settlement*. Center for Agricultural Publishing and Documentation, Wageningen, Netherlands, 1968.

Galjart, Benno. "Old Patrons and New." *Sociologia Ruralis* Vol. VII, No. 4 (1967).

Gilly, Adolfo. "The Guerrilla Movement in Guatemala." *Monthly Review* Vol. XVII, Nos. 1, 2 (May, June 1965).

Goldrich, Daniel. *Toward the Comparative Politicization in Latin America*. In *Contemporary Cultures and Societies of Latin America*, edited by Dwight B. Heath and Richard N. Adams. New York: Random House, 1965.

González Casanova, Pablo. *La Democracia en México*. Mexico: Ediciones ERA, Segunda Edición, 1967.

González Ramírez, Manuel. *La Revolución Social de México, Vol. III, El Problema Agrario*. Mexico, D.F.: Fondo de Cultura Económica, 1966.

Gruening, Ernest. *Mexico and its Heritage*. New York: The Century Company, 1928.

Gurr, Ted. "Psychological Factors in Civil Violence." *World Politics, A Quarterly Journal of International Relations* Vol. XX, No. 2 (January 1968).

Gutiérrez, José. *La Rebeldía Colombiana, Observaciones Psicológicas sobre Actualidad Política*. Bogotá: Ediciones Tercer Mundo, 1962.

Guzmán Campos, German. *La Violencia en Colombia*. California: Parte Descriptiva, Ediciones Progreso, 1968.

Heath, Dwight B. "The Aymara Indians and Bolivia's Revolution." *Inter-American Economic Affairs* Vol. XIX, No. 4 (Spring 1966).

Heath, Dwight B.; Erasmus, Charles J., and Buechler, Hans C. "Land Reform and Social Revolution in Bolivia." Mimeographed. University of Wisconsin: Land Tenure Center, 1965.

Hewitt, Cynthia N. "An Analysis of the Peasant Movement of Pernambuco, Brazil: 1961-1964." In *Latin American Peasant Movements*, edited by Henry A. Landsberger. Cornell University Press, forthcoming.

Hirschman, Albert O. *Journeys towards Progress, Studies of Economic Policy-Making in Latin America*. New York: Twentieth Century Fund, 1963.

Hobsbawm, Eric J.E. "Problemes Agraires à La Convención (Perou)." Communication Présentée au Colloque International C.N.R.S. sur Les Problèmes Agraires en Amerique Latine, Paris 11-16 Oct. 1965.

Holmberg, Allan R. "Changing Community Attitudes and Values in Peru: A Case Study in Guided Change." In *Social Change in Latin America Today*, edited by Richard Adams et al. New York: Council of Foreign Relations, 1961.

Holmberg, Allan. "Land Tenure and Planned Social Change: A Case from Vicos, Peru." *Human Organization* Vol. I (1959).

Horowitz, Irving Louis. "Party Charisma." *Studies in Comparative International Development*, Vol. I, No. 7 (1965).

International Labour Office. *Freedom of Association and Conditions of Work in Venezuela*. Studies and Reports, New Series No. 21, Geneva, 1950.

International Labour Office. *Indigenous Peoples*. Studies and Reports, New Series No. 35, Geneva, 1953.

International Labour Office. *The Landless Farmer in Latin America*. Studies and Reports, New Series No. 47, Geneva, 1957.

Julião, Francisco. *Brazil. Antes y Después*. Mexico: Editorial Nuestro Tiempo, 1968.

Julião, Francisco. *Escucha Campesino*. Introducción de Edgardo Carvalho. Montevideo: Ediciones Presente, 1962.

Julião, Francisco. *Que son Las Ligas Campesinas*. Montevideo: ed. ARCA, 1963.

de Kadt, Emanuel. "Religion, the Church and Social Change in Brazil." In *The Politics of Conformity in Latin America*, edited by Claudio Veliz. Oxford University Press, 1967.

Landsberger, Henry A. "The Role of Peasant Movements and Revolts in Development: An Analytical Framework." *Bulletin*, International Institute for Labour Studies, No. 4 (Feb. 1968).

Landsberger, Henry A. *Latin American Peasant Movements*, Ithaca: Cornell University Press, 1970.

Landsberger, Henry A. and Hewitt, Cynthia N. "Preliminary Report on a Case Study of Mexican Peasant Organizations." Mimeographed. Ithaca, N.Y.: Cornell University.

Landsberger, Henry A. and Hewitt, Cynthia N. "Ten Sources of Weakness and Cleavage in Latin American Peasant Movements." Paper read at the Second International Congress of Rural Sociology, 5-10 August 1968, Enschede, Netherlands.

Letts, Ricardo C. "Breve Historia Contemporanea de la Lucha por la Reforma Agraria en el Perú." *Economica y Agricultura* Vol. I, No. 2 (1963-1964).

Lewis, Oscar. *Life in a Mexican Village: Tepoztlán Restudied*. Urbana: University of Illinois Press, 1963.

Liga de Agrónomos Socialistas. *La Comarca Lagunera, El Colectivismo Agrario en Mexico* No. 15, México, 1940.

Loomis, Charles P. *Turrialba. Social Systems and the Introduction of Change*. Glencoe: Free Press, 1953.

Lord, Peter P. "The Peasantry as an Emerging Political Factor in Mexico, Bolivia and Venezuela." LTC Paper No. 35. University of Wisconsin: Land Tenure Center, 1965.

MacLean y Estenos, Roberto. *La Reforma Agraria en el Peru*, Cuadernos de Sociología, Instituto de Investigaciones Sociales, UNAM, Mexico, 1965.

MacLean y Estenos, Roberto. "La Revolución de 1910 y el Problema Agrario de México," *Estudios Sociologicos*, Tomo II, IX Congreso Nacional de Sociología, México, 1958.

Magaña, Gildardo. *Emiliano Zapata y el Agrarismo en México*, Editorial Ruto México, 1951, 5 tomos.

Malpica, Mario A. *Biografía de la Revolución*, Ediciones Ensayos Sociales, Lima, 1967.

Martínez Mugica, Apolinar. *Primo Tapia, Semblanza de un Revolucionario Michoacana*, Segunda Edición, Mexico, 1946.

Melville, Thomas and Melville, Margie. "Guatemala: The Doing and Undoing of Land Reform." Paper presented to Seminar on Latin America, American University, Washington, D.C., 1969, forthcoming.

Mendieta y Nuñez, Lucio. *El Problema Agrario de México*. México: Séptima Edición, Editorial Porrua, 1959.

Moraes, Clodomir. "Peasant Leagues in Brazil." In *Agrarian Problems and Peasant Movements in Latin America*, edited by Rodolfo Stavenhagen. New York: Doubleday, Anchor Books, 1970.

Nathan, Paul. "Mexico en la Epoca de Cárdenas." *Problemas Agrícolas e Industriales de México* Vol. VII, No. 3 (1955).

235

Neira, Hugo. *Cuzco: Tierra y Muerte Reportaje al Sur*. Lima: Editorial Problemas de Hoy, 1964.

Newbold, Stokes. "Receptivity of Communist Fomented Agitation in Rural Guatemala." *Economic Development and Cultural Change* Vol. V, No. 4 (1957).

Padgett, L. Vincent. *The Mexican Political System*. Boston: Houghton Mifflin, 1966.

Patch, Richard W. *Bolivia: U.S. Assistance in a Revolutionary Setting*. In *Social Change in Latin America Today*, edited by Richard Adams et al. Council of Foreign Relations, 1960, A Vintage Book.

Patch, Richard W. "Freedom and Development, Rural Decision-Making and Agricultural Development." LTC No. 22. University of Wisconsin: Land Tenure Center (1966).

Paulson, Belden H. "Difficulties and Prospects for Community Development in North-East Brazil." *Inter-American Economic Affairs* Vol. 17, No. 4 (Spring 1964).

Paulson, Belden, H. *Local Political Patterns in North-East Brazil: A Community Case Study*. Mimeographed. University of Wisconsin: The Land Tenure Center (Aug. 1964).

Payne, James L. *Labor and Politics in Peru. The System of Political Bargaining*, Yale University Press, 1965.

Pearson, Neale J. "Latin American Peasant Pressure Groups and the Modernization Process." *Journal of International Affairs* Vol. XX, No. 2, Columbia University: School of International Affairs, 1966.

Pearson, Neale J. *The Peasant Movement in Guatemala, 1944-1954*. In *Latin American Peasant Movements*, edited by Henry A. Landsberger. Cornell University Press, forthcoming.

Petras, James and Zeitlin, Maurice. "Miners and Agrarian Radicalism." In *Latin America. Reform or Revolution?*, edited by James Petras and Maurice Zeitlin. Fawcett Premier Book, 1968.

Powell, John Duncan. *The Politics of Agrarian Reform in Venezuela: History, System and Process*. Mimeographed. Ph.D. Thesis (Pol. Sc.), University of Wisconsin, 1966.

Powell, John D. *Preliminary Report on the Federación Campesina de Venezuela: Origins, Organization, Leadership and Role in the Agraria Reform Program*. Mimeographed. Research Paper, University of Wisconsin: Land Tenure Center, No. 9, Sept. 1964.

Powell, John D. *The Role of the Federación Campesina de Venezuela and Related Political Aspects*, manuscript prepared for CIDA study, 1967.

Powell, John D. *The Peasant Movement in Venezuela*. In *Latin American Peasant Movements*, edited by Henry A. Landsberger. Ithaca: Cornell University Press, 1970.

Prebisch, Raul. *Towards a Dynamic Development Policy for Latin America*. Mimeographed. United Nations, ECLA, E/CN.12/680, 1963.

Quijada, Ramón. *Reforma Agraria en Venezuela*. Caracas, Editorial Arte, 1963.

Quijano Obregon, Aníbal. "Contemporary Peasant Movements." In *Elites in Latin America*, edited by Seymour Martin Lipset and Aldo Solari. New York: Oxford University Press, 1967.

Quijano, Aníbal. "El Movimiento Campesino del Perú y sus Líderes." *América Latina* Vol. VIII, No. 4 (1965).

Santos de Morais, Clodomir. "Comportamiento Ideológico de las Clases y Capas del Campo en el Proceso de Organización." Mimeographed. Santiago, Chile: I.C.I.R.A., 1965.

Schmitt, Karl M. *Communism in Mexico, A Study in Political Frustration*. Austin: University of Texas Press, 1965.

Scott, Robert E. *Mexican Government in Transition*, 2d ed., rev. Urbana: University of Illinois Press, 1964.

Senior, Clarence. *Land Reform and Democracy*. Gainesville: University of Florida Press, 1958.

Silva Herzog, Jesús. *El Agrarismo Mexicano y la Reforma Agraria*. México: Fondo de Cultura Económica, 1959.

Simpson, Eyler N. *The Ejido. Mexico's Way Out*. Chapel Hill: University of North Carolina Press, 1937.

Stavenhagen, Rodolfo. "Clases, Colonialismo y Aculturación." *América Latina* Vol. VI, No. 4 (1963).

Stavenhagen, Rodolfo, ed. *Agrarian Problems and Peasant Movements in Latin America*. New York: Anchor, 1970.

Survey of the Alliance for Progress. *Colombia–A Case History of US AID*. Doc. 21-145. Committee on Foreign Relations, U.S. Senate, 1969.

Survey of the Alliance for Progress. *Insurgency in Latin America*. Doc. 86-406. Committee on Foreign Relations, U.S. Senate, 1968.

Survey of the Alliance for Progress. *Labor Policies and Programs*. Doc. 87-782. Committee on Foreign Relations, U.S. Senate, 1968.

Tannenbaum, Frank. *The Mexican Agrarian Revolution*. New York: Macmillan, 1929.

Tannenbaum, Frank. *Peace by Revolution: Mexico after 1910*. Columbia University Press, 1966.

Thiesenhusen, William C. "Grassroots Economic Pressures in Chile: An Enigma for Development Planners." *Economic Development and Cultural Change*, Vol. XIV, No. 3 (April 1968), pp. 412-429.

Torres, Restrepo, Camilo. *La Violencia y los Cambios Socioculturales en las Areas Rurales Colombianas*. Bogotá: Memoria del Primer Congreso Nacional de Sociología, 1963.

Vazques, Mario C. *Hacienda, Peonaje y Servidumbre en los Andes Peruanos*. Monografías Andinas No. 1. Lima: Editorial Estudios Andinos, 1961.

Villanueva, Victor. *Hugo Blanco y la Rebelion Campesina*. Lima: Editorial Juan Mejía Baca, 1967.

Wertheim, W.F. *East-West Parallels*. The Hague: Van Hoeve, 1964.

Wertheim, W.F. "Sociology between Yesterday and Tomorrow," *Comparative Studies in Society and History* Vol. IX, No. 2 (Jan. 1967).

Weyl, Nathaniel and Weyl, Sylvia. *The Reconquest of Mexico. The Years of Lázara Cárdenas*. Oxford University Press, 1939.

Whetten, Nathan L. *Guatemala, the Land and the People*. New Haven: Yale University Press, 1961.

Whetten, Nathan L. *Rural Mexico*. University of Chicago Press, 1948.

Wilkie, Mary E. A Report on Rural Syndicates in Pernambuco, Brazil. Master's thesis, University of Wisconsin, 1967.

Wolf, Eric R. "Aspects of Group Relations in a Complex Society: Mexico." *American Anthropologist* Vol. LVIII, No. 6 (1956).

About the Author

Gerrit Huizer has been active in community development and peasant organization since 1955. First as a volunteer in a village in Central America, later in villages in Sicily in a project directed by Danilo Dolci and from 1962 onward in several capacities with different agencies of United Nations in Latin America and South-East Asia. Through practical involvement with the peasants and their struggle he gained insights which were also of scientific value, disproving some of the ideas held by scholars who claim to use more purely scientific methods of research concerning peasants and their "resistance to change." The insights gained and the methods used are reflected in this book which served as a Ph.D. Dissertation (Cum Laude) supervised by Professor W.F. Wertheim of Amsterdam University. The author is presently working as a visiting professor at the Institute of Social Studies in the Hague.